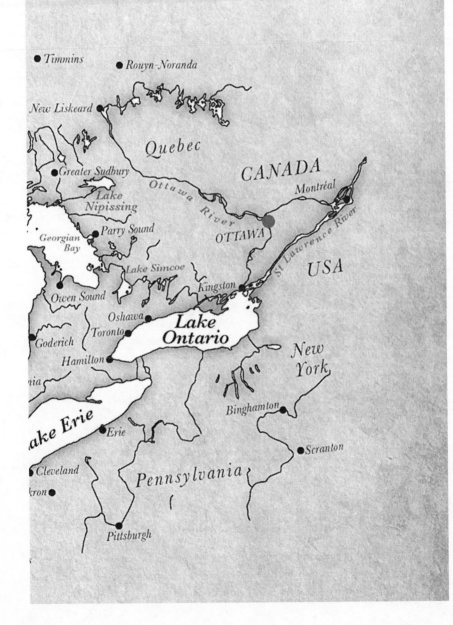

No Roads to Follow

Kayaking the Great Lakes Solo

Michael Herman

iUniverse, Inc.
Bloomington

No Roads to Follow
Kayaking the Great Lakes Solo

iUniverse books may be ordered through booksellers or by contacting:

iUniverse
1663 Liberty Drive
Bloomington, IN 47403
www.iuniverse.com
1-800-Authors (1-800-288-4677)

ISBN: 978-1-4620-5193-9 (sc)
ISBN: 978-1-4620-5194-6 (e)
ISBN: 978-1-4620-5195-3 (dj)

Printed in the United States of America

iUniverse rev. date: 10/21/2011

To my parents, Ron and Brenda Herman,
who gave me the freedom to explore and a heart for dreaming;
and to my wife and best friend, Fleur Pigeon, who makes me feel I can
do anything I set my mind on.

INTRODUCTION

I BELIEVE VERY strongly in synchronicity, the idea that everything happens with a divine purpose and that there are no coincidences in life.

IT WAS NO coincidence to me that I decided to set a goal to kayak the Great Lakes solo, or to support the Canadian Cancer Society in the process. The puzzle pieces of my life had come together perfectly.

In many ways it seems that I had been training my whole life for this trip. I grew up exploring the forests near my family home in Creemore, Ontario. I had always felt completely at ease in nature, and I hiked, snowshoed, and camped on my own as often as my parents would allow me.

As a young boy, I loved to sleep outside. When summer arrived and school was finished, I would trade my comfortable bed for a sleeping bag and groundsheet under the stars in the backyard. Looking up at the sky each night, I would fall asleep dreaming I was living in the wilderness.

I started canoeing when I was seven, and in the last few years before embarking on my expedition of the Great Lakes, paddling had become a passion with me. I loved to paddle. It is freedom in motion. Rarely did a weekend go by that I wasn't canoeing a lake or river somewhere within driving distance of my home. Dreams of leaving on a long canoe expedition began to fill my thoughts regularly, fuelled by books like *Summer North of 60*, *Seekers of The Horizon*, and *Water and Sky*. While paddling with friends, I would tease them with invitations to run away on canoe expeditions.

"Hey, Steve, let's quit our jobs and paddle out the St. Lawrence to Nova Scotia! ... No, let's go to the Gulf of Mexico!" I enthused.

"Mexico?" he would argue. "Let's head for the barrens and follow the footsteps of Franklin."

It was like asking someone how he would spend his money if he won the lottery. I didn't really think I would ever do it; I just loved talking about the possibility.

Making the decision to kayak 3,200 kilometres solo across the Great Lakes in support of the cancer society came easily. Understanding why I made this decision was much more difficult. I believe part of the reason was due to my feeling that I was losing control of my life. I was uncertain where I was headed, with no clear ideas or direction.

Dissatisfied with ethical dilemmas and government policies, I had left a career in fisheries management to which I had devoted ten years. I felt lost. I was struggling to figure out who I was and where I fit in with society without my chosen career. Regardless of all my parents' teachings, I still found myself judging who I was by my work, or lack of it, and my financial position in life. Had it been someone else, I probably would have told him, "You're more than your job or worldly possessions," but for me at that time in my life, many of the beliefs I had previously held to be true seemed weak and without merit.

Beginning this trip was therapy for me. It gave me a purpose, a goal to focus on. However, this was not the only reason and probably not *the* reason that inspired me to take the plunge, or more importantly, to involve the Canadian Cancer Society. The real inspiration came from something I heard on the radio while driving home from a canoe trip. For the better part of two years I had been focusing on what I didn't have, instead of celebrating what I *did* have. I knew then, listening to the news on the radio, that it was time to make a change.

TIME FOR A CHANGE

On Labour Day weekend, 1993, I went on a canoe trip in Killarney Provincial Park with my girlfriend, Fleur, and a group of friends. Fleur and I had been inseparable all summer, dashing away on canoe trips every weekend. She was ten years younger, blonde, fit, and full of life. When the time came for her to leave for her first year at university, we agreed to say goodbye. I didn't think it was fair to expect her to tie herself to me. I thought it would be better for her to start school with a clean slate and a free heart. At the end of the weekend, we kissed and hugged each other at the bus stop in Parry Sound.

It was a difficult time for each of us. She was headed for Lakehead University in Thunder Bay. I was headed back to my job selling life insurance. I hated my job, and my sales record showed it. Although I believed in the idea of owning life insurance, I couldn't muster the enthusiasm to sell it to others. Since leaving a career with the Ministry of Natural Resources a year and a half earlier, I didn't know what career path to follow. I was drifting through life without a purpose.

During my drive home, the news on the radio was about Carlos Costa, a double leg amputee from Toronto, who successfully swam across Lake Ontario for Variety Village. When I heard the news about Costa, something clicked in my head. I felt inspired by his courage, determination, and desire to help others. With each broadcast of Costa's achievement, I felt inspired to do something like him. I wasn't a swimmer, but I could paddle. Somewhere on my drive home, I got the idea to paddle the Great Lakes and raise money for the Canadian Cancer Society.

Choosing to fundraise for cancer seemed like the only logical choice. I didn't have cancer, but I had watched my grandpa Herman and grandma Hill suffer through the disease and treatment. I was very close to both of them, and the tragedy of their experiences had left an indelible impression on me. If that wasn't reason enough, earlier that spring my mom had been scared that she had breast cancer after a questionable mammogram, and Fleur's mom had died of cancer when Fleur was only nine. Although I never knew Fleur's mom, I witnessed how the experience of losing a parent had continued to plague her in her adult life.

For the rest of my drive home, I kept thinking about the logistics of completing a trip on the Great Lakes. When I woke up the next day, I had made the decision. I was going to complete a fundraising trip for cancer. That same morning, I told my manager at Sunlife Insurance that I was quitting my job. Al didn't object. He had watched me putter away my time and fall short of his sales expectations for me during the past six months. When he asked me what I was going to do next, I was non-committal. I wasn't ready to tell anyone what I planned.

Fleur was the first person I told. Our break-up had lasted six days. One quick phone call had morphed into another and another and then the realization that maybe there was more to our relationship than we had originally thought. Fleur was quick to support my idea and never said a discouraging word.

Later that same week, I announced my plan to my parents. They didn't say much. I believe they were stunned by the news. They had watched me flounder aimlessly since leaving my career in fisheries management, and they didn't know what to make of my announcement. I am sure initially my parents didn't take me seriously, but even at that early stage, I was committed.

After living eighteen months without feeling excited, motivated, or proud about the work I was doing, I suddenly felt energized. I barely slept. I was too excited. I embarked on a project that galvanized everything that I had become, including *being* a salesman. I thought I hated being a salesman, yet I quickly learned that I had quit selling life insurance so I could start selling my idea of a fundraising kayak trip.

The methods I used to sell life insurance were the same skills I used to sell my trip—research, cold calls, query letters. The only difference was the product and my attitude. After selling life insurance I was used to rejection, but now, instead of feeling crushed when people turned away, I adopted a feeling that each *no* for support brought me closer to a *yes*.

In the beginning stages of planning I met a lot of rejection. I contacted my local chapter of the Canadian Cancer Society and told them about my idea. Someone I spoke with on the phone told me she would get back to me. She never did. I think they thought my idea for a fundraising trip was a joke. Undeterred, I went ahead with my plans to organize the trip, believing the cancer society would accept my fundraising idea when I looked more organized.

To make money and support myself, I took a job picking apples at a farm near my home outside of Bolton. In my spare time, I compiled a list of all the equipment I would need for the trip. The list was extensive: camping gear, paddling clothes, maps, food. This exercise helped me realize that I needed a sea kayak. Although I considered myself a canoeist and had only sat in a sea kayak a couple of times, I knew it would be a struggle for me to paddle a canoe from Thunder Bay to Toronto in a single summer.

To bridge the financial gap and to help pay for the trip, I started writing proposal letters seeking corporate sponsorship. I wrote to dozens of companies, offering them advertisement space on my kayak (which I didn't own yet), and potential media coverage once my trip was started, in exchange for cash or products. Over the next few weeks and months, replies slowly trickled back with varied responses. The beginning paragraph of each letter was very similar: "We admire your ambitious venture to raise money for cancer ..." With respect to supporting my trip, some simply declined, while others stated that they had already committed their budgets until 1996 or beyond, and that I should contact them for support in 1997. One company said they might be interested, but wanted to know who I was and what credentials I had to tackle such an outrageous endeavor, including letters of reference from fellow kayakers and kayak instructors. Falling back on my life insurance training, all I could think of was *next*, and search for a new company to solicit.

I set mid-May as the date for my departure from Thunder Bay. By the beginning of November 1993, I had not secured a single sponsor, and the Canadian Cancer Society hadn't sanctioned my fundraising trip. Naively, I still felt confident that somehow everything was going to work out. Why I felt confident that I could do the trip, I don't know. Except for Fleur, the initial reaction from my family and non-paddling friends was that I was crazy and that the trip was too dangerous. When I told some friends that I wasn't finding any corporate support, they suggested that I put the trip on hold for a year until I could find a group of sponsors. I flatly rejected their advice. I had become single-minded and determined to start the trip in the spring.

I remember deciding that if I failed to secure even one corporate sponsor for my trip, I was going to do it anyway. This decision included selling everything that I owned. I believe this complete unwavering commitment was the reason for my eventual success. Instead of focusing on possible reasons why I might fail, I continued to charge ahead, writing letters and making plans with the belief that I would succeed. I was living and acting on a philosophy called "the law of attraction," which states that what you think about and *believe* expands to become your reality. I filled my mind daily with a belief that sponsors would come.

At the same time, I took a new job as a janitor for a large hardware store in Bolton. My new job started at two in the afternoon, so the schedule allowed me time in the morning to begin my physical training program and work on finding potential sponsors.

My luck changed in mid-December when I received a fax from Steve Ree, president of Seaward Kayaks in Summerland, British Columbia. The company had received my proposal requesting product support, and they wanted to loan me a sea kayak for my solo expedition. I read the fax half a dozen times, analyzing every word, before believing it was true, and then I danced around my bedroom. I had secured my first sponsor. Now that I had a sea kayak, the trip was official.

I was jubilant, but I sensed that my parents were not happy. They said very little to me but appeared shocked that a B.C. company would loan me a new sea kayak. I suspect they realized then that I was serious, and really planned to do the trip. Until then, with no kayak, I think they saw my idea as only a pipe dream.

The promise of a sea kayak triggered a change in my ability to find sponsors. From that point forward, when I wrote a proposal letter, I could state that I already had an official sponsor (Seaward Kayaks). This fact seemed to soothe some corporate fears of being the first or only sponsor. Just like a dance, nobody wanted to be the first on the dance floor, but now that someone had endorsed me, others wanted to join in the party.

Over the next few months, letters of corporate support came back from Tilley Endurables, Hi-Tec Sports, The Original Bug Shirt Company, Nimbus Paddles, Mustang Survival, Effem Foods, Harvest Foodworks, General Ecology Inc., Mountain Equipment Co-op, Gatorade Sports, Mountain Dreams, and Tim Ingram, the inventor of the 'Sea Wing' self-rescue kayak sponsons.

In early December, I turned my attention to the Canadian Cancer Society, with hopes of gaining its endorsement for me to raise funds on the organization's behalf. My original efforts to speak with someone at the regional office in Brampton had ended with my initial phone call. I don't remember how I heard about Alice Train. Someone I knew must have told me to call her. Alice was a volunteer with the Bolton chapter of the Canadian Cancer Society. She was a cancer survivor and a foot soldier involved with anything the society organized. Whether it was selling daffodils in April, driving cancer patients for treatment, or helping to organize the Terry Fox Run, Alice was heavily involved on a local level.

I remember the day I called Alice for the first time. She had a strong, gravelly voice, like someone who was a pack-a-day smoker, but her passion for anything that involved wiping out cancer was unwavering. Alice listened patiently while I told her my plans and failure to get support from the cancer society. If I needed a champion, Alice Train was the perfect candidate. She knew nothing about kayaking or expedition travel, but she made me feel like what I planned to do was not just possible, but a great idea. Alice gave me the one piece of advice I needed to hear.

"Forget the regional office, Michael. Your idea is beyond them; you have to talk to the people at the top. You have to call the Ontario division of the Canadian Cancer Society in Toronto."

When I called the Ontario division, nobody wanted to hear my fundraising idea over the phone. Instead, I was instructed to send them a written proposal with clear ideas stating what I hoped to achieve. I mailed them my proposal, explaining my idea for a fundraising kayak trip, my reasons why, how I thought the cancer society would benefit, and the list of sponsors committed to my project. While I waited for a reply,

I trained, worked, and continued to mail proposal letters to potential sponsors.

It never occurred to me that the cancer society would turn me down. My fundraising idea made perfect sense to *me*, even though some people thought a solo kayak trip sounded crazy. Every day was spent looking for possible sponsors or thinking of ways to raise funds.

One day I went to the local grocery store and saw something I hadn't noticed in the past. Below the giant IGA sign was the slogan, "Hometown Proud." I stared at the sign and had a revelation. I had been looking for sponsors far and wide when all along I had a hometown sponsor waiting to be asked. I pitched the idea of connecting my fundraising trip with IGA's 'hometown proud' slogan to Mark Knoester, the manager of the Bolton IGA store.

My original hope was to receive some food and a business location to collect cash donations. Mark loved my idea and immediately put me in touch with Jim James, director of marketing for Oshawa Foods. Jim liked my idea too, and he saw its full potential as a marketing tool for IGA and the Canadian Cancer Society. In exchange for advertising space on my kayak, I would receive food coupons redeemable at IGA stores on my route, and IGA would advertise my fundraising trip three times during the summer in their price flyer, which published 1.8 million copies each week. I couldn't ask for better publicity.

In early January, Mark Climie from the Ontario division of the Canadian Cancer Society called me for a meeting to discuss my proposal. I drove to Toronto dressed in my best business suit. To Mark it may have been a meeting to discuss a fundraising proposal, but to me it was a job. It didn't take me long to realize that Mark wasn't convinced it was a good idea for the cancer society to get involved. He saw significant risks and little hope for monetary gain. For the first time, it occurred to me that the cancer society might not want my help.

"Michael," Mark began, "you have to realize I get fundraising proposals sent to me every day. Stacks," he added, holding his hand above his desk to emphasize the point. "Somebody wants to run across Canada. Another wants to rollerblade. What happens, god forbid, if you have an accident? People will hold us responsible for you. We can't afford that kind of negative publicity. How are people going to donate? You need some way to collect money."

The meeting went long into the day as obstacles to the idea of me kayaking the Great Lakes were raised and solutions discussed. I don't know what convinced Mark to agree to my plan. Whether it was my conviction or the fact that I had already secured sponsors, eventually we reached a deal. I had the blessing of the Canadian Cancer Society to raise funds on their behalf. For my part, I promised to radio the Canadian Coast Guard as often as possible so people would know I was safe.

I drove home feeling both ecstatic that I finally had the support of the cancer society and driven to find a way to collect donations. When I left Mark's office, I realized that I couldn't simply ask for donations and expect that people were going to give money.

I approached the question of how to raise funds the same way I tackled the need for corporate sponsors. I focused on my goal and never let rejection or fear of failure take hold of my thoughts. It was simply a matter of exploring ideas until a solution was found.

The solution for collecting donations came to me during a later conversation with Jim James from Oshawa Foods. I had already thought about having a donation can in the Bolton IGA store, so when I learned that the weekly price flyers were shipped out of the Toronto food terminal to one hundred and eighty-four IGA stores across the province, I had an idea. With the support of Jim James and Oshawa foods, I would put donation cans in every IGA store across Ontario. Jim James would secure support for the use of the donation cans from the independent store owners, and I would provide the cans.

I phoned Mark Climie the same day that Jim and I made the agreement. I was excited about the idea, and I wanted Mark to know that I was still developing a fundraising campaign. Mark liked my news and suggested we use donation boxes the cancer society could buy from a supplier. Cardboard donation boxes would cost a dollar each, and plastic boxes would cost two dollars. My mind raced ahead quickly, doing the math. With two cans per store, that added up to a significant expense before we received our first donation. I told Mark that I didn't want to start by putting the cancer society in debt before I raised any money. I needed to find donation cans for free.

When I searched the yellow pages in the phone book, I was shocked to discover that my hometown of Bolton had a manufacturing company that made tin cans. I phoned Bob Carter of Crown, Cork, and Seal. After

I briefly explained my trip and my fundraising plans, I asked him if his company would be willing to donate tin cans to be used for fundraising. Bob was enthusiastic about the opportunity to become involved in my project and donated fifteen hundred cans, each with a customized piggy bank-style slot in the top.

The next step was to make labels that would identify the cans with my "Kayaking for Cancer—A Celebration of Life" fundraising campaign. I designed the label and then faxed it to Mark for approval. He made a few minor suggestions on the lettering and insisted that to be approved by the cancer society; the colour had to be the exact shade of red as the cancer society's logo.

I had the labels made at Leavens Printers in Bolton. The owner agreed to print the fifteen hundred labels at a discounted price of sixty dollars. After considering the previous cost that Mark had quoted me for donation boxes, I was happy to pay the sixty dollars myself as a gift to the cancer society.

The final stage of preparing the donation cans was labeling. My grandma Pat offered to help me put labels on the cans. I brought the fifteen boxes to her house and we spent hours taping labels on cans. When my cousins Jennifer and Owen Smith learned what we were doing, they came and helped too. Some days Jennifer brought her friend Linda Valente. For many nights we sat in my grandma's kitchen drinking hot chocolate and tea, talking while we labeled cans late into the evening. I appreciated their help and enjoyed sharing my dream with them. When we labeled the last can, we let out a collective cheer, and then we taped the box shut.

I never asked anyone for help during the months of planning and preparation. Right or wrong, I saw my trip and fundraising plans as *my* project and *my* responsibility. If someone offered to help, I never turned them away, but I never asked for help, and I never expected it. I later learned that this hurt and upset my parents very much. They felt I had excluded them from my dream. From my side, I didn't think they wanted me to do the trip. I felt that if they wanted to help, they would offer. Our different points of view and feelings around being included created a widening rift between us that eventually erupted in a showdown.

Early one evening they confronted me at the kitchen table and shared their anger and hurt. Feeling that they didn't approve from the beginning, all I could do was sit and quietly listen. My mom was the most vocal, complaining about me making long distance phone calls and fax messages. My parent's phone bill was paid by my dad's company as part of his salary, so I didn't understand the issue they were raising. But phone calls and faxes were not the real issue. The real source of their angst was revealed when they questioned why I hadn't asked them for help, or more accurately, why I hadn't included them in my dream. I don't remember all of the words spoken that day, mostly sentiments, but I do remember my mom losing her temper.

"Michael, you walk around here in your own world without any idea what this plan of yours is doing to us. You are not letting us in. How do you plan to get your stuff and the kayak to Thunder Bay? Did you ever think to ask your dad?"

Their reaction took me by surprise. Since the family condemnation at Christmas over my plan to kayak the Great Lakes, I thought they were against my idea. Feeling attacked, I lashed back in defense.

"You don't even want me to do this trip, so why would I ask you for help? I don't know how I am getting to Thunder Bay, but if I have to, I'll drive my truck and sell it when I get there."

I would never have thought to ask my dad to drive me. That seemed too much to expect or ask. I also didn't understand my parents' need to be needed. I don't remember much more. I do remember a long moment of silence, a kind of collective deep breath and slow exhale. Afterward, we made up. Like close families do, we vented, we listened to each other, and then we moved on. I asked my dad to drive me to Thunder Bay, and he agreed. Family bonds and commitment held us together.

The next week I delivered the donation cans to the Toronto Food Terminal, Oshawa Foods' shipping point for the food and weekly price flyers. My part was done. It was now up to Jim James and the owners of independent IGA stores across Ontario to help collect donations from their customers.

During the time spent seeking support from the cancer society and writing proposals to sponsors, I was also working and training physically to stay fit. My day was a routine. Eat breakfast, go for a forty-five minute cross-country ski that included as many uphill climbs as I could create in a circuit, come home and row for an hour and a half on a rowing machine, stop to plan my trip, and then repeat the exercise regime after lunch before leaving for work in the afternoon. I exercised and trained every day. On Thursday nights, to work on my cardio endurance, I played basketball with guys who were taller than me and pushed myself not to take a break. For toning and developing my arm muscles, I used light hand-held barbells.

The other part of my training schedule included reading volumes of books about kayaking skills and stories about people who had completed long distance kayak expeditions. My plan was to learn everything that I could about kayaking skills from a book. This was not the most practical approach, but it was still helpful when I applied the information to my canoeing background.

From a psychological aspect, I filled my mind with stories about people who had successfully completed sea kayak expeditions. My goal was to focus my thoughts on stories of success. I believed that this would help to form the foundation for a deep belief that my solo expedition was "do-able." I also believed strongly that all achievements are first completed in the mind as an idea, and then from a belief in success.

During the winter, I trained my mind to visualize myself safely kayaking each of the Great Lakes and arriving in Toronto to a crowd of family and friends. Hans Lindemenn, a German doctor who crossed the Atlantic from the Canary Islands to the Virgin Islands, first in a dugout canoe, and then in a rubber kayak, was my inspiration. I read his story, *An Impossible Voyage*, and adopted his technique of using auto suggestions to program his mind for success. Like Lindemenn, I concentrated on phrases such as "I will succeed, I will make it" and "Never give up" during my winter training until my whole being, on a conscious and subconscious level, was convinced that I would succeed.

By March, my efforts to secure sponsors had ended, and I was busy each day working on the logistics of the trip. I planned menus and purchased maps and gear. I established contacts with radio and television stations and with people living in towns on each of the Great Lakes who were willing to store food for months until I arrived. While I worked on planning the trip, my mind wandered in search of new, additional ways to collect donations. It was the memory of selling chocolate bars in grade six for a school fundraising that sparked my next idea.

As I remember it, all of the students in my school had competed to sell the most chocolate bars, and the winner was promised a new sailboat.

My idea was similar. I would approach local schools for students willing to collect donations for Kayaking for Cancer, and the prize for the most money collected would be a family pass to watch the Toronto Blue Jays. After the team won back to back World Series in the previous two seasons, 1992 and 1993, Jays tickets were a valuable prize.

If this sounds outrageous or presumptuous on my part, the oddest thing was that I didn't feel this way. I had a goal to raise money for the Canadian Cancer Society, and I explored every possible idea without self- doubt or embarrassment. I had become the thick-skinned salesman my insurance sales manager had hoped I would be.

I sent a proposal letter outlining my idea to Peter Cosentino, manager of community relations for the Toronto Blue Jays. Two weeks later he called me. He couldn't get involved in a fundraising effort that used kids, but he did have an idea of how he could help. Peter offered to promote my fundraising trip during the pre-game show at the SkyDome. I would be introduced to the spectators and information about the trip and requests for donations would be shown on the Jumbo Tron. I didn't need to think very long about the idea before I accepted. It was great publicity, and although I wasn't a huge baseball fan, the offer was thrilling.

I arrived at the SkyDome with my parents and my younger sister, Crystal. We entered the stadium through a high-security service door in the belly of the dome and were escorted onto the field near the Blue Jays' dugout. The experience was surreal, more dreamlike than anything else.

I remember at one point looking up at the Jumbo Tron and seeing words move across the screen: Michael Herman, Kayaking for Cancer, Thunder Bay to Toronto from May 14–September 17, please make donations at your local IGA store, or contact your local Canadian Cancer Society office. I also remember standing at the pitcher's mound and receiving a Toronto Blue Jays' sweatshirt and autographed ball cap from Mike Huff, a new member of the Blue Jays team.

After I received my shirt and hat, the team photographer took a few pictures of me and my family before we were escorted to our seats to watch the game. Unfortunately, the Jays lost to the White Sox 9-2, but the details are etched in my memory: me standing in the infield of the 1993 defending World Series champions. For a baseball fan, it was an enviable experience.

During the month of April, I was busy completing the final preparations. I had divided my route into thirty-kilometre daily sections and recorded map reference points such as, Stony Point and Boogey Beach, so family and friends could follow my progress. I purchased last minute gear with money given by close family members wanting to express their love and support.

By the end of April I had completed all preparations for my trip. There was nothing to do but train, and wait to leave for Thunder Bay.

Saying Goodbye

================

On Tuesday May 10, after eight months of planning, my dad and I began our drive to Thunder Bay with my kayak and a mountain of gear and boxes of food. Our first stop was in Parry Sound, to say goodbye to my friends Mark, Cathy, and Peter and enjoy a bon voyage barbecue dinner. The three of them were my closest and dearest friends, and it meant a great deal to me to have the chance to spend the evening with them before leaving for Thunder Bay. After dinner, Mark produced a bottle of champagne to toast my kayak and the trip. We gathered around the kayak while Mark made a gesture to smash the bottle over the bow of the boat. Thankfully, he decided against the nautical tradition and we settled for pouring a few drops of champagne over the bow before drinking the rest. I could only imagine what the neighbours were thinking if they were watching the five of us on the street passing around a champagne bottle.

No one shared any feelings of fear for me that night, but I could sense they were worried. Peter said the most of anyone before he left. He told me that it felt strange that I was going without him. After all of the canoe trips that we had done together, he told me that he felt that he should be coming too. I sensed that he wanted to say more to me. Perhaps he wanted to tell me to be careful, or say something like, "Don't be stupid out there." He never found the words, but I knew anyway. We had been friends a long time.

The next morning my dad and I ate breakfast with Mark and Cathy before we left for Sault Ste. Marie. Mark offered to be my *go-for* for anything I needed when I reached Parry Sound in July. I was deeply touched by the support. That night, I wrote in my journal, *It felt good to have friends who care so much. The feelings warmed my heart, and will give me support when I am alone on my trip.*

My dad and I arrived in Sault Ste. Marie around three in the afternoon, and I immediately called the MCTV news director, Greg Vanasperen, to arrange an interview. It was going to be a few weeks before I kayaked into town, but I wanted to create a buzz about my trip so people would be looking for me when I arrived. I met a reporter and cameraman at the Roberta Bondar Park on the St. Mary's River and gave my first interview. Afterward, my dad and I dropped off a food cache with Kirk Kinghorn, a cousin of a family friend, and then checked into the Skyline Motel. After ordering take-out pizza, we drank a few beers and watched TV, neither of us mentioning my trip. We were only halfway to Thunder Bay but we had already retreated into our own thoughts to cope with the fact I would soon be kayaking alone on Lake Superior.

We stopped only a few times on the way to Thunder Bay. In Katherine's Cove, the bay was blocked solid with ice, so we stopped to have a look. Mark Climie had told me on Monday that he had heard that Black Bay on Superior's north shore was still iced in. He had suggested that I postpone my departure date until the ice on Superior melted, but I had declined, stating that I was determined to start and finish on my fixed dates. The ice in Katherine's Cove was solid, and I wished that my dad hadn't seen it. We left food caches at the Lake Superior Provincial Park office at Red Rock Lake and with Madeline Watt in Marathon. Each box contained three weeks' rations of food and camp fuel for my stove.

We arrived in Thunder Bay at five thirty, on the doorstep of friends just in time for supper. Cindy and Jim Rusak were old friends that I had known when I worked for the Ministry of Natural Resources in Dryden and Ignace. Cindy and Jim were both biologists, and we had shared fishing and camping trips together over two summers in the late eighties. I had not seen them since their wedding three years earlier, but they had offered me a place to stay when I told them about my trip. My dad and I felt completely welcome, even though their house was small, and they had twin boys aged four that were as wild as tomcats.

The following day was a whirlwind of excitement, confusion, and last-minute preparations. At nine in the morning, I had an interview with Mickey from *The Post* newspaper. At ten thirty I had an interview with CBC radio host Fred Jones. I filed a sail plan with the Canadian Coast Guard so that I could check in and let people know that I was safe. Filing a sail plan had been a condition for me to receive endorsement by the Canadian Cancer Society. The society was worried that something could happen to me, and they wanted some kind of safety net in place. When I met with Terry Nishibata, the Canadian Coast Guard representative, he wanted me to file a sail plan and call in every day. This way, if something prevented me from contacting the coast guard, an emergency response would be triggered and a search and rescue plane would be dispatched. I couldn't accept those terms, and after much debate we agreed that I would call every five days with my VHF radio. I didn't think I was very likely to call the coast guard in an emergency. With the ice just melted, I expected the water temperature to be somewhere between 0 and 4 degrees Celsius. If I had a serious accident on the water, I was going to have to rescue myself. The only practical help I believed the coast guard would be able to offer would be if I was stranded and my kayak was lost or broken.

When we started to fill in the official document, the form asked for a vessel name, which would become my official call signal. Initially I was stumped, and then I thought of the famous ship the Mayflower, which carried the pilgrims from England to Plymouth, Massachusetts in 1620. I named my kayak the *Mai Fleur*, combining the French words Mai (the starting month of my trip) and Fleur (which was my girlfriend's given name). Hoping to borrow some luck from the Mayflower, I thought the name was perfect.

At four o'clock I had a last minute interview with CKPR radio before rushing back for dinner at Cindy and Jim's. Their sons, Mathew and Aaron, and a couple of bottles of red wine were good distractions from talking about the thick ice still evident on Superior.

My dad had become increasingly quiet during the day, and before supper he had asked Jim if he would take me and my kayak to the marina in the morning. He had decided not to be there when I began my trip, explaining that he wanted to leave for home early in the morning. By nine that evening my dad was asleep, snoring on a foam mattress on the living-room floor. I could tell he was stressed about me starting my trip, but there was nothing I could do.

My mom called after supper to wish me luck and tell me that she loved me. I had never thought about how my decision to do this trip would affect my parents, but that night I felt deeply guilty. I was now fully aware that, even though I was an adult, my parents were worried about me. A little while later, Fleur called me on a CB radio phone from her tree-planting camp north of Sioux Lookout. I never expected to hear from her, and the surprise was a wonderful gift. Fleur exuded so much enthusiasm and excitement for my trip that my spirit felt lifted simply from hearing her voice. We spoke for only a few short minutes, but her message to me was clear: *I love you. Be careful. I will meet you in Sault Ste. Marie.* When I hung up the phone I felt as though all of my emotional loose ends were tied. I felt ready, but I stayed up organizing my gear. Packing a kayak is much different than loading a canoe. Instead of packing everything into a large canoe pack, items need to be organized into smaller bags that can be stuffed into the small storage space in the kayak's hull. During my dry run packing that afternoon, I realized that I didn't have enough stuff sacks, so Cindy stayed up with me and sewed five nylon bags with drawstrings so they could be tied closed. It was midnight on May 14 when I eventually went to bed.

A Journey Begins

===================

MY DAD'S ALARM clock went off at 6:00 a.m. He quickly dressed and prepared to leave. I knew he wanted to say goodbye before anyone got up. He was very emotional and hugged me tight to hide his face. During the few minutes we had together, my dad didn't say a lot, but his feelings were obvious. He told me he loved me and to trust my instincts. It was a difficult goodbye for each of us. I wished I had a crystal ball so that I could show him that I would be okay. I felt guilty for causing him to worry about me. Then he left for home.

I ate a quick breakfast and then Cindy, Jim, Aaron, Mathew, and I headed for Marina Park. Soon after we arrived, people started to join us. There were cancer society volunteers, curious onlookers, and local residents who had heard me on the radio and wanted to see me leave. People talked with me while I slowly packed the kayak from end to end with food, camping gear, warm clothes, and personal items. Packing a kayak is a thoughtful process. Each item had to be packed in order of need, but consideration also had to be given to weight distribution. It wouldn't work if the bow was heavier than the stern. More than once, someone would jokingly ask, "Is all that stuff going to fit?" and I would reply with a grin, "I hope so." I finished packing shortly after nine and by then there was a small crowd. I hugged Cindy and Jim and thanked them for their help. A few people walked up and wished me luck, but most simply watched from a distance. Jim and I struggled to carry the loaded kayak to the edge of the lake. The weight was staggering—my food and gear easily weighed more than a hundred and fifty kilograms. I climbed into the cockpit, stretched the spray skirt over the opening, and silently waved goodbye.

As I dipped my paddle into the water for the first stroke, I felt like a child taking my first tentative steps into a new world. I could feel everyone's eyes on my back, not judgmentally, but nervously, caring, encouraging. Just as the little boy sets his toy boat adrift in the story *Paddle to the Sea*, they too were setting me adrift. My fate was out of their hands now. Breaking the rhythm of my paddle strokes, I stopped and turned around to wave. I had only paddled a dozen strokes but already the group on shore appeared much smaller. I felt a great sense of relief at leaving behind the worries of others. Their fears had felt like I was wearing a heavy winter coat. Now, as I paddled away from shore, I was shedding their worried thoughts and fears. I felt lighter, empowered, and free. Strangely, I had no doubts or fears about the journey ahead of me. I was exactly where I wanted to be, doing what I wanted to do. The dark sky hung low overhead, but I didn't care. Leaving the marina was already the fulfillment of a dream.

Paddling outside the breakwater, I headed northeast towards the top of Thunder Bay. After twenty minutes of paddling, it began to rain and fog moved in around me. At first the rain drops fell undetected except for the ring that formed when they hit the water. Then, drop by drop the rain began to fall harder. Strangely enough, I enjoyed the sensation. I was bonding with my new environment. Each sound and sensation I experienced brought me closer to a world I gladly welcomed. For the first time in a long time, I was alone—alone with my thoughts, dreams, and prayers. Unlike some people, I enjoy being alone, not as a hermit who prefers to live in private isolation, but alone for the opportunity to truly explore my inner thoughts.

Including Others

A FTER ALMOST FOUR hours of continuous paddling in the rain, I felt the sudden need to pee. Studying my topographic map, I decided I must be at Silver Harbour. The problem was that I couldn't relieve myself while sitting in my kayak. The double layers of underwear and sealed dry suit made the idea completely unthinkable. Seeing homes and cottages on shore made me leery of landing the kayak and peeing in front of someone's window.

Pushing onward, I hoped the buildings would disappear before my bladder exploded. Another ten minutes of paddling forced me to do something. I had to go pee. Immediately! I saw a thin column of smoke rising from the chimney of the next cottage, and I decided to land there. Changing course toward shore, I quickly noticed sand beneath my kayak. Fifteen metres from shore my paddle blades began to touch bottom with each stroke. A couple of half strokes and it was too shallow for me to continue. Climbing out of the kayak, I grabbed the bowline and dragged the kayak inland. The last seven metres were only a few centimetres deep, so I left the heavily loaded boat beached in the shallow water.

As I walked up to the house, I noticed faces staring out from a large picture window. I stood in front of the side door and rehearsed my lines. I looked down at myself and realized that I must look strange to them. My red and blue nylon dry suit looked like the space suit worn by Robin Williams in the '70s television show *Mork & Mindy*. My feet were covered in black neoprene booties, and my head was covered in a black neoprene diving hood and wide brimmed Tilley hat. Laughing nervously to myself, I knocked on the door. Instantly, the door opened and a young man appeared.

"Hi, my name is Michael Herman. Do you have an outhouse I could use?" I asked sheepishly.

He looked at me with an awkward stare showing his disbelief of my question. Then he turned his head and shouted, "Dad, he wants to know if we have an outhouse he can use."

"He can use your uncle's next door," the hidden voice from inside called out. Turning back to me, the young man stuck his head out of the door and pointed toward a small square building.

"You can use my uncle Bill's next door," he offered.

As I ran off to the outhouse, I realized I couldn't have waited much longer. The call of nature can be very impatient when put on hold for too long. I wasn't sure if I could get my clothes off in time. Tilley hat, neoprene diving hood, life jacket, unzip the dry suit, gently pull the sleeves off, slip my head through, pull the suit down, then two layers of underwear. *Oh my god, hurry up before you piss yourself,* I thought to myself. *Ahhh! How am I going to control this for the next month?* I wondered. I redressed in reverse order. Walking back toward the house I decided to stop and thank the family for the use of their outhouse. Seeing me standing outside the open door, a woman came over to greet me.

"Hi. Are you the guy we heard on the radio this morning who's kayaking to Toronto?" she asked.

"Yeah, I guess I am," I answered, not knowing what else to say.

"Would you like to come in for lunch?" the woman asked. "We just sat down," she added. As I peeked inside, I could see that the place looked warm and inviting, with cushioned couches, central heating, and a dining table covered in food.

Usually I would refuse once out of politeness, not wanting to impose. That day I didn't. In that split second I decided to share my trip with as many people as I could.

"Yes, thank you, I'd love to join you," I answered.

Two hours later I pushed myself away from the Halabisky family dinner table. Warm and stuffed to contentment, I felt a little reluctant to leave. During the course of my visit I had been warmly embraced by Rick and Lorraine and their two children, Brad and Tanis. Listening to family stories of summer life at Silver Beach seemed much more pleasant than re-entering the cold rainstorm outside. However, I knew it was time to leave.

Once I was fully dressed, the Halabiskys escorted me outside to my kayak. Huddled together arm in arm, my hosts stood in the rain as I walked the kayak into deeper water before climbing inside. Nestled in my seat with the spray skirt tightly fastened to keep out the water, I turned and waved to four human figures that had touched my life. Instantly they waved back in unison. Silently, I slipped my hands into the neoprene mitts that were attached to my kayak paddle. As I paddled away I thought about the sociology of human relationships and connection. A day ago I could have walked past this family on the street or in a shopping mall without any connection. Depending on the circumstances we might not have even acknowledged each other. Today we were acquaintances, and I felt enriched and comforted from our meeting.

I doubt there is anything more powerful than human touch and a feeling of connection with others. It seems as basic a requirement to our survival as food and shelter, yet so many people go without. Looking at my own life, I felt truly fortunate to have so many caring people whose presence I could feel even now.

Icebergs

S OON AFTER I left Silver Harbour, thin traces of fog began to appear again. Drifting by like trails of white smoke, the fog quickly grew thicker until it filled in around me. Everything was white except for the grey images of the trees on shore. As I paddled, I felt the cold wind against the bare skin around my eyes. The rest of my body was covered against the cold, but these areas were bare and they felt the harshness of the weather. Steam escaped from my mouth and nose with each new breath. I felt certain the rain would change to snow at any moment, but instead of feeling unhappy, I felt like I was in my glory. *Man, this is great,* I thought to myself. *I'm actually here, doing it!* So many people thought I was crazy or that I couldn't plan this trip, let alone do it, that I felt in my glory just to be there. I didn't care about the rain or the cold. The weather was just part of the adventure, and I wanted all that I could get.

Due to the fog, I was unable to measure my progress by matching points of land with references on my map, so I simply paddled parallel to shore. As long as I could distinguish the trees through the fog, I knew I was headed toward the top of Thunder Bay, where I hoped to camp for the night.

After an hour of steady paddling, I noticed thick chunks of ice the size of dinner plates floating in the water beside me. With each new paddle stroke, the ice began to get bigger and the wind, which had merely been a discomfort, was now creating an endless series of onshore waves. In a matter of minutes, I was paddling among thick ice sheets bigger than dining room tables. Pushed by the increased wind, the ice was a real danger to my fragile kayak, and I knew I needed to find safety quickly.

I studied the shore through the fog but could not see any place to escape onto land. The lakeshore was a fortress of large boulders and ice, preventing me from going to shore. I was stranded, with no choice but to continue paddling through the ice. Sometimes I was forced to paddle quickly between two colliding islands of ice. My mind raced with questions. *Where am I going? What's ahead? What if I get trapped inside a circle of ice?* Yet, even with those concerns to think about, I also loved every minute. Somewhere inside me was a kid saying, "Bring it on. Scare me some more. I want a real adventure." So I kept paddling.

Slowly through the fog a grey silhouette of land and trees appeared on my right. An island? Hopeful for an escape route, I changed my direction and wove my way through the large chunks of ice. After twenty minutes of slow progress, I finally reached the island and was surprised to discover a small natural harbour. Created by a rocky, peninsula that stretched out from shore like an arm bent at the elbow, the harbour offered safe access to shore. Slipping past the mouth of the harbour, I breathed a sigh of relief. I was out of the ice.

PRIVATE PROPERTY

INSIDE THE PROTECTION of the small harbour, I slowly navigated the kayak to shore, trying not to scratch the virgin hull. Still unscathed from any contact with rocks, I felt determined to keep the *Mai Fleur* in mint condition for as long as possible. My kayak and I had a long way to travel together, and safety was imperative to my success. Stepping out of the kayak was a great relief. Still unaccustomed to sitting for long periods of time, my legs enjoyed the freedom of movement.

As I dragged the kayak up onto a grass clearing at the head of the harbour, I was reminded how much stuff I was carrying. The weight of my loaded kayak was crazy. The chance of having grass available each time I needed to come ashore was very small, and I worried about the imminent problems it would cause. The kayak was both my vehicle and home, which meant that everything I needed I carried with me in the kayak: food, clothes, camping gear, camera equipment, books, maps. The list seemed endless, yet everything was essential; there was very little I could discard to lighten my load.

Anxious to find a place to set up camp, I left the kayak and explored the island on foot. I hiked up a rocky slope and discovered a beautiful house standing on a flat clearing high above the lake. My heart sank in disappointment when I saw *No Trespassing* signs nailed to several trees. Immediately, I felt uncomfortable being there. I expected to have some difficulty finding unoccupied land to camp on in southern Ontario, but not this early in my trip. The thought of the owner discovering me increased these feelings, so I decided to announce myself and ask for permission to camp. Walking toward the building, I noticed it appeared empty. Lifeless. No lights. No smoke escaped from the chimney. No human activity. I walked around the building and tried to peek inside. The drapes were pulled shut on each window. This was obviously someone's summer cottage. Satisfied that no one was there, I walked back toward the kayak.

Interested in seeing more of the island, I chose a different route and saw something that caught my attention. Almost invisible in the fog and camouflaged by branches, was a silver-grey dome tent. I stopped dead in my tracks. Maybe someone is inside, I thought.

"Anyone in the tent?" I called out. No answer. Maybe they hadn't heard me over the sound of the rain. "Hello! Anyone in the tent?" I shouted again. Nothing. Hmm. The oddity of a lone tent set up this time of year made me hesitate before jerking the zipper door open. The inside was empty except for a cardboard box with a cook pot inside and a small portable radio the size of a pocket novel. Small puddles of water had formed in two corners of the tent. The rest of the tent was dry. I stepped inside out of the rain.

The tent was much bigger than my own, with a higher ceiling. Four people could easily sleep side by side without any discomfort. I picked up the small transistor and turned it on. Instantly, static hissed from its speaker. I turned the tuning dial and magically, Garth Brooks' voice escaped into the tent. Listening to the music, I pondered the moral ethics of camping in the tent for the night.

It's pouring rain, this tent is already up, and it's already wet.

Yes, but it's not your tent, I argued with myself. *And you don't have permission.*

I was torn by the choice. I didn't like the thought of setting up my dry tent in the rain, but I wasn't overly comfortable using someone's tent without their permission. Eventually, I gave in to laziness and defended my decision with the argument that the owners wouldn't mind.

Later, after a couple of trips to the kayak for supplies, I was dressed in warm, dry clothes and eating bread, chunks of Gouda cheese, and a chocolate bar. The rain fell hard and relentless. I felt little enthusiasm to cook dinner outside the comfort of the tent. My kayak clothes were damp, and unlike in my tent, there was no way to hang a clothesline inside for them to dry. I crawled into my sleeping bag feeling cold, tired, and lonely. For comfort, I listened to music and people talking on the radio until the tent was dark. With darkness soon around me, I quickly fell asleep with the hope of sunny skies in the morning.

Early Wake-up

A T 5:30 A.M., I woke to the sound of people talking outside of the tent. Afraid to be found on private property, I quickly pulled on my damp clothes and scrambled outside to explain why I was there. Standing in my long underwear and neoprene boots, I listened carefully. I heard nothing. Convincing myself that my conscience was imagining things, I returned to the tent. I slipped off my boots and crawled back into my sleeping bag to get warm. Unwilling to get up so early, I curled myself into a ball and went back to sleep.

An hour later, I woke again and decided to check on the weather. The sky was filled with grey insulation that blocked out the sun, but the fog had finally disappeared. Realizing the day might not get any better, I quickly packed my belongings and ate a hurried breakfast of cold cereal and an orange.

The tiny harbour where I had pulled my boat ashore yesterday was calm, and I easily launched my kayak into the water. I paddled around the west side of the unknown island and instantly I could see Caribou Island in the distance. For the first time since the previous afternoon, I knew where I was.

As I skirted the west side of Caribou Island, I could see the rock cliffs of Sibley Peninsula calling out to be noticed. Towering above a mixed stand of trembling aspen and white birch trees, the jagged rock faces beckoned me to hike to their crown. *Maybe another time,* I promised myself as I continued to paddle toward the tip of the peninsula known as the Sleeping Giant because it resembles the profile of a giant lying on its back.

Pushed by a northwest wind, gentle, rolling swells moved under me and carried the kayak toward land. As each new wave grew bigger, I suddenly found myself surfing down the backside of rolling waves three metres high. Uncomfortable with the kayak's sudden burst of speed, I back-paddled in an effort to slow down. Each time a large swell grabbed and pushed me toward shore, my kayak would turn sideways, threatening to roll. The conditions were dangerous and worrisome. Nervously, I steered with the rudder and my paddle blade. By the time I reached Hoorigan Point, the swells had died down enough for me to relax and enjoy the help of the wind. Without any impending dangers to think about, I began to notice that my feet felt like two blocks of ice. Even though they were protected by a pair of wool socks and aging neoprene boots, my feet screamed at me for warmth. I wanted desperately to go ashore and get warm, but I couldn't see an easy place to land the kayak. The shoreline was fiercely guarded by large boulders which threatened to damage my boat's hull if I got too close. Uncomfortable with my choices of where to go ashore, I reluctantly pushed on to Sawyer Bay five kilometres away.

Northern Hospitality

W HEN I REACHED the shelter of Sawyer Bay an hour later, I was desperately cold and hungry. Still worried about cracking the hull on the large rocks, I anchored the boat in the water three metres from shore. By the time I finished unpacking the stove and food for lunch, my hands and feet were begging for relief from the cold. My hands were too cold to light the stove, so I ran along the shoreline flapping my arms like an albatross taking flight. Scrambling clumsily over the rocks, I forced myself to stop before I slipped and hurt myself.

A slow fifteen minutes later my hands were wrapped around a steaming mug of tomato soup trying to unthaw. I looked at my watch and couldn't believe it was May 15. Regardless of the date, winter weather had not left, and I wondered how long it planned to stay. After eating my soup and a frozen chocolate bar, I cleaned my dishes and repacked the kayak.

As soon as I stepped back into the water, the cold sucked all of the precious heat from my body. Instantly, I felt cold again. I left the bay and followed the shoreline to Thunder Cape at the foot of the Sleeping Giant. From there I had a clear view of Isle Royale. I thought about the first time I heard about the island. It was during a high school biology class while watching a film by Bill Mason called *Death of a Legend*. The Canadian National Film Board documentary was filmed at Isle Royale and described the life history of wolves and their misunderstood role within the food chain.

Looking across the open water, I wondered how long it would take me to paddle to the island. It didn't look that far across the water, but I knew the distance was deceiving. Opening the spray skirt, I grabbed the map from the shelf above my knees. A quick glance was all I needed to realize the idea was out of the question. Without measuring, I could see it was well over twenty-five kilometres to the island. All alone, the exposure to sudden changes in wind or wave conditions could be catastrophic. I put the map away and decided to continue on my planned route.

In the late afternoon, I arrived at Silver Islet. There were no signs of any people as I paddled my kayak into the shelter behind the small rock breakwater. Cold and a little tired from the steady use of weak muscles, I beached my boat on shore near a weather-beaten wood building. Pulling my legs free of the kayak, I stood up and rubbed my buttocks like a saddle-sore cowboy. The place looked deserted. I climbed the grassy slope and walked to the front of a large two story building with a sign that read "general store" and displayed two metal soda pop ads nailed to the outside wall. Interested in how the store looked on the inside, I pressed my face against the window and strained for a peek between the newspaper and curtains that blocked the windows. Unable to see much, I stepped back and suddenly heard voices coming from further up the hill.

I was anxious to meet anyone from the area, so I followed the sounds of the voices to a small cottage with a wrap-around porch facing the lake. I was met by two friendly middle-aged couples who had just returned after the slow pass of winter. Anne, Rudi, Lenard, and Joan were summer residents of Silver Islet. Happy to be back for a new season, they were sitting outside toasting their homecoming while enjoying the view of Superior. Dressed in thick wool sweaters, they were modern pioneers who seemed to fit the landscape. Intrigued by my unusual suit, they were quick to ask what I was wearing and where I had come from. After explaining myself, I asked for permission to set up my tent down near the water.

"Hell, you can put your tent up anywhere you want for the night," Rudi offered while gesturing his arm with a wide sweep. "No one around here will mind."

"Would you like to join us for dinner?" his wife, Anne, invited. "We're having a barbecue in a little while."

"It's only hamburgers and baked potatoes, but we have lots of it!" Lenard added.

The genuine friendliness of the group made it difficult to say no. A part of me that felt too tired to socialize just wanted to crawl into bed, but an opportunity to talk about the area with seasoned residents was too good to pass up. After accepting their invitation and promising to return, I walked back to the kayak and changed into some dry clothes.

An hour later, after sponging out the excess water from inside the cockpit of the kayak and removing the foam seat cushion to dry, I returned to my gracious hosts. They were quick to offer me a drink, and as I sat on the balcony, I could feel the warmth of the brandy spreading through my insides. Not a big drinker, I sipped my drink slowly, worried that someone would fill my glass if I emptied it before dinner.

The group spoke lovingly of Lake Superior and the north the way city dwellers talk of a favourite restaurant or night club. To each of them, Lake Superior and Silver Islet was the jewel of Canada.

"All those people in the province of Toronto can have the city. We have everything we need right here," Anne stated emphatically. Looking out onto the endless stretch of water, it was difficult to argue with Anne. The view was breathtaking and the serenity relaxing.

After dinner I walked across an expansive grass lawn to the Cheadle residence. I was trying to save the batteries for my VHF marine radio as much as possible, and I was told the Cheadles would have a portable telephone that I could use to call the coast guard and relay my location. Silver Islet is so far off the beaten path that telephone lines had never been installed, and the residents rather enjoyed the fact.

Upon reaching the house, I was greeted warmly by Beverly and her son, Greg. I had interrupted their dinner, and they insisted I join them for a glass of red wine and tell them all about my trip. Exhausted with my own story, I prompted Greg to relate the history of Silver Islet for me instead. Greg explained that Silver Islet was once the largest community on the north shore of Lake Superior due to a silver mine that started on a tiny offshore island during the late 1860s. Deemed the biggest silver mine of the time, steam powered pumps ran twenty-four hours a day to keep the mine shafts dry. The two-story framed homes and log houses used as cottages today were once owned by company officials and married workmen and their families. Single men were forced to live on the island

31

to keep them away from the married women, Greg explained with a smile. Supposedly against all efforts by the mine managers to control any theft, miners still managed to sneak their own small fortunes by floating silver to the mainland in small wooden barrels. Then as Greg explained it, a ship's captain and crew got drunk in Cleveland, Ohio, and didn't make it to Silver Islet with the winter supply of coal before the lake froze up. Eventually the pumps ran dry and water flooded the mine shafts. Attempts were made to re-open the mine but the grade of ore had been decreasing, and with mining costs rising, the profits were marginal. When the mine closed for good, the community quickly emptied.

Greg stopped and took a drink from his wine glass, signifying the end of his story. I enjoyed his narrative so much I wished he would continue, but I needed to call the coast guard and advise them on my location before it was too late in the day.

Feeling bad for leaving my previous hosts for so long, I jogged back and arrived just as everyone was settling inside for the night. Anne's father, Sam, invited me to spend the night in his spacious cottage instead of setting up my tent. A recent widower after fifty-two years of marriage, this was his first spring at the cottage without his wife. Walking inside, I saw that his cottage was everything I could ever imagine a lakeside retreat should look like. Large windows faced Superior, attracting warm sunlight, while a stone fireplace commanded attention over the entire room. He explained it had taken him and his wife two summers to complete the stone work for the fireplace. Each stone was hand-picked and fit so comfortably together that I could visualize the thought that had gone into placing each rock. Nestled side by side in front of the fireplace were two, high-backed winged chairs, evidence I was certain, that Sam and his wife had done everything together. Seeing the empty chair, I felt sad for him. I couldn't imagine losing my partner after fifty-two years together. The longest relationship I had ever had was two years, and even that was hard to let go of. We sat in the big chairs before bed. Out of habit, Sam sat in his chair and I sat in his wife's. Talking and staring at the fireplace, I imagined this was how they planned and dreamed a life together.

Later that night, while lying in my sleeping bag, I thought about my girlfriend Fleur and the possibility of us spending fifty-two years together. After a while, I stopped feeling sorry for Sam and decided that he was lucky to have experienced something greater than many people ever achieve—a long and lasting love.

I woke at 6:00 a.m. to the buzz of the alarm clock Sam had given me. We both got up and ate breakfast together. Sam made me what he called the breakfast of champions, a peeled grapefruit and a large bowl of bran flakes with raisins, pumpkin seeds, and sunflower seeds topped with milk. He promised me I would have energy all morning.

Sam helped me launch my kayak back into the water and suggested that I stay the night in a cabin on Swede Island. I left Silver Islet at eight thirty. Once I was out past the small breakwater, I was hit by a strong headwind. I decided to make my first distance crossing from Silver Islet across the Montreal Channel to Point Porphyry on Edward Island. The distance was approximately ten kilometres. Although I felt a bit anxious at leaving the safety of shore, I was cutting off all of Black Bay, which still had lots of ice, and the shortcut would save me hours of paddling.

My plan for the day was to island hop along the south shore of Black Bay Peninsula and camp at Swede Island. The paddling was very difficult, and my arms complained about the constant strain from fighting the wind. By the time I reached Magnet Island, I was hungry beyond words. It was too difficult to go ashore because of large boulders, so I ate lunch sitting in my kayak. The water gods claimed their first prize during lunch. A cotton glove that I wore when I wasn't paddling blew into the water and sank quickly. I watched my glove sink out of sight in the crystal clear water.

When I started to paddle again, I discovered a cabin, and a place to go to shore, that was tucked into a pocket in the rocky shoreline. I landed the kayak on a gravel beach and warmed myself in a sunny clearing out of the wind. My clothes were damp with sweat, so I stripped naked and hung my clothes to dry. When my clothes were warm and dry, I set out and paddled on the backside of Shaganash Island and then completed the crossing over to Swede Island.

Sam had told me there was a cabin on the island that I could use, but he didn't mention which side it was on. Feeling cold and tired, I followed the western shore and almost circumnavigated the entire island before discovering the cabin on the southeast corner. *Damn!* I arrived at 7:45 p.m., exhausted. My arms were dead tired and felt like Jell-O. I had paddled thirty-seven kilometres that day.

The cabin was rustic, but well-kept and clean. I made a fire in the woodstove, and the cabin quickly glowed with warmth. I ate my dinner quickly and had just enough energy to check my maps and write a few lines in my journal before falling asleep.

The next morning I slept until 8:45 a.m. In the previous two days, I had paddled seventy-seven kilometres and I didn't want my eagerness to wear my body down too quickly. My muscles were only starting to grow accustomed to the demands of the trip. I started paddling at 11:44 a.m. under a sunny sky with calm water. The scenery surrounding the islands fronting the Black Bay Peninsula was breathtaking—high rocky hills, rugged granite boulders, and green water. I wanted to stop and explore Otter Cove, but I missed the entrance and it was too windy to backtrack. It's difficult to find friendly places to go ashore with a large kayak. Much of the shoreline was blocked by jagged rock or large boulders, and I feared for my fiberglass hull.

In spite of my tired arms, I paddled two more hours in search of a safe place to land my kayak. My arms ached and felt heavy as I pushed and pulled my paddle with each stroke. I found a place to stop on Bowman Island at six that evening. My arms were dead. I believed quick amputation would offer the only immediate cure. I had also pulled some muscles on my left side below my armpit, and I hoped it wasn't serious. What I wanted was a massage, but there was no time for lounging, so I started my daily routine. I changed into warm, dry clothes which included wool mitts, hat, socks, hiking boots, fleece top, and outer nylon pants and jacket. When I was warm and dry I hung a clothes line for my lifejacket and paddling clothes and lit the stove for a hot drink and dinner. While my meal was cooking, I set up the tent and took care of my kayak. I removed my foam seat to dry in the wind, re-filled empty water bottles, and sponged all traces of water and sand out of the cockpit. Afterward, I muscled the kayak beyond the high water mark and secured a canvas cover over the cockpit opening. While checking the gear that was tied or secured on the top deck of the kayak with bungee cords, I noticed two lengths of rope were missing—two more offerings to the lake gods.

Inside the tent that night, I studied my maps. I had paddled forty-four kilometres that day and was now working from the second topographic map on my route of Lake Superior. When I joined the two maps together, I was pleased to see the progress I had made in only four days.

Lip Balm and Bears

THE NEXT MORNING was bright and sunny, but the air was cold. During the night the temperature had hovered close to zero. I was moving slowly again today, and I didn't start paddling until 10:30 a.m. My arms were a bit tender, but the muscles on my left side below my arm pit were unbearably sore. Each paddle stoke brought a sharp stab of pain. I feared that I had strained a muscle. My ass was also beginning to ache. There was not enough cushion for the long periods of sitting in the kayak. I tried to wiggle my cheeks to get comfortable, but there was no change, and I hoped my butt would soon develop muscles for coping with the long days ahead.

The water was dead calm with barely a wind as I set out, flanking the south side of islands that made up Black Bay Peninsula. I decided that the gods must be favouring me because of the gifts I had given them—or else my family must be praying a lot.

I saw a white-tailed deer standing on a rock ledge near shore, so I paddled closer and was able to quietly approach until I was only the length of my kayak away. The animal was much smaller than the better fed southern Ontario deer I was accustomed to seeing. It was a nice change from the usual sighting of rocks and trees, trees and rocks.

I felt the pain in my side while I kayaked the entire day, and the discomfort followed me into my tent that night. I had only paddled five consecutive days, and already my body was feeling the strain of travel. Although I had trained all winter by cross-country skiing, rowing, and exercising to prepare my muscles for the demands of this trip, there was no substitute for *real* paddling. Without the opportunity to kayak during the winter I still had some muscles to whip into shape, and until that happened, their complaints would continue.

Fortunately, the next day was a scheduled rest day. Sitting on my Thermarest sleep pad, I studied my progress from a topographic map under the glow of a small flashlight. As best I could determine, I was on tiny Dunmore Island near the southwest coast of Simpson Island. In five days I had travelled a hundred and eighty kilometres, exceeding my schedule by one day. I felt pleased to be ahead of schedule, but I was also aware of how quickly things could change. Wind and weather conditions could change swiftly on Superior, making paddling difficult or impossible. Information I had read about the dangers of paddling Superior advised travellers to expect to be stormbound one out of every three days. By those odds I was already faring better than expected.

Later, lying in my sleeping bag, I could hear the rope creak from the strain of the food pack. Up until then I had forgone the chore of hanging my food, partly due to the huge amount, and also because it was stored from end to end inside the hull of the kayak and would be difficult to unpack each night. However, that night I had seen my first bear track around my camp. Left in the soft black mud near the lakeshore, it was larger than my outstretched hand. The imprint was enough of a sign that maybe I should try to hang at least some of my food.

Thoughts of bear encounters filled my mind while I lay in my sleeping bag. I didn't have any strong fear of black bears, but I did have a great deal of respect for them and their abilities, especially their tremendous strength and power. Sensing my lips were sore and chapped, I pulled my lifejacket out from under my head and searched a pocket for a small stick of cherry-flavoured lip balm. The strong smell of cherries reminded me of a story I had heard from an acquaintance, a tree planter who had a black bear rip through his tent because he had a box of cherry-flavoured bubble gum inside. Unwilling to put the theory to a test, I tossed the lip balm out into the darkness.

Better safe than sorry, I figured.

A Day to Reflect

The following morning I woke to the loud throaty calls of two ravens talking above my tent. Comforted with the thought that today was a rest day, I lay there listening and wondering what they were talking about. Ravens have always been a favourite bird of mine because of their unique language. Many people are left mystified by the mysterious sounds, atypical of regular "bird talk." Their unusual vocal antics, which include mimicking other bird calls, impart a feeling in me that these birds possess a devilish sense of humour, a character trait I can easily identify with.

In time, I was rousted out of bed by a hungry stomach and was greeted by another beautiful day. The sky above me was powder blue with a light blush of orange toward the east where the sun was rising above the trees. The air was cold and crisp. After quickly eating my breakfast of hot oatmeal with almond slivers and apricots, I decided to spend the day exploring the lakeshore by foot. Looking at my topographic map, I saw a smooth straight line defined the edges of the world's largest freshwater lake. But here its shores were crooked and bent with tiny coves and bays that concealed hidden treasures waiting to be discovered. Slinging my camera over my shoulder, I left my campsite and began to wander the shore. It was the first day for me to stretch my legs, yet I soon found myself missing my kayak. If it weren't for the cold wind off the lake, it would have felt hot. Thankfully, there were no bugs. It was still too cold at night, and I was grateful for their delayed arrival.

As I hiked the shoreline, I discovered a giant block of ice larger than

37

a minivan resting against a rock beach. Angel white, with a hint of blue near the base where it sat in the water, the iceberg was a reminder of how cold the lake really was. Thinking about the cold water reminded me of last Christmas when my extended family learned of my plan to kayak Lake Superior. Aunts, uncles, cousins, and grandparents were all gathered at my aunt Carol and uncle Joe's house for dinner when my mom opened up a hornet's nest of angry confusion.

"So Michael, are you going to tell everyone about your big plans for next summer, or should I?"

With that introduction, faces turned to me with anticipation. Unprepared, I weakly explained my plan to kayak the Great Lakes and raise funds for cancer. The backlash was swift and harsh. Confused and sometimes angry voices questioned that I would dare to think of kayaking alone on a lake made famous for its deadly cold water and merciless storms. Although I tried to ease their concerns with explanations of my preparations, it was impossible to respond to their worries and hostile objections. What I remembered was promising them that I would return home safely and asking that they believe in me.

Looking at the aqua-green water, I wondered how long I could really stay in the water if an accident ever occurred. Sure, I had my dry suit, but how well would my two layers of fleece long underwear keep me insulated from the cold water? It was a question I had struggled with all winter during preparations. Now that I was here, the relevance of my decision was paramount. Undoubtedly, I could never dress too warmly for the water. The real challenge was dressing so that there was a balance between warmth, freedom of movement, and keeping from getting so overheated that my clothes were sopping wet with sweat. Looking once more at the frigid cold water, I knew I didn't want to find out if I had achieved that balance or not!

Curious about what lay along the shoreline, I walked its border, eager to exercise my legs. The edge of Superior's shore was naturally protected by constantly changing features—cobble beaches created from countless waves shovelling fist-sized stone from its inner depths, giant boulders often taller than myself that had broken away from solid land masses, and fractured or fissured rock walls that sometimes rise hundreds of feet above the water.

After an hour of exploring, I rounded a point of land and discovered a small sandy bay with an endless supply of firewood. Hundreds of trees that once floated freely were now trapped twenty feet from the water's edge in a tangled pile, victims of a vicious wind storm that had shoved the dead trees out of the water's reach. Stripped naked from continuous battering against the rocks, they lay there exposed, bleaching in the sun. I walked over and touched one. It had been a towering tree, its body almost twice as thick as mine. Its roots were broken away, leaving only roughly polished stubs.

When I returned to my campsite, I called the coast guard and informed them of my location. I didn't feel lonely, yet it would have been nice to have a companion there to share the experience. I saw a ring around the sun in the afternoon. I would have to watch and see what became of the weather, I told myself. I feared a storm was on its way. The evenings were very cold; the wind rarely stopped blowing its icy breath. I planned to wake early the next morning and get a good jump on the day. If a storm was coming, I wanted to be packed and on my way before the rain started. I dreaded the thought of loading the kayak in the rain.

When I opened my journal that night to record my day, I found a wonderful surprise. Sometime in Thunder Bay, or maybe in Sault Ste. Marie, my dad had taken my journal when I wasn't looking and written a short note at the top of the page for day six, May 19. His simple words said, *Love you, son—Good luck!* His thoughtfulness and encouragement warmed my heart. My dad and I had often struggled to talk to each other, but over the years he had offered helpful written words, always at the right time. His note was a precious gift to me.

LEAVING MORE THAN
BREAD CRUMBS

================

O N MY SEVENTH day, May 20, I woke early, as planned, at five thirty and tried to get away as quickly as possible. In my haste to pack up, I rolled up the tent with my watch still hanging from the ceiling, so I don't know what time I started paddling. There was a heavy cloud front in the east, but it moved west, leaving a clear sky in all directions. Unfortunately, the weather brought a strong headwind from the east, which made my crossing from Copper Point across Schreiber Channel to Mount Gwynne seem extra long. Headwinds and white-capped waves fought my progress all day, but the *Mai Fleur* handled well. She seemed to love the rough water, rising over the bigger waves with ease.

There was an interesting lighthouse on Battle Island. I observed the beacon from my cockpit while I ate my lunch. Later, while I was brushing my teeth in the kayak, I knocked my tube of toothpaste off the spray skirt and into the water. As with my glove, I watched it sink far down into the clear water.

"Another offering to the gods. Much more of this and I'll have a trail all the way to Toronto," I warned myself.

When I neared Terrace Bay, I saw a group of people fishing along the banks of a river. They were dressed in bright yellow and orange chest waders and life-jackets, and it seemed odd to see so much unnatural colour after many days alone.

The batteries on my VHF radio had died before I had remembered to ask the coast guard to phone Mark Climie at the cancer society, so I asked a fisherman named Bill if he would call the 1-800 number and let the staff know I was okay. Eager to help, Bill promised me he would call when he got home.

I camped on the outskirts of Terrace Bay on a sandy beach, the first time I'd seen a beach when I was ready to make camp. Unfortunately, there was a creek emptying into the lake and it seemed to have discharge water, likely coming from the local pulp mill. I was forced to breathe in the sulfurous, rotten-egg smell all night.

TRUST YOUR COMPASS

================================

I GOT UP at 6:30 a.m., packed up, and ate breakfast under cloudy skies. I felt great. My arms and side had stopped hurting, and I was beginning to feel like a *real* kayaker. I paddled non-stop until Bottle Cove. By then the skies had been blue for hours. I went to shore at Bottle Cove for a pee and lunch break. It was a beautiful site with only a slight breeze, and a white-throated sparrow sang continuously. Thankfully, there were still no bugs, and I was able to take off my top and soak up the sun's heat without being bitten.

After lunch, I attempted my longest single crossing, from Bottle Point across Ashburton Bay to Guse Point, a distance of seventeen kilometres. When I was planning my trip I had thought that long solo crossings of "open water" were crazy and too dangerous and that I would paddle close to shore. But as my confidence grew and my muscles got stronger, I decided that the weather and my speed were the only limiting factors to consider. It took me three hours to complete the crossing, which included a fifteen-minute rest break to eat a chocolate bar.

That night I made camp in Devil's Cove. It was by far the best campsite I had seen, a beautiful sand beach for landing my kayak, sheltered from the wind, and lots of driftwood for a fire. Something had gone wrong with my stove, and I was forced to cook over a wood fire. I made camp late. By the time I had eaten dinner and finished my chores, it was too dark to hang any food. I hoped there were no hungry spring bears nearby.

The sound of raindrops drumming on the tent fly coaxed me from my dreams. Laying in the darkness, it took me a few seconds to remember where I was. Like a drunk waking up from an all-night binge, I searched my memory for an answer to the question, "Where am I?" Tent. Lake Superior. Kayak trip! I was amazed that my mind could wander so far from my experience that I could forget where I was. I checked my watch. Five twenty. It was too early to get up, so I scrambled outside and retied the tent and kayak in case it stormed. Afterward, I returned to the warmth and comfort of my sleeping bag, hopeful I could re-enter my dream.

The next time I woke it was light, and I could easily read the numbers on my watch. It was Sunday, May 22. I checked my map and estimated that the town of Marathon—and my first food cache—was less than fifteen kilometres away. I felt confident in my ability to travel the short distance and decided on a leisurely breakfast, cooking whole wheat and raisin pancakes in a pan over a fire. I liked eating pancakes. They reminded me of when I was a kid and my mom would make me pancakes when I came home for lunch. As a kid, I had an ongoing competition with myself to see how many I could eat. I think my record was fifteen. I don't know where I put them all back then, because now I was stuffed after only three.

I packed the kayak with all my belongings, then walked back to check that I hadn't left anything behind. It was eleven o'clock and the sun was high in the sky when I paddled out of the protected cove. The lake was dead calm and reflected the hazy blue and grey sky into my eyes. I knew the town of Marathon was somewhere across Peninsula Bay, but studying my map, I couldn't recognize any shapes. Everything across the bay was a cloudy haze. I used my compass and measured a bearing from Detention Island to Hawkins Island, a large landform fronting the prominent peninsula that the town hid behind.

I paddled steadily for one hour, when thin traces of fog swarmed around my kayak. It surprised me how quickly the fog had started. I continued to paddle and hoped I would escape. I reached forward with my paddle blades and pulled the kayak through the water as though I were in a race. Stroke! Stroke! Stroke! Within minutes the fog had completely surrounded me. The fog blocked out the sun until all I could see was my kayak. Most of the lake and all of the Superior shoreline was gone from my view. Uncertain where I was, I continued to paddle and trusted that my kayak compass would know the way. My eyes stared at the compass mounted on the deck of the kayak, watchful for any slight change in direction. Instead of keeping me on a straight course, however, the kayak swayed left and right from my constant overcorrecting. The fog continued to thicken, creating an eerie mood around me. I felt completely swallowed, as though the fog was a great empty space that allowed nothing to escape. After a while, the fog began to play tricks on my mind. For no sound reason, I began to question my compass. My internal compass began to tell me I was going the wrong way. I began to panic that I was going off course. I knew that a variance of five degrees to the south would put me a day's paddle from Marathon. Concerned that I couldn't rely solely on the kayak compass, I retrieved a second compass from my lifejacket pocket and was shocked to discover the two disagreed on where I should be headed! Nervous and somewhat anxious for a definitive answer on where to go, I threw my paddle down in frustration.

"Where the hell am I going?" I shouted. The minutes passed slowly while I sat motionless in my kayak. The silence was suffocating. Then, out of my childhood memories came something my dad had told me years ago.

"Relax. Eat your lunch. Take your mind off the problem and remember, always trust your compass, unless you have good reason not to."

I listened to his old advice and ate my lunch in the fog. I used the spray skirt as a table and spread out an assortment of bannock, gouda cheese, cucumber, dried apricots, and gorp in front of me. Silently, the *Mai Fleur* and I floated while I ate my lunch.

When I had finished eating, I felt more relaxed and ready to continue the crossing. Feeling rejuvenated with a clear mind, I followed the original bearing from my kayak compass. Time seemed to pass slowly, but each paddle stroke brought hope that I would soon see shore. Ten minutes passed. Fifteen. Twenty. Twenty-five. Then gradually, I could see the faint grey outline of trees through the fog. Excited by the discovery, I increased my speed and raced ahead. As I moved closer, I could see that I was approaching an island. It must be Hawkin Island; I was right on course! When I passed the southern tip of the island, it didn't bother me to paddle back into the white empty space. I now felt confident that I would reach the mainland shore safely.

Have You Seen a Turtle?

TWO AND A half hours after leaving Devil's Cove, I reached the point of land called The Peninsula. Judging from my map, the town of Marathon was built north and south of this peninsula, so I decided to paddle the southern shoreline in search of a town dock or marina. I paddled for twenty minutes and stopped. I was confused because I hadn't seen any sign of the town. As I studied my map, I saw the faint outline of a man walking through the fog on shore. Hopeful for directions, I paddled closer and waved to catch his attention. When I was close enough, I shouted above the loud crash of waves on shore and asked for directions to Marathon. The man was unable to hear all of my question and simply agreed that I was at Marathon. After I had failed repeatedly to make myself understood, I decided the man must be partially deaf. I asked him where he was going and he told me he was looking for his pet turtle. His answer amused me, so I asked him where his turtle had gone.

"The turtle ran away from me the day before," he explained with complete seriousness. "While we were out for a walk," he added, as though that would explain everything.

I wanted to laugh, but the man seemed serious. Uncertain what to think, I wished him luck and paddled away.

This time I headed north in the direction from which I had come. As I rounded the north side of the Marathon peninsula, I couldn't help but notice the pulp and paper mill. Humming and barking with activity, its tall, slender smokestacks belched thick grey gas fumes into the sky, just

45

like the mills I had seen in Thunder Bay. I stared with bitter contempt as I remembered reading the McGuffins' description of this same scene in their book, *Where Rivers Run,* so many years ago. Back then, I had naively thought how things would change when people learned what was happening to our greatest freshwater lake. As I smelled the same noxious sulfuric stench, my heart ached with sadness. How could we continue to poison a lake that was the envy of the world, one which holds one fifth of the world's fresh water? A part of me knew there were two sides to the story. I understood the argument that people wanted paper, and that jobs from the mill provided a livelihood for families. Yet as I watched the smog from the mill form toxic clouds in the sky overhead, I thought about the mill's effluent pipelines secretly discharging into the lake, and I felt deeply moved. As with many things, Superior was changing with the effects of humans. The lake would never be the same again.

It was three o'clock when I arrived at the town of Marathon. The first thing I noticed was that there was no marina or public dock. Instead, a small, narrow boat ramp had been crudely constructed on the rock and gravel shore to help boaters launch and retrieve their motor boats. I didn't care that there wasn't a marina. My boat had a draft of only a few centimetres and could easily dock along shore. It just seemed odd to me that a town built on the shore of Lake Superior didn't have a dock. As I studied the area more closely, it seemed evident that maintaining a dock along this exposed shoreline would be very difficult. Exposed to crashing waves and crushing ice without the protection of a breakwater, a dock would be lucky to last a year or two before becoming a disfigured mass of broken concrete and twisted metal. It was nice to know that the lake still had control over some things.

I paddled twenty or thirty metres past the boat ramp and parked the kayak on a small stony beach. I didn't know what to think of my arrival. Marathon was the first town on my route, a stop born out of necessity rather than choice. During the months of planning, I had decided to carry as much food as I could manage while travelling the eight hundred kilometres of remote Superior shoreline. I had read the accounts of paddlers who had become stormbound for days on Lake Superior without enough food, and I didn't want that to happen to me. In preparation I had arranged a food cache in Marathon and at Lake Superior Provincial Park. The Canadian Cancer Society had helped me make contact with a woman named Madeline, and she had agreed to hold my food and stove fuel until I arrived on May 24. Looking at my watch, I knew I was two days early, and I worried that she might be away for the Victoria Day weekend.

The town was built back from the lake, which meant that I would have to leave my kayak unguarded while I searched for a phone. I had known there would come a time when I would have to abandon the kayak, but right then I felt terribly uncomfortable with the idea. I worried about vandals or thieves, yet I also knew this was something I would have to accept. I had brought a cable lock for the nights I would stay in the bigger towns and cities, but there wasn't a solid object on shore that I could lock to the kayak. I told myself that I would just need to have faith in people. I held a strong belief in the philosophy that you receive what you expect, so I made the decision right then that the kayak would be safe for the duration of my trip. To believe anything else was simply inviting problems.

The town seemed deserted as I followed the empty streets to Madeline Watts's apartment complex. A half hour later, I pushed the buzzer below her name and waited for a reply. A few seconds later a scratchy recorded message told me that Madeline wasn't home but that I could leave a message after the beep. I left a message that I had arrived and would be waiting at the lakeshore. I hoped she hadn't gone away for the weekend.

I walked back to my kayak and found it sitting exactly where I had left it. I felt a warm sense of relief, but I was trapped. With no place to go, I sat on an enormous, dark copper-coloured rock and wrote in my journal. At five thirty, a minivan pulled up in front of my kayak and I was greeted by Madeline and her friends, Ellison and Joyce Mackenzie. They were noticeably confused and surprised that I had arrived two days early, but Joyce and Ellison kindly offered me a place to stay for the night. Since it was late, I gladly accepted. Ellison brought his truck down to the lake shore and I emptied the kayak, and then we transported my kayak and gear to his house. The McKenzie family made me feel immediately at home. Joyce offered to do my laundry, and they made a bedroom available for me where I could dump my things and charge the battery for my VHF radio.

During dinner, I learned that Ellison and Joyce were both from

Prince Edward Island. They had come to Marathon for work and had ended up staying and raising their children there. Their son-in-law, Jack, came by after dinner and helped me fix my camp stove. He had some better tools than I had and, with some tinkering, found a tiny grain of sand in the stove's generator. Just before bed, Ellison offered me the chance to read a trip journal he had on his bookshelf. In 1988, he had helped a voyageur canoe group from the United States that had stopped in Marathon. The journal was called *The Montreal Grand Portage Canoe Expedition*, and I read a few pages of the journal before bed. The writing was very good, and the book shared a lot about the dynamics of keeping a large group motivated and happy—a challenge I gratefully did not share, being both captain and crew of the *Mai Fleur*.

The next morning I stayed in bed and read more of the voyageur canoe trip journal until I heard Ellison and Joyce get up. After breakfast, Joyce and Ellison drove me to Madeline's to pick up my food and then to the local radio station, CFNO 93.1 FM. Marty Lecours interviewed me and asked about my trip, where I got the idea, and what I hoped to achieve. I thought the interview went well. I felt he asked me some interesting questions and hoped it would motivate someone locally to donate to the cancer society.

After the interview, we went back to the McKenzie house and I began organizing my food for the next two weeks. At the end of a long day paddling, the last thing I wanted to do was sort through my food and decide what to eat. It took me a long time, so I was invited to stay for lunch. Most of Ellison and Joyce's kids and grandchildren had arrived while I was working, so I ate my last meal with the entire McKenzie family. It was a wonderful meal and everyone treated me like a visiting relative.

At one thirty everyone joined me at the beach to say goodbye. The kayak was too heavy to transport loaded, so I had to repack the kayak while everyone watched and waited. Just as in Thunder Bay, packing the kayak took me a long time. Everything had to be packed in sequence of need and weight. After an hour of packing mixed with some talking, I still was not finished. When it started to rain everyone except Ellison said goodbye and left. It took me until three thirty to finish packing, and I had extra clothes I couldn't fit. I gave Ellison some money and asked him if he would mail the clothes to my parents. When we shook hands, I couldn't thank Ellison enough for his help and kindness.

Hockey, a Canadian Game

I PADDLED AWAY from the Marathon shore under heavy rain, but by the time I was past The Peninsula, the rain had stopped and the skies had cleared. I paddled for three and a half hours without a break and eventually stopped at the mouth of the Pic River. I had travelled twenty kilometres and my body felt great. After the twenty-four hour break, the paddle from Marathon seemed like an easy day. I was getting stronger.

The Lake Superior shoreline at the mouth of the Pic River was an expansive sand beach littered with drift logs and uprooted trees left there from storms and river floods. I entered the river mouth and paddled upstream twenty metres until I found a calm spot to beach the kayak. I opened up the cockpit and climbed out. My legs felt stiff and awkward as I stood up for the first time since leaving Marathon. I grabbed the handle on the bowline of the kayak and dragged it further up onto the beach until the hull was level. Since it had been restocked with food, I could feel the added weight in the boat. It was reassuring to know I had plenty of supplies. My next food cache wasn't until Agawa Bay, which left a long stretch of water in between where I could go hungry.

I opened up the front hatch and pulled out a change of clothes. I couldn't wait to put on fresh dry socks. Just then I saw the silhouette of a man standing on the hill overlooking the beach. Surprised to see another person, I stopped unpacking and stared up at him. Who could that be, and where did he come from? While I stood and stared in disbelief, the stranger started to walk toward me, slow and deliberately. The rhythm and style of his walk told me he was accustomed to the terrain. As he

49

drew closer, I could see his face was naturally tanned and weathered. Just then, I remembered that there was a Native Reserve somewhere in the area, and I began to worry I was on native property. Maybe he's come to evict me? Or worse, charge me for trespassing? In a panic I began to formulate a story in defense. I expected him to start talking to me once he was closer, but he never said a word. I felt uncomfortable with the silence between us, so I said, "Hi." The man nodded his head and said hi back. After another long pause he spoke.

"What kinda boat is that?" he asked, looking past me to my kayak.

"A kayak," I said, happy to talk about anything other than whose land I was camped on.

"I've never seen one before," he admitted. "Where ya going?"

"I'm paddling from Thunder Bay to Toronto," I explained proudly.

"You're goin' to Toronto in that small boat?"

"Yeah. I left Thunder Bay ten days ago."

"How long do ya think it will take?" he continued.

"A hundred and twenty seven days."

"That's a long time." After a few seconds to think he added, "How far is it?"

"Ah, approximately thirty-two hundred kilometres."

He looked south for a long moment. It seemed as though he was trying to picture Toronto off in the distance. "You should have a motor," he advised. "Are you all alone?"

"Yeah, there's just me," I said with a grin. "I wanted to travel alone."

"Why are you doing this?" he asked, obviously puzzled by my answers.

"It's a fundraising trip for the Canadian Cancer Society. But I'm also doing it for the challenge," I admitted.

"Are you gettin' paid?" he asked.

"No, it's just something I want to do."

"You should get paid," he stated emphatically.

By this time I was feeling pretty confident that he didn't care that I was camped there, so I asked him his name and where he lived. He told me his name was Reno and that he lived at the nearby reserve. Reno then pointed up river and explained that the boundary to the reserve ended a few miles away. I was happy to hear that. Reno began to talk a little about his fifty-some years on the reserve and how he used to run a trap line until the fur market collapsed. Suddenly, in mid-sentence he stopped talking and looked at his watch. Before I knew what had startled him from our conversation, he explained that he had to leave to catch the playoff hockey game.

I watched him walk away and reflected on his perception of my trip. It seemed ironic to me that a native elder would find the idea of my trip so foreign. His comments, such as "you should have a motor," seemed far removed from his heritage. There was a time when his ancestors would have travelled by foot and canoe for weeks or months to trade goods with other tribes. I suppose that was a different time, long before automobiles, powerboats, and playoff hockey.

Pukaskwa Pit Stop

THE NEXT MORNING I awoke before dawn to the sound of the tent fly flapping in the wind. Thinking that a rainstorm could be approaching, I stuck my head outside for a quick look. The sky was dark and overcast and the wind had a familiar threatening edge. Not ready to get up, I crawled back inside the warmth of my sleeping bag and returned to sleep. I woke again at seven thirty. This time, roused by a hungry stomach, I slowly dressed and went outside to prepare something to eat. The sky to the west was black and threatened a storm. It seemed as though the clouds hung only a few feet above the water. It was bitterly cold. I sat on a sun-bleached drift log and ate my breakfast dressed in my warmest clothes and drinking hot chocolate. An hour later, a cold west wind was blowing metre-high waves against the rushing river current that exploded upward in a fury. I watched the two forces meet. My mind filled with nervous excitement, knowing that I had to pass through the waves.

Sliding into the kayak, I stretched the neoprene spray skirt cover over the cockpit and checked the edges to be sure it was tight. The waves off Superior were building and driving steadily into the mouth of the river. I paddled straight into the waves. The long slender dolphin-shaped kayak bow dove into the wall of water and punched a hole big enough for me to follow through. Instantly, I was past the barricade and riding over top of the rolling waves on Superior. The wind pushed against my face and tugged at my Tilley hat, and I felt the freedom of travel once more.

I arrived at the mouth of Pulpwood Harbour fifteen minutes later.

Bordered by two rocky points that stretched out into the lake, the natural harbour was a maze of small islands and false channels that lead into numerous coves. As I paddled close to shore, my eyes searched the rock and trees for a sign of the hidden entrance leading into Hattie Cove and the Pukaskwa National Park visitor centre. Reminiscing about tales of pirate's hideouts, I eventually slipped through a narrow passage in the rock wall and entered the sheltered cove. Untouched by the harsh winds and crashing waves from Lake Superior, the water was calm and peaceful. Inside the cove, the park visitor services building stood out as a welcoming beacon. My plan had been to register my trip with the park staff and then continue further down the coast. I had a letter from the park superintendent granting me free passage through the park, but I felt obligated to talk with someone and let them know I had arrived.

The pine building looked quiet and still as I approached the shore. The drapes were pulled across the windows and the stone chimney showed no signs of life inside. It appeared that the place was still closed for the winter. I sat down on a big log that rested on the walkway in front of the cabin. Almost one year ago, I had sat on the very same log while my friend Peter filmed the completion of our White River canoe trip. We had started at Sagina Lake, where the river crosses the Trans-Canada Highway, and paddled for ten days before reaching Superior and then Hattie Cove. I had no idea then that I would be back so soon attempting this trip. Arriving at Hattie Cove again was simply another surprise in my life.

The sweet smell of wood smoke lured me across an empty parking lot and into the forest campground. I walked along a narrow gravel road that snaked its way around huge jack pine trees toward a row of campsites. Sitting huddled together on top of a picnic table were two young women watching orange and red flames dance inside a stone circle. Not wanting to startle them, I called out a morning greeting and was met by two smiling faces that invited me to join them beside their fire. Deb and her friend Sue were on a special holiday to celebrate their graduation from university and the start of new jobs as physiotherapists. Close friends after years of academic struggle together, they shared with me their feelings of disappointment over accepting positions in separate parts of Ontario.

"I never thought we would have to move so far apart to find work,"

Deb explained. "I know I should be happy to have a job so quickly, but it's hard to say goodbye. I don't have a big family and Sue feels like a sister to me."

"Good friends are hard to find," Sue proclaimed with a hint of sadness. Listening to the two of them talk reminded me of my own life and the struggles I had faced while separated from family and friends in pursuit of a career with the Ministry of Natural Resources. Someone once said to me that life was full of daily compromises. Unfortunately, sometimes the choices are not always easy to make.

When I told them my reason for being in the park, their eyes widened in disbelief, until they realized I wasn't joking. Then, acting like embarrassed hostesses who had forgotten to offer their guest something to drink, they asked if there was anything they could do to help. A few minutes later I was in the backseat of an aging red Volkswagen bug crowded with two large hiking packs and an assortment of cassette tapes spread across the backseat. The drive to the park office took less than ten minutes, but the walk would have taken me four times as long and I was very grateful for their help. When they parked in front of the office, I thanked them for the ride and said goodbye, but they insisted on waiting.

I met with the assistant park superintendent and completed the park's mandatory registration form. "Just in case you run into any trouble," he said with a smile. "The important thing is that you call us after you leave the park so we know you made it out safely. Otherwise, we have to come looking for you." As I walked out of his office I kept hearing the words, "otherwise we have to come looking for you." I had planned to be through the park in three days. To be safe, I told him it would take me ten. By the time I reached the car, I was wondering if I had given myself enough leeway in case I had any problems. I knew of people who had been windbound on Superior for nine days in a row. Realizing the commitment I'd made, I promised myself I would be out in plenty of time to call. Following the rules was sometimes difficult. It would have been a lot easier not to contact the coast guard or register my trip with the park. Lake and river travel isn't an exact science, and it's difficult to make concrete promises that you will be somewhere at a certain time.

My drivers brought me back to the campground in time for lunch. I didn't want to impose myself any further, so I thanked Deb and Sue for their help and said goodbye. They explained that they were happy to help and invited me to join them for an evening campfire if I decided to stay the night. After eating a peanut butter and jam sandwich, I shoved a Mars bar into my pocket, grabbed my camera, and followed the road to the start of the Halfway Lake hiking trail. I decided that rest and reflection was the key to fully experiencing my trip. Otherwise, I would arrive in Toronto with only a blurred memory of everything I'd seen, a case of too much too fast.

It would be like the time my grandma Hill went to Europe and visited seven countries in twelve days. Afterward she couldn't remember one city from the next. "We boarded a new train each morning and ate dinner in a new city each night. How can I remember where I'd been?" she complained when I questioned her about the trip.

Hours later, after my hike, I returned to the kayak and began unpacking my stove and cook-set for dinner. Hungry for something quick and easy to prepare, I decided on a falafel sandwich with salsa and tahini butter. When it had finished cooking, I sat down on my wool mitts with my back against the wall of the visitor building and ate my sandwich. Eating my meal in silence, I watched as thin traces of fog drifted into the cove and blurred my vision. It had only been two days since my crossing to Marathon, but I was still amazed at how quickly the fog could move in without any warning. Alone in a world all its own, I was startled to suddenly see two figures walk into view, each carrying a plastic sea kayak on his shoulder. I stood up to greet them and stared with disbelief, realizing that I might actually know one of them. Noticing my stare, the man stared back and began to smile when he realized that he recognized me too.

"Well, I'll be, if it isn't one of my Sir Sandford alumni," Gary announced while shoving his hand outward to meet mine.

"How ya doing, Gary, what are you doing here?" I asked with astonishment.

Gary and I had studied fish and wildlife management together at Sir Sandford Fleming College during the early eighties. When we were in school, everyone said he looked like a young professor. As I looked at him, he seemed to resemble a young David Suzuki. Even though we were roughly the same age, his black hair and goatee were flecked with strands of grey, which added to the resemblance. Gary introduced me to his friend Rob and then went on to explain that he was a full-time park warden involved with wolf and caribou studies inside the park. As we talked, the two of them slid their kayaks into the water and began pulling on their nylon spray skirts. Fascinated with his work, I didn't mention my trip until Rob saw my kayak.

"Looks like you're on a trip. Where you headed?" Rob asked with interest.

When I explained that I was paddling solo to Toronto, I could sense their immediate envy. It wasn't that I was doing something that they couldn't do, but because I had the time and opportunity to do something they would have loved to do too.

"We're going out for a quick paddle before dark. Do you want to join us?" Gary offered.

"No, thanks. I've got a lot of chores to finish before dark," I explained. "But if you have time when you get back, I'd love to hear what you know about the coastline south of here."

"If you don't mind waiting until we get back, you can spend the night at our staff residence and we can talk all you want," Gary offered.

Anxious to learn more about the area, I eagerly accepted his offer. Gary and I stayed up until twelve thirty and studied a collection of marine and topographic maps and talked about Superior and sea-kayaking trips.

"Have you ever paddled around Isle Royale?" Gary asked with a smile. Immediately I thought about the giant island that had beckoned me to visit at the start of my trip.

"A friend and I took the ferry across with our kayaks last summer," he continued. "We spent four days exploring the coast but it would take you weeks to see the whole thing." Looking at a map of the regal island, I could see why. The shoreline snaked in and out, creating an endless number of bays to explore.

After we said goodnight I lay awake inside my sleeping bag resting on top of two Sealy coil spring mattresses. "Synchronicity," I told myself. How else could I explain the chain of events that brought me to meet Gary after all these years?

Despite being a national holiday weekend, May 25 was a regular work day for the staff at Pukaskwa National Park. As I woke, I heard voices and the sound of heavy boots shuffling down the hall. Worried that I was holding Gary up, I dressed quickly and walked to the dining room. Seated at a messy table with a cup of coffee, Gary was calmly reading a magazine while a feeding frenzy of staff whirled around him.

"If you hurry, there's enough time for a bowl of corn flakes," he said, looking up from his magazine. Since they were short on kitchen chairs, I held my cereal bowl in one hand as I stood a few feet away from the confusion. When I had rinsed my bowl in the sink and placed it on top of a mountain of other dishes stacked on the counter, we left.

Gary brought me to the park office and introduced me to Keith Wade, a fellow park warden and kayaker. Keith had seen a lot of the Pukaskwa coast and suggested places to camp or stop and stretch my legs. Afterward, I phoned Cindy in Thunder Bay to tell her that I was okay. Cindy was really happy to hear from me. She told me she hadn't really comprehended the task I was embarking on until I paddled away from her in Thunder Bay. She offered to call CBC in Thunder Bay and see if they wanted to do an interview. Fred Jones called me at the park office at eleven and we taped an interview for the afternoon show that day.

Later, Gary stood and watched me as I squeezed into my narrow kayak. I forced my legs out in front and my feet touched the familiar foot pedals that controlled the stern rudder. Once again, the water inside the cove was calm, but I found myself wondering what waited for me beyond its protected rock walls. Gary was quiet while I settled into my seat and arranged my lunch bag between my legs. I thought I understood how he felt. As much as he enjoyed his job, I could tell that he would have liked to come with me.

"I haven't kayaked all of the park coastline," he had confided with me the previous night as I asked him questions about my route. "You're doing something I've dreamed about for the past few years."

Sensing that I was ready to go, Gary wished me luck with a handshake and stepped back from the water. Sometimes it's difficult to be the one that stays behind.

DISCOVERING KAYAK MAN

I T WAS ALMOST noon as I pushed away from shore, paddled through the passage in the rock, and raced out to meet Superior. The fresh winds caressed my bare face and awakened my senses. I felt alive and free once again. I was happy to be back on the water, pushed by an excitement for what lay ahead and the anticipation of being somewhere new.

When I was young, my family would spend a few weeks each summer exploring Ontario in our Coca-Cola red 1969 Ford Econoline van. Each summer my dad would take the rear bench out, and we would fill the back with enough camping gear to drive across Canada. We never went that far, but my parents rarely told my sister Angela and I where we were going, so it was always a mystery.

"Where we going, Mom?" we'd ask.

"I don't know," she'd say. "We're gypsies; half the fun is never knowing where we're going. That way we're always surprised when we get there!" By some standards it may have sounded like a boring way to spend a family vacation. Yet for me it awakened an explorer's spirit in my soul that still yearns to see new places.

I paddled with renewed energy and vigor after my day off. I could tell that the muscles in my arms and chest were getting stronger, and I liked the feeling. It felt empowering, as though I were transforming into a modern superhero with unnatural strength and an ability to paddle forever. *I am Kayak Man,* I told myself as I sprinted ahead and paddled as fast and as hard as I could. I concentrated on a distant tree on the horizon and continued to paddle even after my heart began to pound against my chest and begged me to stop. Feeling excited by the new speeds that I was able to achieve, I pushed myself until I felt as though something inside me was going to explode. Only then would I gradually slow my paddle strokes back to my regular rhythm. Eventually, sprinting became an ongoing escape from the boredom of paddling the same speed all day long. Whenever my body felt tired or lethargic, I paddled as fast as I could to rejuvenate my muscles and awaken my mind.

The sky was clear and blue as I paddled south along the coast toward Willow River. According to my notes, I was still a day ahead of schedule so I decided to listen to Reno's earlier advice and camp there for the night. He had told me about a beautiful sand beach that offered a wonderful place to camp and watch the sun slowly slip into the lake. Anxious to see Willow Beach, I paddled steadily and only stopped briefly to eat a handful of peanuts and raisins or drink some water. At two o'clock I arrived at the mouth of the Willow River and stopped for a break. I ate a cold cheese sandwich and walked down the length of the sand beach. The beach sand was a light golden yellow, the colour of straw, and reminded me of raw sugar. It would have been a nice place to camp for the night if it had been later in the day, but the conditions were too good to stop early so I decided to abandon my plans to camp and keep going. Without a need to hurry, I poked along the edge of the shore and examined anything that caught my eye—driftwood shaped like ducks, faces in the rock, aging moose tracks.

A few hours later I passed between a group of small islands and immediately enjoyed the shelter from the wind and waves. Identified as Morrison Harbour on my map, the water there was calm and in places shallow enough that I could see the bottom of the lake. I peered down into the water as I paddled, almost with hope that I would see some kind of treasure. I had no reason to expect this, yet I felt the urge to look anyway. "Who knows what's down there," I convinced myself. "Just waiting to be found. Native artifacts, dropped muskets, voyageur cargo." The bottom was mostly sand. Occasionally, I would see a sunken log or a small group of clams buried on their sides like fat cookie wheels pushed into a bowl of ice cream, but they were rare.

Without the threat of a rolling surf crashing on shore, I gently nudged the bow of the kayak onto the beach and then slowly pulled myself out of the cockpit. My feet ached pins and needles. After sitting for hours motionless, my feet had turned to lifeless blocks of ice at the end of my legs. I jumped up and down, trying to send warm blood back to my feet with slow results.

The beach was quiet and empty as I unpacked my camping gear and sponged the water and sand from the cockpit. Far away I heard the faint chorus from a flock of migrating Canada geese. Cupping my hands around my eyes, I stood and stared southward in the direction I heard their voices. Unable to see them, I waited and listened while their travelling song grew nearer. To me it was a song of inspiration. Thinking about the thousands of miles they had come reminded me of my journey, and I began to wish I had a song to sing too. Eventually they passed high overhead in a giant V formation and disappeared into the northern sky. I chose a campsite underneath a stand of towering jack pine trees with branches that seemed to droop down along their sides. The park had constructed a rectangular tent site with four logs around its perimeter to encourage people to use one area for camping. Obediently, I set up my tent in the middle of the square and tossed my sleeping bag and Thermarest pad inside the tent.

When the sun dropped a bit lower in the sky, the air turned cold and penetrated my light jacket. I ran to the kayak for something warmer and returned wearing a thick fleece pullover.

I lit the stove and set a large pot of water on to boil. The stove hissed and growled loudly, almost in defiance as the blue and white flames licked around the base of the cold pot. When the water began to bubble, I removed the lid and added a package of dehydrated vegetables and a small handful of rice, bulgar wheat, and vegetable protein. When it was finished cooking, I ate my dinner on the beach and watched the golden sunlight mix and flow on the surface of the lake. Absorbed in my surroundings, I felt thankful to be able to see and hear and eat the beauty of life's offerings.

When I thought back to the months that led up to my being there on a fundraising expedition, I knew it had a lot to do with changing my attitude. Sometimes I can get so caught up in the small problems and battles in life that I forget that every day someone else is struggling for something I take for granted. The quiet meditation each day on the trip was a helpful reminder to "enjoy the moment" and to be grateful for what I had.

I stayed on the beach until the moon came up from behind me and cast shadows through the trees. I wanted to stay out longer, but the air had become uncomfortably cold and my thoughts turned to the comfort of my sleeping bag. Inside the tent, I opened my journal and discovered my dad's writing at the top of the next empty page. *Hope the weather has been kind!! Take care, we send love.* When I had discovered a message from him in my journal a few days earlier, I had thought it was a solitary effort for encouragement. Reading the new message a second time, I realized it was my dad's way of being with me on my journey.

REMEMBERING A WATERWALKER

HE NEXT MORNING, I crawled out of my tent and was greeted by a blast of cold air that licked at my face and sent chills across my shoulders and down my back. Each morning had been cold, but today's strong northeast wind felt more like winter than ever before. I walked over to the kayak and discovered that the beach was frozen solid below the high water mark, and a thin layer of ice had formed on the outside of my kayak. I tried to open the hatch covers but they were frozen closed and I worried that if I forced them open, the rubber seals would tear. Hungry and dejected, I went back to the tent and attempted to read a book. Twenty minutes later I returned, more hungry and determined, and with considerable care I slowly removed the half-thawed hatch covers from the kayak.

Two hours later I left the shelter of Morrison Harbour and paddled south along the Pukaskwa coastline under a clear blue sky. Cold arctic air followed me as I picked my way between groups of small islands, some still covered with ice and snow. I paddled hard and steady to keep warm and soon felt clammy and wet from sweat. I hated the feel of damp, itchy, underwear and stinky neoprene, but there was little I could do. Trapped inside the dry suit from my neck to my ankles, my body slowly suffocated in the heat while my feet froze. "This is what you wanted?" I asked myself out loud. "Ha!" When I realized that I was talking to myself, I shook my head. "Hell, you're going crazy," I announced.

Despite the cold, the sun was a comfort that helped to keep my spirits up. I couldn't feel any heat from the sun, but the blue sky and sunshine made everything around me seem vibrant and alive. The water was emerald green, reminding me of pictures I'd seen of Caribbean holidays on the covers of travel magazines. To help me forget the cold, I dreamed that I was exploring warm tropical islands. It was May 26, but I had seen snow each day since I had left Thunder Bay.

After lunch, the wind picked up and blew more fiercely than I had seen yet, creating two- and three-metre waves. The shoreline along this stretch of coast was breathtaking, and I stayed close to shore so I could marvel at the small coves, harbours, and islands.

Late in the afternoon, I stopped at the mouth of Newman's Bay. The rough water forced me further away from shore and the crashing surf. Riding low in the water, the kayak rose and fell with each new wave as I studied my map. Originally, I had hoped to camp beside Cascade Falls, but the strong winds and cold temperatures were wearing me down. Based on my crude measurement, I had paddled twenty-seven kilometres already, and I couldn't decide if I wanted to paddle the additional ten kilometres to the falls. I studied the map for possible campsites but my eyes kept returning to the words *Cascade Falls* printed beside a thin blue line. I had never been to the falls, but I had watched Bill Mason paint them dozens of times in the film *Waterwalker*. Every time I watched him crumple his painting of the falls and throw it into the campfire, I wanted to reach forward and save it from the flames. Now was my chance to finally see the falls, and I didn't want to let it go.

I heard the roar of the rushing river falling into Lake Superior minutes before I was close enough to see anything. The falls were hidden behind a bend in the shoreline, but the thundering roar of the river intensified my desire to be there, and I paddled steadily toward the sound. It was the first time since the start of my trip that anything could compete with the sound of Superior's crashing waves.

I followed the shore from a distance. Huge waves were driving against the rock wall and rebounding back out towards the next assaulting wave, causing violent, angry water that seemed ready to swallow or topple anything that got too close. Eventually I rounded a large bend in the shoreline, and my eyes were drawn to three white chutes of water that spilled over a high rocky ledge and into the lake. I sat and watched the white water flow over the ledge. For a moment my time schedule had no meaning while I gazed in awe at the natural beauty.

I paddled towards the falls, aware once again of the powerful waves that pushed me from behind. As I got closer, I could see that the crashing surf was dumping onto a rock and rubble shore. I back-paddled cautiously, and let the waves roll under my kayak while I eyed the shore for a safe place to land. Pictures I had seen of this place showed a sand and gravel beach with lots of room to come ashore, but what I saw was different. The higher water had buried the beach.

I decided that if I chose to land, I would have to time the wave so that it carried me to shore and gently let me down on top of the watermelon-sized rocks. If I timed it wrong, the kayak would be pushed roughly onto the rocks.

I counted the swells and looked for a pattern that would tell me when a smaller wave was coming, but each wave seemed the same. I was nervous about landing. I felt responsible for the safety of the *Mai Fleur*, and I worried that I could damage the hull. Minutes passed while I held my position and debated my choices. In the end, I decided to try. I pulled up the stern rudder and edged the kayak slowly forward. I back-paddled and studied the beach, suspicious of hidden dangers I hadn't noticed. I turned in my seat and looked behind me and saw a big wave moving toward me. I waited for the wave to pass, and then I chased it towards shore.

My hope was to ride the back of the wave without getting pushed forward out of control. Luckily, I timed it right and was carried on a cushion of water and left resting on the bed of rocks on shore. Aware that a new wave was on its way, I slid out of the kayak just as a wall of water dumped onto shore and filled the open cockpit. I tried to move the *Mai Fleur* but it was too heavy. Then a second wave dumped over the kayak, and I cringed at the sound of fiberglass grating on rock. Seeing a pile of driftwood six metres away, I thought about creating a ramp but decided the kayak couldn't wait for me to find two pieces of wood from the tangled pile.

From where I stood holding my kayak, I could see the place where Bill Mason had sat by his campfire and painted. I wanted desperately to camp there too and feel his spirit at this special place. A third wave washed over the kayak, dumping more water and gravel into the cockpit, and I knew then that I had to leave. I slid the boat backwards into the water as another wave came crashing into shore. I held onto the edge of the cockpit and struggled in a tug of war with the retreating wave. Frantic, I turned the kayak completely around to face the waves and climbed inside before another wave could dump over me.

The cockpit was full of water and gravel, and I couldn't seal the spray skirt because my marine radio was floating in the water and had jammed itself under my butt. Desperate to get the spray skirt on before the next wave, I twisted, turned, and pulled until the radio came free, then sealed the cockpit just in time for the next wave to crash on top of me. Moving quickly, I paddled through the breaking waves towards deeper water. With each paddle stroke, the water inside the cockpit sloshed back and forth, and slowing my progress. Thankful to have escaped unharmed, I cursed myself for being foolish enough to go ashore in the first place. *That was a dumb idea,* I scolded myself repeatedly.

I was unsure where to go next. It was after eight, and the sun was dropping steadily on the horizon. If I didn't make camp soon, I would be left to paddle the waves in the dark, and that worried me. I had paddled in the dark before, but never with big waves. Always, it had been on calm summer nights, sometimes under the glow of the moon to help guide my path. The next cove was five kilometres away, too far to reach before dark.

At the park office, Keith had told me there was a lighthouse and wharf on Otter Island. He also mentioned that they keep one of the houses open for people in need of shelter. I stared at Otter Island lying motionless in a sea of rolling black swells three kilometres away. Between the island and me was rough open water. I knew it would be a difficult crossing with a headwind and waves, but I felt confident that I could cover the distance before dark. With a quick decision, I started a steady pull toward its safe shore.

As I paddled, rolling hills and deep valleys rose and fell beneath my boat. Each approaching wave loomed above me as though it threatened to close over top like a lid. For a brief moment, I was forced to look straight into the cold, black water and visualize being buried deep below the surface. The threatening swells reminded me why I had heard of the island lighthouse in the first place, and I began to laugh, filled with a sense of morbid black humour. I had been told the lighthouse keeper was the last person to speak with the crew of the *Edmund Fitzgerald* before it sank during a cold November storm.

"Not today!" I shouted into the wind. I had faith in the *Mai Fleur*. Strained by the heavy rocking motion from the water inside the cockpit, she still moved through the water like a dolphin eager to play between the waves. Feeling confident with my kayak helped me stay calm, and I concentrated on steady, efficient paddle strokes. The roar from Cascade Falls grew softer the more I paddled, and I wanted to turn around for one last look, but I couldn't. Turning in my seat was awkward and made me feel vulnerable to the rolling waves. The conditions were forcing me to sit squarely and brace my legs against the inside hull of the kayak.

As I paddled to safety, there was a sadness that comes with the realization that something important had been lost. "Next time," I told myself in an effort to be cheerful. I had always wanted to canoe the Pukaskwa River, and I promised myself that when I did, I would canoe to Cascade Falls and stay the night.

THE LIGHTHOUSE KEEPER

OTTER ISLAND WAS long and slender and sloped higher on its
west side, giving it the illusion that it was much larger than it
really was. Uncertain where to go, I paddled straight towards
the most northerly tip. My map didn't show a lighthouse, but I imagined
that it had to be on a prominent westerly point, and I prayed that there
was a safe place to bring my kayak ashore.

The huge waves rose in front of me and often blocked my view of
the island. When I eventually rounded the north end of the island, I
witnessed the heavy assault of waves against the rocky shore. Each wave
crashed loudly against the rock and exploded into the air in a fury of
white froth and spray. High above, a red and white coloured lighthouse
stood tall and proud as a symbol of safety, but unable to offer me any
help. The island's western shore was a rock fortress, and the realization
that I didn't see an obvious place to land was unnerving.

Still clinging to the hope that there was a protected cove or harbour
near the lighthouse, I followed the shoreline south. Now with the wind
and waves at my back, the kayak surfed recklessly down the front of each
passing swell. Almost immediately, I knew there was no place to escape
from the wind and waves, and I turned around.

It was late. The sun was a golden amber ball suspended above the
horizon. I paddled hard into the wind and climbed over the top of each
wave. Near the island's northern tip I discovered what I had been hoping
for all along, an opening in the shoreline. With each paddle stroke, the
shore opened wider and revealed a hidden passage. Inside the opening,

I was surprised to discover it was a channel between Otter Island and a smaller island to the north. Somehow the train of rising swells had hidden the channel from me when I had passed by the first time, making the two islands appear as one.

The islands were positioned at just the right angle to block the force of the wind and waves. Once I crossed the invisible threshold, the water turned calm and peaceful. I felt both elated and exhausted from the experience. The crossing had been tiring and had required constant alertness to my surroundings. Mentally and physically drained, I turned in my seat and watched thankfully as a glowing red sun gracefully slipped into the lake. The sight was true magic, but also a reminder that no matter what I did, the sun would go on rising and setting each day with or without me.

On the smaller island on my left, a group of dilapidated buildings stood permanently slouched from years of heavy snow. Long wooden walkways and boat docks with rotten and missing planking also stood crippled along shore. Judging from what I could see, someone had built an impressive fishing camp that was now abandoned and forgotten. The place looked like a junkyard, and it made me feel angry that anyone would leave such a mess.

Opposite the fish camp on Otter Island, a large two-storey house painted white with red trim stood on a solid stone foundation. I wasn't sure how long the lighthouse keeper had been gone, but it was easy to tell it had been a long time. The house looked dark and quiet; it had lost the warmth that comes from people living inside its walls. Tired and hungry, I was anxious to see if I could get inside. I knew I could set up my tent, but I was cold and tired and looking for an easy shortcut.

I stopped the kayak in front of the house and stepped out onto a concrete boat ramp. Daylight was fading quickly into shadows. A concrete breakwater blocked my access to shore, so I decided to empty the boat and carry it to dry land. My feet ached while I stood in the icy water and filled my arms with gear. Tent, sleeping bag, cooking pots, food, clothes, everything had to be unpacked to make the boat light enough to carry from the water. When my feet became too cold to bear, I stopped unpacking and stood on shore doing jumping jacks or running on the spot. When the kayak was empty, I lifted the shell to my shoulder, carried the boat to shore, and rested it on the ground in front of the house.

I climbed the small narrow steps to the front door of the house and checked if it was locked. The doorknob turned easily and the door opened into a dark room. Excited, I jumped down from the top of the stairs and ran to the pile of gear beside the kayak. Searching the pile, I found the stove, cooking pots, and daily food bag and rushed back to the house to start dinner. Armed with a small flashlight, I walked inside the house and immediately felt an eerie chill race from the base of my spine to the top of my head.

The room was black as night, except for a small beam of light shining from my flashlight, which created lingering shadows on the edge of the darkness. The room before me was too big for my flashlight so I followed the narrow band of light until I saw a table. I placed my belongings on a chair and slowly shone the flashlight around the room as though I expected to see someone. The room was arranged with a wooden table, chair, bench, and two couches. The table was empty, except for a half-burned candle stuck in the neck of an old stubby beer bottle. I lit the candle with a match and watched the darkness creep back into the corners, away from the light.

A narrow, closed door was on one wall and darkness led into two other adjacent rooms. I felt unnerved, and for a brief moment I thought about leaving the house and setting up my tent. Instead, I teased myself for acting like a baby until I screwed up enough courage to stay, even though I continued to feel that I was not alone. While dinner simmered on the stove, I moved my gear inside and lit my candle lantern for more light. The extra light took away the mystery of the dark, but it couldn't eliminate the strange feeling I had.

I chose to sleep in a small bedroom equipped with two spring mattresses just inside the front door. Opposite the bedroom was another narrow door I suspected led upstairs. Normally, I would have eagerly explored the passage, spurred by a need to know what lay beyond. I did not go upstairs. Instead, I crawled into my sleeping bag with childhood memories of being alone in the dark. I still remembered the rules. Monsters and demons can't touch the bed. As long as your body is covered with blankets, *they* can't get you. I told myself repeatedly that I was being silly, but the feelings wouldn't go away. I was genuinely spooked. Everyone had asked me before I had left for Thunder Bay how I would handle being alone.

"Aren't you afraid of the bears? Wolves? Psychotic killers?" they all asked. I told them I was in complete peace in the wilderness.

"Animals won't usually bother you, and psychotic killers hide in cities," I assured them.

I lay beneath the protection of my sleeping bag listening and waiting for something I couldn't explain. I didn't see or hear anything threatening, yet I was certain I could feel something was there, watching, listening, and waiting. Put me in a tent surrounded by wilderness a thousand miles from the nearest person, and I'm completely relaxed. Move me to an old abandoned house, and I'm afraid to fall asleep.

"You are a big baby," I told myself out loud. Thankfully, I was too tired to stay awake, and I quickly fell into a deep sleep.

Finding a Mate

Wᴴᴇɴ I ᴡᴏᴋᴇ in the morning, the house was bright with sunshine, and the creepy feelings from the night before were gone. Hungrily, I dressed and began preparing a pot of oatmeal for breakfast. The house was damp and cold, and hot steam escaped from my nose and mouth with each breath. I stepped outside for a pee and found that my water bottles were frozen solid.

"So, old man winter is back," I commented to myself. Curious about the lighthouse on the other side of the island, I decided to spend the day exploring. I was travelling faster than expected, and since I wasn't able to camp at Cascade Falls, I decided to use the time to enjoy Otter Island. Given the possibility of eventually having bad weather, it was a gamble, but I decided to be generous with my time and see as much as possible. "Besides," I told myself, "the trip is young, and my body is still adjusting to the daily demands of travel. Better to ease into the trip rather than burn out halfway through."

I found a trail behind the house and began climbing a long, sloping hill toward the other side of the island. Minutes later, I heard a male ruffed grouse drumming his wings in the air. Immediately, my thoughts switched from lighthouses to watching grouse courting. I followed the sound slowly, stopping regularly to look through the trees for the bird.

Fifty metres away, I spotted him standing proudly on top of a large boulder. The feathers around his neck were puffed out and his tail feathers were fanned open in a brilliant display. He was looking for a mate. I watched and photographed him for two hours while he went through his routine. First, he stood up straight and proud and flapped his wings up and down, faster and faster until they were only a blur. Thirty seconds later, he sat and listened quietly. Occasionally, he would turn around and look in the opposite direction. Each time he heard a twig snap, or the leaves rustle, he cocked his head and stared intensely with the *hope* it was a female making her way toward him. Usually, it was only a chipmunk, and I sensed his frustration and disappointment each time.

After a few minutes of waiting, he stood up and beat his wings again, still hoping a possible mate was close by and would come to investigate. Eventually, I quietly slipped back through the trees toward the trail, but my thoughts remained with him and his chances of finding a mate.

For some reason, the grouse reminded me of my girlfriend, Fleur, and the series of events that brought us together. I had almost given up on finding the right person for me until one day I saw an ad in the Mountain Equipment Co-op store in Toronto. I had been reading the used gear bulletin board when a small ad caught my eye: "Looking for someone to go canoeing with. I don't have a car or canoe, but I am willing to share expenses. If interested, call Fleur." From that brief ad came two canoe trips, two winter camping trips, and a friendship that grew into love. Thinking back to the determined grouse, I wished him luck. One never knows what the future holds.

Becoming Grateful

I LEFT OTTER Island late in the afternoon so that I wouldn't have to spend a second night alone in the house. Real or not, I was certain something occupied the house, and I was in no hurry to discover the truth. I paddled back to the mainland and into Otter Cove looking for a place to camp. At the far end I found a park warden cabin with a grassy clearing large enough for me to set up my tent. Before I could slide out of the kayak, a cow moose stepped out from the trees and into the water ten metres away. Unaware that I was watching, she walked further from shore and began swimming across the narrow bay. Feeling blessed, I watched the large animal swim effortlessly with her head high above the water, looking and smelling for danger. When she reached the other side she stepped from the water and shook like a giant dog, the sunlight highlighting each water drop like sparkling diamonds.

That night in the tent, I examined my feet with concern. During the day my feet were always wet in my neoprene boots, barely able to breath. Studying my toes I discovered dead skin and toe jam between my toes. I had a first aid kit, but I didn't have any foot powder. My feet were slowly rotting and the smell was putrid inside my small tent. What my feet needed was powder and a chance to dry out and breathe, but the nights were too cold and the smell was horrible, so I covered them up with wool socks. I decided that my feet would have to wait until I reached Sault Ste. Marie, where I could buy some foot powder.

The next day, I paddled blindly without a topographic map. I was missing the section from Otter Cove to a few kilometres north of the Julie

River. The distance was a day's paddle. Somehow, the way the topographic maps joined together, one map only covered thirty-five kilometres of Lake Superior shoreline. Topographic maps were expensive, so I had decided for this small section that I could figure out where I was going and save some money. *How difficult could it be?* I told myself. *All you have to do is follow the coastline.* I don't know if it was because I didn't have a map, but the day passed in a blur without any noticeable events.

I had noticed that over the past week I had been regularly blessing the essential equipment and clothing that I was using. This wasn't something that I consciously decided to do, it just started one day and continued. It began with my dry suit. The water was so deadly cold that I knew that I wouldn't last long in the water without it. When I put the suit on in the morning, I realized that I was blessing the suit for protecting me and keeping me warm. I also blessed the people who helped to make the suit, the designers, and the people who chose the materials, sewed the fabric, and glued the seams. I prayed that they were happy and that they took pride in their work, because I knew that this suit was all that separated me from the icy cold water. After the dry suit, I started to bless many of the items I used each day: the kayak, my paddle, VHF radio, tent, and stove, most of my gear. Everything that I had with me was important and had been made by people—individuals who lived far from where I was, with lives of their own. It occurred to me then that, in a way, a part of all those people was with me on my trip, helping me to succeed.

That night after supper I sat near the shore studying the new map, and listening to the crash of the surf and chorus frogs singing wildly behind my tent. I was camped approximately ten kilometres south of the Pukaskwa River on a secluded sand beach. When I arrived, there had been large wolf tracks in the sand but no other sign of visitors. The beautiful beach was so isolated that very few would ever see it.

During the day, a coast guard helicopter had flown low over the water, as though it were looking for someone. When I was at the park office three days earlier, the park wardens had been talking about a group of canoeists that were late coming down the White River. Seeing the helicopter, I wondered if the wardens had started to search for the missing paddlers.

It was raining steadily the next morning, so I stayed in bed and read a few chapters of my book by Wayne Dyer, *You'll See It, When You Believe*

It. The book was an inspirational guide about how to transform a person's life. It seemed a fitting topic for someone who was seeking change by quitting his job and embarking on a summer-long expedition.

When the rain stopped, I packed up and left the beach under cloudy skies and paddled like I was set on cruise control, hard and steady against the wind.

I ate my lunch in the kayak and only went to shore to go for a pee. My shoulder and back muscles were finally in shape, and the only discomfort I felt was when my bladder was full. Often, the weather was either too rough or the shoreline was too rocky when I had to pee, and I was forced to *hold it.* Sometimes the pain was so intense I thought I would die. Trapped in the kayak with no way to go to shore, I was sometimes forced to paddle for hours. No matter how painful it got, I wouldn't allow myself to pee in my dry suit.

I pushed on all day, finally stopping in a small bay with a stream running down from a hill, a few kilometres west of Point Isacor. It rained slowly and steadily while I set up camp but stopped long enough for me to cook dinner. When I crawled into the tent, a thick fog blanketed the outside world. I fell asleep to the peaceful sound of waves crashing on Superior's shore.

When I awoke to more fog the next day, I decided to wait and see if the weather changed before I committed to leaving. Worried I might miss something interesting if I left in the fog, I spent the day reading in the tent and exploring the forest around my campsite. When the weather hadn't changed by noon, I cooked whole grain pancakes and ate them with maple syrup in the quiet fog.

While I was cleaning my dishes, I saw a kayaker in my bay. I waved at him, and he paddled over to greet me. We talked awhile. He was headed for Hattie Cove. I thought he was crazy. Not because he was paddling alone. Who was I to say anything? What shocked me was that he wasn't wearing any cold weather clothing or a lifejacket. He said he was too hot, which I totally understood. Dressed in my own dry suit and neoprene diver's hood, I had struggled with overheating and sweat running in my eyes, but the alternative, if I made a mistake on the water, seemed far worse.

The lake remained fogged in all day. I contemplated moving to the mouth of the Dog River, but decided to stay. I was only five kilometres from my planned campsite, so I decided it was best to wait. I cooked lots of flatbread in the fry pan, went for short hikes, and took photographs of spring flowers.

Late in the afternoon I was reading on the beach, when I noticed an ant trapped in a depression in the sand. I put my book down and watched for a minute. Each time the ant got close to the top, it would slide back down; the incline was too steep. Wanting to help, I reached down and made an opening for the ant to escape. The ant remained perfectly still, afraid to move. When I nudged the ant from behind it ran in the opposite direction from the opening. Amused, I made a second opening in the sand and again the ant stopped moving and remained still. Determined to help, I nudged the ant again, and this time it scrambled out the opening and didn't stop to look back.

As I walked away feeling good about helping the ant, I thought about the similarities of our two worlds. I wondered what the ant's perception was of the situation, and of me. Don't we as humans experience similar encounters of help, oblivious to its origin? Don't I also freeze, or run away from situations of opportunity in fear, creating a need to be pushed or gently nudged in the right direction? The similarities intrigued me, and I wondered what the ant had to say about his adventure in the giant sand trap. Good luck, Mr. Ant.

That night after dark, a storm swept across Lake Superior and ravaged my camp with hurricane-force winds. Thunder cracked and rumbled loudly overhead until my ears were ringing, and lightning flashed and lit up the inside of my tent. Never before had I witnessed greater anger in nature. Rain pounded relentlessly against the tent, adding to the noise and making it impossible to feel completely safe. Restless, I sat up every few minutes with my flashlight and inspected the ceiling and floor for water.

A month earlier, I had spread the tent and fly on the floor in my basement, dabbing seam sealer over all of the stitches. The tent manufacturer label explained that this would make the tent one hundred percent waterproof. Lying in my sleeping bag listening to the rain pound against my tent, I hoped they were right. Years of camping had proven that in time, something would give in to the rain. It would usually start as a tiny trickle, almost like an innocent bead of sweat. But the water drops would eventually grow bigger, until a steady flow of water was seeping through the inside walls or floor and pooling in a large puddle on the floor. In desperation I would be forced to form an island with my body in the middle of the tent to keep my sleeping bag dry. Once the water reached my island, there would be no escape from a wet bed.

After half an hour of steady, pounding rain, I began to feel more confident that my little tent would stay dry. Bolstered by a renewed trust, I lay peacefully in my sleeping bag and listened to the thunder rumble and roar around me.

There is something very satisfying and fulfilling about living outside. While I lay there listening to the wind and rain with a full stomach, I felt true comfort. This was not the same kind of comfort I felt while lying on the couch watching television and eating a bag of potato chips. This feeling was more basic. Primal. The focus of my life had been reduced to the very basics of survival. Food, water, and shelter. I felt content knowing that I was surviving comfortably. I wondered if prehistoric man experienced these same feelings while living in a cave. As for me, there was no other place I wanted to be right then.

I fell asleep easily, but woke often through the night from the loud crack of thunder and flashes of light inside the tent. I couldn't remember any storm that had lasted as long or with as much intensity. It was definitely a *superior* storm to anything I had ever seen before.

When I woke the next morning, the storm had ended but it was still foggy, and heavy winds were driving huge rolling waves onto the beach. I wanted to leave, but I didn't like the conditions. Travelling in wind or fog wasn't a concern for me, but the two, combined with the dangerous crossing of Point Isacor, could be dangerous. Although I felt anxious to go, I decided to wait and see if the weather improved. By noon the fog had cleared, but the wind was unchanged and showed no signs of subsiding. I couldn't decide. I hated the thought of packing up. If I could have instantly been in my kayak and on my way, I would have left immediately. The debate on whether to leave continued late into the afternoon. I didn't understand my reluctance to leave when part of me was so eager to paddle. I decided there must be a reason for my hesitation. My inner voice must be sending me a message, I told myself. I wanted to fight the feelings and go, but I decided to listen to my gut and stay another night.

It started to rain in the afternoon and continued during my supper hour, so I ate peanut butter and jam sandwiches in the tent. I didn't like to eat in the tent, but I didn't feel like sitting out in the rain, so I broke my cardinal rule about no food in the tent. Well aware of the risks, I picked up every dropped crumb before retiring to write in my journal. When I opened my book, I found another message from my dad at the top of the page for day eighteen. I enjoyed the surprise of discovering the messages, so I hadn't looked ahead to see if there were more. The note said,

Remember your quest!! Things should get better by now!

BIG SKY. BIG LAKE. SMALL ME.

EARLY ON JUNE 1, I awoke to a blue sky and a heavy frost. Eight Canada geese were on the beach when I climbed out of the tent, and they didn't move when I approached. I decided they were too cold to fly, and gave them the beach out of pity. I ate a huge pot of hot oatmeal, packed my gear, and left before something could prevent me from leaving. I had seen enough of the beach. I had been at the same campsite for two days and three nights, and I was happy to let the geese have it.

Anxious for new scenery, I headed east toward the Dog River twenty kilometres away. After an hour of steady paddling, I reached the point of land known as Point Isacor. Everyone I had spoken with who knew this section of the coast had warned me to watch out for this area.

"If the wind is up, you don't want to be hugging the shoreline near Point Isacor," they warned. Towering rock cliffs rise up from the water and extend for five kilometres along the coast. A former naturalist at Pukaskwa National Park emphasized the warnings.

"You run into any problems out there, and there's nowhere to go. I got caught in my kayak near that point once. The waves slammed me up against the rocks. The only thing that saved me was luck and that my boat was made of plastic; anything else, and my boat and I would have been smashed to bits."

The wind was still building momentum when I paddled past the vertical rock wall from a cautious distance. I tried to imagine what it would be like to be caught next to the wall while giant white-capped waves raged towards me. Remembering the wind and fog of the last couple of days, I was happy I'd stayed put.

I stopped for something to eat in a small, sheltered bay near False Dog Harbour. I had lost my watch the day I crossed over to Otter Island, and so I ran completely by my body's clock. When I woke up. When I was hungry. When I was tired.

I had wrestled with the dilemma of whether to bring a watch before the trip and had decided it would be useful to arrange my communication with the coast guard. Now that my watch was gone, I didn't miss it. Although it was useful for timing crossings and estimating travel speed, I always felt it ran my day. I wondered if, subconsciously, I had lost it on purpose.

Floating in the bay while seated in the kayak, I ate my lunch while looking out the narrow mouth of a bay toward Superior. Between quiet daydreams, a large steel boat materialized at the mouth of the bay. Coughing black diesel fumes, it chugged slowly in front of me and then disappeared as though it simply melted into the shoreline. Intrigued by the mysterious ship, I quickly stuffed my lunch under the spray skirt and paddled out of the bay. The boat seemed to have disappeared. Somehow it had vanished into the rock shoreline.

A hundred metres away, I discovered a secret passage in the rock like the one at Hattie Cove, but smaller. Inside the natural harbour, I found the fishing boat tied to a dwarfed pine tree and resting against the rock shore. The steel boat looked old and rusted. I couldn't see a name, which made me wonder if maybe I had stumbled onto something illegal. Smugglers? Poachers? Drug runners? Before I could decide to leave, a metal door slid open and a man stepped out onto the deck and stared at me in surprise. He looked to be about thirty and was dressed in a thick grey wool sweater and aging yellow rain pants with a bib that covered his chest. Although his clothes were the gear of a fishermen, he seemed out of place, as though he was following someone else's calling. I felt like a kid caught spying, until the man smiled.

"Where'd you come from?" he asked.

After I had briefly explained my trip, I asked the man what he was doing on Lake Superior. He told me his name was Kelly and that the boat's owner and second crew member were inside untangling sticks from their gill nets. I asked him the name of the boat, but he didn't know, which surprised me because I thought everyone named their boats. Even I had given my kayak a name.

I learned that Kelly was from Batchawana Bay, and that each morning, the three men drove their truck to Michipicoten Harbour and were on the water by six, rain or shine, windy or calm. Kelly didn't say much unless I asked him, so I stopped asking questions, fearing that he thought I was being too nosey. When the silence became noticeable, he went back inside but returned a minute later and asked me if I wanted a fish for dinner.

"Sure!" I responded, almost too quickly to be polite.

"What would you like, a whitefish or lake trout?" he asked.

I decided on a lake trout. I never saw the other fishermen, but I could hear them talking while Kelly chose a fish for my dinner. A few minutes later, he came back offering me a three-pound lake trout. I was expecting something smaller, but felt it would be rude to say anything.

"Here ya go, fresh this morning," he said as he passed the fish down to me over the side of the fishing boat.

I hadn't thought about where I was going to put the fish until I had it in my hands. Cold from lying on a cooler of ice, the fish had that familiar smell, and I immediately thought about bears. I must have had a confused look on my face while I sat there holding the fish, because Kelly went back inside the boat and returned a moment later with a plastic milk bag. Worried the smell might get inside the kayak, I strapped the bagged fish under a bungee cord on the deck of the kayak. Seeing that I was okay, Kelly explained that he had to get back to work and said goodbye. I thanked him for the fish and paddled away, feeling lucky for the chance encounter.

I stopped in the next bay and cleaned the fish on the beach to keep the smell away from my campsite. I removed the head and organs and left them in a pile on the sand for the animals to eat, then returned the fish to the milk bag.

A short time later, I arrived at the mouth of the University River, also known as the Dog River. Rolling swells crashed against the cobblestone and boulder shoreline, and large standing waves blocked the entrance into the river where the shorebound waves met the outgoing river current. Neither option seemed like an easy alternative to get to shore and I sat and studied the situation while eating a chocolate bar.

Eventually, I chose to paddle through the standing waves and up the river. I charged toward the wall of icy cold water and straight through the entrance, then paddled against the river's current. When the current became too strong to paddle up, I zigzagged a course from one side of the river to the other, eventually ending in a calm pool on the east side of the river. When I looked further upstream, I saw that the river curved gently to the left and then disappeared to the right behind a sharp bend. Somewhere up there was Denison Falls, another Superior landmark I had learned about from reading Bill Mason books.

I pitched my tent among a cluster of short willow trees, close to the river and protected from the prevailing wind. Except for the wind-pruned willows, the area was bare of vegetation and the ground was covered with layers of small, flat rocks, each one oddly shaped, as though it were a piece from a giant stone puzzle.

Lured by the familiar sound of the crashing surf, I walked to Superior's edge and watched the rolling swells rise toward shore and collapse in a curling wave onto the rocks. Never tired of the lake's company, I walked along the shore looking for new treasures. Each foot-step sank in the bed of stones and sounded like glass bottles rubbing together. Chink. Chink. Chink. Chink.

Half a kilometre from my camp, I sat on a big drift log and looked out over the lake where the water and the sky met. Every day Lake Superior dominated my waking senses. Even when the lake appeared still, gentle waves would roll and collapse onto shore like a heavy sigh. The sound was constant, and it was soothing to my spirit. Already, I couldn't remember what it felt like to live without the lake near me. I always felt its presence, even in my sleep. Each day as I paddled I felt its vast open space spread out before me.

Since I couldn't see land to the west, it was easy to believe there was no end to the great lake. Without science and geography, I could have believed the earth was flat. The sky and lake fought for dominance, each so big and endless it was difficult to decide who was greater in size and power. Big sky. Big lake. Small me.

I returned to my campsite hungry and ready to cook the fish. Well aware of the smell and the potential for spring bears, I decided to cook the fish without using a pot or frying pan. I had learned this method of cooking fish as a child watching *Sesame Street*. When I was growing up, there had been a regular segment on the show that featured a young Native American boy and his grandfather. Hungry for knowledge about nature and the traditional skills of North American Indians, I learned from that boy and his grandfather how to prepare and cook bannock on a stick, harvest wild rice, and cook fresh fish over an open fire. Many times I had watched the young boy with his grandfather and wished I was native. I wanted to know what he knew and live a life connected to nature.

I lit a small fire and burned driftwood until I had a thick bed of glowing red coals. While a pot of rice steamed near the heat, I cut a willow branch a metre long and as thick as my thumb from a nearby bush. Using my Swiss Army knife, I sliced the branch lengthwise down the middle, the same length as the fish. Afterward, I cut the fish's body down its spine until I had two fish fillets. I placed one half of the fish on a plate and the other fillet between the two sides of the sliced willow branch so it was sandwiched between my makeshift cooking tongs. To hold the fish in place, I tied the sliced end of the branch closed with a metal twist tie. The grandfather had shown the boy how to use thin strips of green bark, but I decided to improvise.

Once the fish was covered with an assortment of spices, I propped the stick against a stone so that the fish was suspended over the hot coals to cook. Hearing and smelling the flesh cook and drip juices into the coals made my mouth water in anticipation. Just as someone would attempt to cook the perfect marshmallow, I checked the fish regularly. When the orange meat had turned a paler shade and droplets of fatty juices dotted the surface, I pulled the stick from the coals.

With reverent appreciation I sat near the fire and ate my meal while the other half of the fish began to cook over the coals in the same way. The fish tasted delicious, firm textured, moist, seasoned perfectly with a hint of parsley and dill. For dessert I ate butterscotch pudding. It was a memorable meal that deserved friendly company.

When I had finished eating, I sat close to the fire feeling fat and full and scribbled notes about the day into my journal. The sun had already set behind the tree line, and pink and mauve clouds stretched across the western skyline. A small flock of Canada geese honked while they flew overhead. Fish were rising and sometimes jumping at flies hatching from the river. This was one of my favourite times of the day. Dusk. A time for peaceful grace and quiet reflection.

DENISON FALLS

THE FOLLOWING MORNING, I woke early with the anticipation of hiking to Denison Falls. The sky was clear, but the sun was still behind the trees, and the air was cold against my bare skin. Covered by two layers of fleece and a wool toque Fleur had knit for me, I quickly ate my breakfast of cold cereal and bannock. Loaded with a full camera case and tripod, I left my campsite with great excitement. Like Cascade Falls, Denison Falls was an image I had been carrying in my mind for a very long time.

The trail started out very flat and easy to follow. Within a quick ten minutes from my camp, I arrived at an old established campsite beside the river, complete with rotting tarps, makeshift logs, and plywood tables. Disturbed by the mess, I hurried past the site, almost missing two sleepy porcupines that were moving slowly near my path.

Past the campsite, the trail continued to follow close to the river, and I stopped regularly to study the rapids and imagine myself running them in an open canoe. Minutes later, the trail followed into the trees away from the river and became less defined and more rugged. Several large trees lay across the path and forced me to crawl under or over their sharp, pointed branches. Hindered by ice and snow, I scrambled up and down steep rocky slopes, grabbing for small trees or branches for support.

After an hour and a half of continuous climbing, the trail veered back toward the river, within sight of a beautiful five-metre waterfall. At first I was confused and thought this falls was Denison Falls, even though it looked different than the pictures I held in my head. As I walked closer, I felt more certain that it couldn't be Denison Falls, so I continued to follow the vague rocky trail until the route was blocked by a rushing stream. It was too wide to jump, so I searched for a way to cross. A hundred metres downstream from the trail, I took off my pants and boots and carefully waded across the icy water. Goosebumps formed instantly on my legs as I stepped away from the water and hurriedly dressed. Still numb and tingling from the cold, I slowly maneuvered my way through the thick web of trees and branches in search of the falls.

Unable to see very far through the thick tangled mass of branches, I hiked to the top of a high hill and walked across its ridge. Faint sounds of water rushing and falling far off in the distance drew me closer, until I could see partial images of the falls through the trees. Closer to the edge of the hill, the trees separated and allowed me to see the entire falls from top to bottom. I stared with astonishment. The waterfall was bigger and higher than I had imagined. A torrent of wild white water rushed and splashed, and fell hundreds of feet over and around ancient rock, ending as two separate chutes dropping over a ledge into the river below.

For a long time I simply stared and listened to the loud roar of the water falling and crashing onto rocks and into the river water below. I was happy I had taken the time to hike there. The falls felt alive. The rush of the roaring water was like the river's pulse. Its heart was beating very fast, excited with the advance of spring. By mid-June, its pulse would slow considerably as it paced itself for the long hot summer.

Standing near the falls with my eyes closed, there was still so much to *experience* with the senses: the sound of rushing water, the gentle breeze created from the falling water, and the mist raining on top of me and moistening my face and hair, the smell of fresh water, rock, driftwood, balsam fir trees and damp moss. I felt that the falls were as much alive as I was.

While I enjoyed the peace that came from being at the falls, I thought about the animals that lived nearby and wondered whether this place held any special meaning to them. Many people I know would dismiss my ideas as anthropomorphic, but I'm not as certain that animals are less evolved than humans. I have come to believe that all things—the trees, water, rocks, animals, and people—are mysteriously connected by some divine force that some call God or Great Spirit or a number of different names. Places like Denison Falls are not just a visual treat. They have an energy and feeling that is peaceful to be near and nourishing to the soul. And if *humans* can sense pleasure from being near places like Denison Falls, why wouldn't animals?

I stayed at the falls for a couple of hours, taking pictures, exploring rock formations, and simply sitting very still and listening. When I felt it was time to go, I hiked back to camp and packed my tent and gear. It was difficult for me to leave. Much of me wanted to stay longer and become more familiar with the river. I was aware that time and opportunities were fleeting, and although I made promises to myself to return someday, I also knew that plans could change with the unknown demands of my future.

A Hot Shower

s excited as I was to see new scenery, I also felt like a slave to my schedule. *You have to be in Toronto on September 17,* I told myself. Knowing this and the likelihood of unexpected delays on Lake Superior, kept me moving.

I left the Dog River mid-afternoon on June 2, and paddled steadily against the wind toward Michipicoten Bay. I arrived south of the Michipicoten River at eight thirty in the evening, feeling tired and without any plans for where I would camp. After being free to stay wherever I wanted, I was suddenly surprised to see so many homes and cottages evenly spaced along the shoreline. I knew there was a settlement at the mouth of the Michipicoten River, but I hadn't realized there were so many homes. During the height of the fur trade, the Michipicoten River was used as a travel route from Lake Superior to James Bay, via a series of inland lakes and the Missinaibi River. Now, Michipicoten Bay was home to a small community of local residents and cottagers.

I sat in my kayak and studied the beach for a possible tent site, aware that the sun was dropping steadily behind me and feeling uncertain about my arrival. To the people who lived there, Superior was home, and I felt like I was an intruder.

One house built close to the beach stood out to me more than the other homes. The house was small, yet even from a distance, I could imagine that it was cozy on the inside. Instead of making a plan for where I was going to sleep for the night, I started dreaming what it would be like to live there next to Lake Superior. A large picture window faced the lake, and I decided that if I lived there, my kitchen table would sit next to it so that I could look outside while I ate my meals or talked with friends. On the outside, a wooden deck stretched across the front of the cabin. This is where I would sit in the evening with a relaxing drink, watching the setting sun painting the sky and clouds soft shades of orange, purple, and red. After dark, I would curl up in a blanket under the stars and listen to a symphony of crickets and waves washing up on the beach.

While I dreamed about living in the house, a young woman walked out the side door into view. Pulled from my dream, I paddled closer and called out a greeting when she looked my way. Minutes later, Carol and I were talking about my trip, and she had given me permission to camp in a clearing thirty metres from the house. Explaining that she had to leave for a while, she told me her husband, Joel, would be home soon and that I should tell him we had spoken.

Once Carol left, I busied myself with the daily chores of unpacking, caring for the kayak, and cooking my dinner. When Carol's husband came home, I introduced myself and extended my gratefulness to him and his wife for allowing me to camp on their property. We spoke for a few minutes but soon parted so that I could finish cooking my dinner.

Later that evening while I was writing in my journal, Carol returned and invited me into their house for a hot shower. After a week of sponge-bathing in the lake, the offer sounded heavenly. Carrying a change of clothes and my toiletries bag, I followed Carol into the house. Once inside, I was quickly ushered toward the bathroom with orders to use whatever I wanted. When I stood in front of the mirror, I realized I looked like a stray dog. My face was hidden by shaggy whiskers and my hair was now curly and windblown. Only my clean white teeth showed signs of daily care.

In the past, hot showers had been a luxury I had enjoyed at the end of a long canoe trip. Modern conveniences and food cravings like ice cream, pie, or a cold beer usually waited until I had returned, but this trip wouldn't end for another four months. Enjoying the feeling of warm water pummeling my body, I stood under the shower nozzle and let the heat from the water seep deep inside my body.

Showers are like a daily baptism to me. The water washes away my problems or past mistakes, preparing me for a fresh start to try again. When I break away from the daily cleansing routine, showering makes me feel like a new person, as though the old me was washing down the drain with dead skin and dirty water.

I wanted to stay under the hot water forever. The shower felt so good I could have fallen asleep standing up, yet I felt conscious of my hosts waiting for me to finish. I also worried that I was using all of their precious hot water, so I reluctantly turned off the shower and wiped myself dry with a towel. After brushing my hair and putting on clean clothes, I cleaned the tub, sink, and floor, removing all evidence that I had been there.

When I stepped out of the bathroom, my hosts greeted me again, as though I were someone new.

"Well, hello. Do you feel better?" they asked. After describing feelings of rejuvenation, I accepted an invitation for tea and sat down on a cushioned couch that faced the large picture window and the lake.

Seeing the room for the first time, I noticed the kitchen and living area flowed together without borders, creating a relaxed and comfortable setting. Immediately, I liked their home. Unpretentious, everything within sight, it was an affirmation of their characters. Collections of books and magazines were stacked in piles on every available table, a camera was mounted on a tripod beside the window, green house plants scattered about, and a wooden canoe paddle stood in the corner. These were kindred spirits, enjoying a life I often dreamed of living.

Sipping our tea, we talked about my trip, what I had seen already, what I hoped for, and the magnificent beauty that envelopes Superior and everything that it touches. When I described the violent and exciting thunderstorm that pounded rain against my tent a few nights before, Joel explained that it was typical of many storms on Lake Superior.

"Moving back and forth from land to water, thunderstorms can rebuild and storm again, making them last for hours along the coast," he added.

This surprised me, because I was accustomed to storms on Georgian Bay blowing inland violently with a vengeance, and then quieting down. Learning this new insight about the lake added to my already swelled respect for Superior and the control it had on its environment and inhabitants.

At midnight, I left Carol and Joel and walked back to my tent. The night sky was bright with stars and a faint glow of northern lights danced and shimmered above the towering pine and spruce trees like shapeless ghosts rejoicing in the beauty of the night. I stood on the beach hugging myself for warmth and stared up at the sky. This was the time when the sky truly dominated the lake, after dark, when Superior had disappeared into the shadows, its true size hidden from view.

Cold Day to Old Woman Bay

FROST COVERED THE tent when I got up the next day and my bare hands ached while I lit the stove to cook breakfast. The calendar noted that it was June 3, but it felt like early April in Southern Ontario. I moved slowly from the effects of the cold and staying up too late with Carol and Joel. In no hurry to leave, I waited until the sun dried the frost water off the fly, cooked extra flatbread, and wrote in my journal.

Carol and Joel had left for work before I got up, so I tucked a thank-you note inside their screen door. When I started paddling, the wind had picked up, and I fought headwinds all day. There was no shelter from the wind. As I struggled to reach Beauvier Point, it felt as though I was barely moving, and much of the time it seemed as though the next point of land was backing away as I paddled towards it.

Most days, there was some kind of distraction from the physical exertion of paddling. On that particular day it was the smell of my neoprene hood. Fitted tightly over my head similar to a winter balaclava, the neoprene hood was another clothing item I wore as a precaution to keep me warm if I ever fell into the water. After a few hours of paddling, the smell of dirty neoprene began to turn my stomach. The oils from my hair, beard, and skin had been absorbed into the neoprene material, and the smell made me want to throw up. To fight my gag reflex, I covered my lips with cherry-flavoured lip balm in an effort to mask the odor.

I felt ready to make camp long before I could find a safe place to paddle to shore. The wind had been blowing all day, and the waves near shore were rough and intimidating. Too exhausted to attempt a dangerous landing on rock, I decided to push myself and camp near the beach in Old Woman Bay. I had only paddled twenty kilometres, but the cold wind had drained me. I went to bed that night exhausted, but woke up early, afraid to be discovered camping in a restricted area. I was inside the boundary of Lake Superior Provincial Park.

Old Woman Bay was one of the most spectacular sights on the entire shore of Lake Superior, and it can be seen from the Trans-Canada highway. Sheer granite cliffs rise two hundred metres up from the water, and some people say they can see the face of an old woman in the rock. I hadn't planned to camp there when I made my trip itinerary, although I had thought about it each time I stopped along the Trans-Canada to stare up at the cliffs. The problem was that I couldn't find a suitable campsite sooner, and when the sun began to set, I eventually paddled into the bay too exhausted to go any further.

Even though my tent was covered in a thick white frost, I packed it away to hide the fact that I had stayed the night. I had received permission to camp in the park months ago from the provincial government, but this didn't include exemptions from park regulations. The solid metal sign that stood near my tent was very clear, *No Overnight Camping!* When I had moved all of my camping gear beside my kayak, I unpacked my stove and food for breakfast. A short time later, I was seated at a picnic table warming my hands around a cup of hot chocolate when a conservation officer drove into the Old Woman Bay picnic grounds. I felt as though he had heard my thoughts and knew someone was camping there. When he saw me, he stopped his truck in the middle of the road and began walking toward me.

"Shit!" I said under my breath. My heart began to beat faster while my brain started to formulate an excuse.

It was late, I didn't have anywhere else to go, I ...

His sudden smile put me at ease. Even before he spoke I recognized his face. In 1988 I had spent the summer leading aquatic lake surveys for the Ministry of Natural Resources, based in nearby Wawa. The officer's name was Wally. He was tall and broad in the shoulders, with short rust-coloured hair, and he wore heavy metal-framed glasses. I would guess he was in his early to mid-forties but his face was happy and youthful, a sign of someone who still saw life as something fun.

As soon as he asked me if the kayak on the beach was mine, I began telling him that we had worked at the same office six years ago. I hoped that my memory of his name and familiarity would help to create a bond and protect me from the fact that I was camped illegally. Instantly, we were talking about where I went after leaving Wawa, my trip, and about the slow demise of the Ministry of Natural Resources. When we both concluded that our beloved ministry was dying a slow, painful death from endless budget cuts and massive layoffs, he announced that he had to get going. After he was gone, I wasn't sure if he knew I had camped there, or he just didn't see a need to make an issue of it. Regardless, I felt lucky and decided someone, somewhere must be watching over me.

As I left Old Woman Bay, I paddled close to the rock cliffs that rise up from the water. There was something about the rock that drew me near and made me want to touch it. Rough, choppy waves driving toward shore made it impossible for me to get close enough to run my hands over the polished rock. Instead, I settled for paddling beside the giant old woman, enjoying her quiet, knowing company. The indigenous people of North America believe that the trees and rocks can speak to us if we listen carefully. Moments like these help me to believe it's possible. Words and voices unfamiliar to my own drifted into my mind like lingering wood smoke.

The section of shoreline between Old Woman Bay and Bushy Bay offered many surprises. Small caves and crevices begged to be explored, but without easy access I was forced to look only from my cockpit, with growing frustration.

To make matters worse, my camera was packed behind me in the rear compartment. When I was unable to fit my camera case with me in the cockpit, I packed it there for safekeeping. Inside the kayak compartment, the camera was safe and dry, but totally useless, and it made me feel both frustrated and sad that I was missing so many opportunities to make pictures. I thought often about keeping only the camera and one lens with me in the cockpit but was terrified of the chance it could get wet. I had already lost two other cameras on whitewater canoe trips and I couldn't force myself to take the chance. I could have kept the camera in a small dry bag, but I didn't trust the dry bag enough. I kept asking myself what if?

What if the camera gets wet? What if you drop the camera in the lake?

You won't be able to take any more pictures! I warned myself. And what about the insurance company? I had already submitted one claim for my first Nikon camera. I asked myself, *What if they won't replace this camera?* Thoughts like these kept the camera packed out of reach. Safe. Dry. But completely useless!

I struggled against strong headwinds for the second day in a row. Cooled by the cold water and large snowdrifts on shore, the wind was icy and made the physical effort to paddle more difficult. To help me forget my struggles, I focused my attention on the scenery around me. It was the first day I'd noticed that the leaves on the aspen and birch had started to unfold, and it changed the landscape from a dull grey to spring green. From a distance, the forested hillsides were a collage of different shades of green and purple. Days before, the forest had been bare, then suddenly, overnight, the landscape had become alive with fresh new shades of sprouting green leaves. I liked the colour of spring. Spring green is different from summer green. It's more vibrant and luscious.

I camped on a beautiful, secluded beach on the north side of Warp Bay. It was the first beach I'd seen all day. Most of the shoreline had been rough, jagged rock or high cliffs, so a beach seemed like a gift, a safe haven where I could drag my fragile boat ashore for the night. This was how I chose my campsites. Each day I asked myself the same questions: how easily can I get to shore? Are there rocks that could gouge the hull? Where will the wind be coming from when I want to launch in the morning? The beach in Warp Bay was like a scene from a postcard: fine white sand without a trace of another human footprint, framed by a border of blue sky and water.

Later that evening, the air turned remarkably warm. The change was so dramatic, it felt as though someone had turned on the heat. It was the first night that I couldn't see my breath inside the tent, and it brought hope that spring would soon arrive. I set my maps out on the floor of the tent and studied my progress. It comforted me to look back and recount my progress from Thunder Bay. In twenty-two days I had paddled five hundred and thirty kilometres. The distance measured in kilometres didn't mean anything to me, but when I looked at the distance on the maps spread across the tent floor, I could see that I was making progress.

Toronto, here I come.

Agawa Bay Food Cache

IT RAINED A lot over the next couple of days. Once again it felt more like April than June. Kayaking through cold, pounding rain showers kept me thinking of the song "April Showers Bring May Flowers," but there were no flowers in bloom. It was too cold. The warm temperatures I felt in Warp Bay hadn't lasted. I felt sorry for the trees that had been tricked into opening their buds with the promise of spring. What an evil betrayal, I thought.

Light rain and mist filled the air and dampened my face while I paddled toward Agawa Rock. Agawa Rock was the local name for a thirty-metre high rock wall covered with native pictographs. From the water, the wall towered over me, rising straight up out of the water like a towering building.

I had visited Agawa Rock by canoe once before, but time had erased the emotions attached to this unique site. When I arrived, the mystical and reverent feelings flooded back to me. Seated in my kayak, I looked up toward the native pictographs painted on the rock: blood-red images of five people in a canoe, water serpents, and a mythical creature with two horns and spines down its back and tail. I had read somewhere that these images were ancient. This fact amazed me because the images were still bright and clear after years of exposure to rain, ice, wind, and sun.

As I admired the images, I wondered what the purpose was of these paintings. Maybe appeasements to a god? Stories? Recorded history? I'm sure anthropologists have their theories, but what were the artists really thinking when they created these images? I looked up at the magical

95

paintings and thought how exciting it would be to talk with the artists today. It rained hard while I sat and stared at the pictographs, so I didn't have a chance to take any pictures.

Light fog and drizzle swallowed me and my kayak as I paddled slowly away from Agawa Rock. Through the dampness, the sweet, pungent scent of wood smoke filled my nostrils and flooded my mind with warm images. Hungry for bigger gulps of the sweet air, I searched blindly through the rain, losing and then finding the scent at Ganley Island.

Through the fog, I met Jack Miner, a long-time resident of the island. Though we were separated by water, Jack told me how he loved to explore the shoreline even after a lifetime of coastal trips by canoe and motor boat. He explained that the shoreline was always changing, so you can see something different or new each time you explore. Friends called him Relic, after the CBC television show *The Beachcombers*, because he was always looking for something to bring home.

The rain and fog had thickened by the time I arrived at the Agawa Bay campground, which made it difficult to see beyond the cobble beach. The lake was uncommonly still and quiet when I arrived on shore. The Agawa Bay campground office had been closed when my dad and I came through on our way to Thunder Bay, so I had left my food and fuel cache at the Red Rock office. The park staff had promised that they would move my boxes to Agawa Bay when the park office opened.

I left my kayak on the beach and walked through the campground and across the Trans-Canada Highway to the park office. Fortunately, it was a short hike, and it took me only a few minutes to find a staff person who could help me. The staff was very friendly and helpful, offering me a bed, hot shower, and laundry facilities at their staff house.

When I was settled, I called the cancer society and then my mom and dad. It was great to talk with them. They filled me in on family news that my grandma Pat was sick in the hospital. It was the first time on the trip that I wanted to be somewhere else. My grandma had always been an important person in my life, and I really wanted to offer her my love and support. I told my parents a bit about my trip but was careful to only mention the high points without mentioning any of the dangers. I was well aware that they were worried enough about me.

Afterward, I called Cindy and Jim in Thunder Bay. Jim called Fred Jones at CBC and arranged for Fred to call me at nine the next morning.

By the time I had finished my phone calls, I was exhausted. I went to bed in the spare room I was offered for the night.

The next morning, I woke to the sound of light rain. Hungry and nervous about being separated from the *Mai Fleur*, I dressed and walked back through the campground to the beach. I filled a large bowl of cereal and perched myself comfortably on a drift log facing the lake. I had become so accustomed to the sounds of the lake, I missed its voices even for a night.

After breakfast, I walked back to the park maintenance building to organize my new food supply. When I opened the boxes, I was amazed to discover what I had packed: gorp, chocolate bars, soup, hot and cold cereal, bannock batter, dehydrated fruit, new dinner meals, tea, and hot chocolate. I picked through each of the items and was pleased I had packed so much food, especially the chocolate bars.

After refilling my stove and empty fuel bottles, I began to make trips back to the kayak. By the third trip, I realized I was going to need help getting the kayak to the water. Optimistic that someone would be around to help me when I was ready, I continued my job of packing.

Twenty minutes later, an older man came over and asked me if he could help with anything. I was amazed at his timing, since I hadn't seen anyone around the campground all morning. Thankful for his offer, I told him I would need help moving the kayak to the water once I was packed and had eaten some lunch. He explained that he was going out for a while but would be back in an hour to help.

As he walked away, I smiled and thought about the synchronicity of him arriving at the right moment. It seemed that every day something happened to reaffirm my belief that people and events were all perfectly orchestrated to come together.

An hour later, the man returned and invited me to his camper for tea. Neville and his wife, Doris, shared that they had driven from Hornepayne, Ontario, planning to stay until the urge hit them to move on.

"That's the luxury you have when you reach our age," Neville boasted proudly. When I asked them how long they would stay before going home, Doris quickly added, "Oh, we won't go home. We'll just go to another park!" Excited by their chosen lifestyle, I asked them where they would go next.

"We stay a few weeks here, then go up the coast to Pukaskwa," Neville explained.

"We don't like the small inland lakes some parks have to offer. We like the rugged shoreline of Superior," Doris concluded. The couple had been beachcombing and hiking the shores of Lake Superior for fourteen years and were still in awe of its raw natural beauty. Doris served tea and Peek Frean shortbread cookies. Confessing my fondness for sweets, I thanked her and apologized ahead of time, just in case I made a pig of myself. We discussed life and the importance of taking time to reflect and appreciate nature in our everyday life. I felt we were kindred spirits forming a bond even though we were decades apart by age.

At two o'clock, I reluctantly announced I had to leave. Neville helped me carry the *Mai Fleur* to the edge of the lake while Doris packed me a care package of cookies and candies. I dressed and squeezed myself into the cockpit while Neville filmed my departure with a video camera. I waved goodbye and left Agawa Bay for Montreal River Harbour, twelve kilometres away. My goal was Mica Bay, an additional nineteen kilometres.

A Helping Hand

D URING THE CROSSING to Montreal River my right arm began to ache increasingly with each paddle stroke. There had been days earlier when my shoulders and back had felt tired and sore, but not like this. Not knowing the cause of the pain made the situation seem worse.

Intent on making up for a late departure, I unfeathered my paddle and pushed on. I hoped this would help relieve the pain. It didn't. Each push and draw of the paddle put a strain on my arm.

What could be wrong? I felt great yesterday; how could this happen so suddenly? The pain intensified with each paddle stroke until I was forced to ease up and use short, childlike movements until I reached the towering rock cliffs at Theano Point. I had only come twenty-one kilometres, but I felt that I should stop and rest my arm. I glanced at the map and discovered that Alona Bay was just around the point, so I decided to camp there for the night.

There were no waves when I entered the bay and paddled my kayak onto the gravel beach. My arm ached but was functional, so I managed to slowly set up camp. Once my chores were done and dinner was eaten, I sat near the water and wrote in my journal. After I had described the earlier events of the day, the pain in my arm became so severe I had to stop writing. A sharp, stabbing pain started at my wrist and travelled up my forearm. The symptom was a new experience for me, but I felt certain it had to be tendonitis.

I had read a lot about the hazards of tendonitis on kayak trips. I learned there are sheaths that cover the tendons in our arms that can become stretched from overuse. If the sheaths become stretched and aggravated from repetitive tasks like paddling, rest is the only medicine. If the sheaths covering the tendons become overstretched, permanent, irreversible damage can occur.

Seated on the gravel beach I cradled my sore arm for relief and wondered what I was going to do. I didn't have the time to wait a week or two for my arm to heal. I had a schedule to keep. I felt defeated and angry at my body for letting me down. Unable to stand the pain any longer, I took two Tylenol tablets and crawled into the tent. While I lay in my sleeping bag, unable to sleep, I thought about my options and the possibility of not reaching Toronto. I was one day ahead of schedule. If the pain was still bad in the morning, I decided I would rest for the day. After that, I'd have to take it one day at a time. That night, sleep was the only escape from the pain and the fear of being forced to abandon my trip.

When I woke in the morning, the pain in my wrist was still there. My prayers to take the pain away had gone unanswered. Feeling restless, I walked to the base of a rock cliff at the end of the beach. I found a dry section of rock in the sun and sat down to meditate. For the first time since I had conceived the trip, I felt vulnerable. Fear was at my door, fighting to get in—fear of the unknown, my ailment, and the consequences if I pushed on in spite of the pain, and fear of not finishing what I had started. The feeling sat heavy on my chest.

I tried to escape my situation through mediation, but I couldn't quiet my mind. I quit after five minutes and made myself a mug of hot chocolate. The fact that it was sunny annoyed me even more. If I had to stay and rest, why did it have to be such a perfect day for paddling? The water inside the bay was calm and inviting. Invisible waves that washed gently on shore were the only sign the lake was breathing. I felt trapped.

When I remembered that I was due to contact the coast guard, I unpacked the radio. I had tried calling the day before without any success, so I was anxious to let them know I was okay. I held the mic in front of my mouth and spoke slowly.

"Sault Ste. Marie coast guard, this is the *Mai Fleur*, over." After a long moment of silence, I repeated my signal again and waited. Still no answer.

Now what? I thought. I had recharged the battery overnight at Agawa Bay, so unless there was something wrong with the radio, I should have made contact.

"Sault Ste. Marie coast guard this is the *Mai Fleur*, over." Pause. Nothing. Feeling angry about my sore arm and my failure to contact the coast guard, I turned the radio off. My arm had become uncomfortable again, so I decided to go back to the tent and rest. Inside my sleeping bag, I was overcome with dread until I eventually fell asleep.

A few hours later, I woke feeling stiff and lethargic. The sun's heat was baking the walls of the tent, making the inside unbearably hot. The pain in my wrist seemed less severe but still nagging, like a dull toothache that wouldn't go away. Forced out of the tent, I ate a chocolate bar in hopes it would lift my spirits. Engaged in the delight of chocolate, I felt my problems disappear until I had finished the last bite, and then all of my problems and fears came back to me. Injury, delay, and communication problems.

I set up the radio once again and tried to call the coast guard. My transmission was answered by a metallic growl of static. I adjusted the squelch and volume and called again. More static. After three attempts, I quit trying. I figured either the radio was damaged or my signal just wasn't getting through. What I needed was a clear line of sight towards Sault Ste. Marie.

Looking out on the water, I felt confident that if I could get in my kayak and paddle out of the bay, I would likely get better reception. But my wrist was too sore; I couldn't even hold my paddle, let alone take a stroke. Intent on making contact, I decided to climb the rocky hilltop at the end of the beach, hoping my signal would be heard from a higher vantage point.

The sun had shifted to the southwest so I knew it was past noon. Feeling hungry, I scooped two large handfuls of gorp into my mouth and washed it down with lukewarm water. Slinging my camera around my neck and shoulder, I packed the radio in its watertight canister and headed for the hill at the end of the beach. From its base, a steep slope rose upward more than three hundred metres in two terraced stages. The lower level was green with white pine and birch trees. Further up, the slope changed into a granite wall, bare to its summit except for the occasional tuft of grass that had grown out of cracks in the rock.

I climbed over huge boulders that blocked my path and entered a darkened forest. Shaded by the cover created by the trees and rock, only small shafts of sunlight touched the forest floor. Accustomed to the bright light on the beach, I removed my sunglasses and waited for my eyes to adjust.

The hike up the hill was slow. I took my time, careful not to twist an ankle on the rock rubble. When I could, I climbed up by holding onto young trees for support. Eventually, I reached the first plateau and stepped into the sunlight. From there, the view of Superior was magnificent. Sunlight danced on blue water below me. I was standing at the tops of the same white pine trees I had walked past at the end of the beach. After taking a few pictures with my camera, I earnestly assembled my radio.

"Sault Ste. Marie coast guard, this is the *Mai Fleur*, over." I waited expectantly for the familiar sound of the radio operator's voice. Nothing. I adjusted the squelch control and called again, with no response. All hope began to fade. I had felt certain I would get a response. I was closer than my last broadcast from the Dog River and considerably higher in elevation. What could be the problem?

I decided that a point of land must be blocking my signal, and I chose to climb higher. The next section of the slope was more rocky, with fewer trees and more plants and shrubs. Blueberry plants still bare of fruit covered much of the open areas. In only a few short minutes, I reached the next plateau and the edge of the tree line. Desperately, I set up the radio and called again. Still nothing. My heart sank with disappointment.

What could I do? The coast guard was expecting me to call by six that evening. If I didn't contact them, they would think I was in trouble and begin a search. I began to think about the problems that would cause ... unnecessary fear and expense. Questions would likely be raised about my ability to be out there alone, not to mention the bad publicity for the Canadian Cancer Society. Unhappy with any of the possibilities, I decided to climb all the way to the top of the hill. If the radio was damaged, I argued, nothing would help. But, if my signal was being blocked by land, I'd never know unless I climbed to the top.

The fact that the rest of the cliff was bare rock and becoming more vertical didn't seem to be a big concern to me then. From where I was standing, the climb looked relatively easy. I could see handholds and crevices in the rock much of the way up, so I convinced myself that I could make it.

Overconfident that I could climb up from where I was, I stuffed the radio canister inside my waist belt and started to climb. Favouring my right wrist and arm, I climbed with my left hand as much as possible. The first fifty or sixty metres were easy. There were plenty of crevices and ledges to hold on to. As the face of the rock wall became more vertical, however, places to grab and hold onto became fewer and more difficult, until I finally reached a dead end.

I had climbed myself into an area where there was nowhere to go. Suddenly, I was caught on the rock wall and couldn't climb any higher. When I looked between my legs, or over my shoulder, I couldn't see my last hand and footholds. I was stuck. I couldn't go forward, and I couldn't climb back down. I was pressed against the rock, hanging by my fingertips with the toes of my boots gripping bare rock. Without a ledge or crevice under my feet there was nothing supporting my weight. Immediately, I knew I was in trouble. I began to think about how dangerous my position was. My hiking boots were nearly slipping off the bare rock and I was hanging by my fingers. What was the likelihood that I could hold on if my feet slipped? For the next few seconds I panicked and cursed myself out loud for being there.

"What are you doing here? Are you fucking crazy? What, there wasn't enough danger in this trip that you had to create more?"

"I needed to contact the coast guard. I didn't think it would be this dangerous," I screamed back, as though I was talking to someone else. At that moment, fear of falling had completely taken control of my thoughts as I began to sense I was losing my grip. My hands became sweaty and my feet scrambled to stay gripped to the rock. The radio that was stuffed inside my waist band started to slip down my left pant leg. I looked over my shoulder toward the ground. It looked like a long way down.

I thought about the outcome of falling. I knew that even if I was lucky enough to survive the fall with only a broken hip or back, no one would ever find me. I could call for help all day and no one would ever hear me. While these thoughts raced in my mind, my arms and legs began to tremble and shake. Climbers call this *sewing machine legs*. How long can I hold on? An hour? More? Less? The situation seemed hopeless. I couldn't see any place to grab hold above me, and I felt afraid to move for fear of falling off the wall.

"Fuck! I don't want to die yet," I yelled.

Then, without any conscious thought or decision, I suddenly reached up with my left hand and jumped. It happened so fast that it caught me completely by surprise, but at the same time, it felt like everything happened in slow motion. In a split second, I was hanging from a rock ledge that only seconds before I was certain didn't exist. How did that happen? I never saw that ledge a moment ago. I was utterly in shock. At the same moment that I jumped, it felt as though a giant hand had come up from underneath my butt and shoved me to safety. The idea sounded crazy, yet it had felt *real*. Confused and shaken, I quickly scrambled to pull my chest and belly over the small ledge. With my legs still hanging over the side, I rested a moment before crawling further away from the void. When I looked over the edge, the bottom was out of sight.

Once I fully realized what had just happened, my body began to shake. I couldn't remember ever being so scared. Pushed by adrenalin, I climbed the last forty metres in a few short minutes. At the top of the hill, I stood and surveyed the landscape below me. The view was unequalled anywhere on earth. High above the trees, I felt as though I could touch the sky. I was free and safe once again. The trees and water were lifeless forms of colour below me, endless expanses of green and blue for as far as the eye could see.

Both anxious and hesitant to try the radio, I attached the antennae and held the mic nervously toward my mouth. Worried that no one would hear my message, I put the radio down. What if no one answered? What if my message didn't get through? At that moment I believed that the remainder of the trip depended on the call reaching the coast guard.

I held the transmitter down and repeated the call. Instantly, a voice screeched over the radio receiver, telling me to switch channels. The response was so quick and unexpected I had to wait for the message to be repeated. Listening intently, I heard the same voice call again and direct me to switch to channel forty-two. Excited about finally making contact, I tuned the radio to channel forty-two and called again. Like an echo, the coast guard radio operator returned my call. "Yes!" I shouted, excited to have made contact. After I had identified my camp position, I explained my difficulties with the radio.

"We could hear you loud and clear," the operator explained. "I guess your receiver was just too small to hear us." Elated that my radio was still working and filled with adrenalin, I talked non-stop until the operator had to beg off to clear the channel. What a relief. While I packed the radio into the waterproof canister, I thought about the events that had taken place during the day. To say I was happy to be alive didn't begin to convey my real feelings of joy.

Full of enough excitement for one day, I hiked down the easier north facing slope and bushwhacked through the forest to my camp. The terrain was rough, with steep slopes, car-sized boulders, and fallen trees, but still much safer than my original route. When I arrived safely in camp, I ate a banquet style dinner of rehydrated beef stroganoff and noodles with butterscotch pudding for dessert to celebrate.

A Bittersweet Farewell

WHEN I GOT up in the morning there was frost on the tent, but the day was clear and sunny. The lake was unusually calm, as though it was inviting me to paddle by saying, "Come on, I'll go easy on you today." My wrist was still sore, but the conditions were too good to stay and wait. I packed up and left, setting a slow but steady pace. Eager to make distance, I veered away from shore and headed toward Pointe aux Mines and then Mamainse Point, cutting kilometres off my route.

All my attention was focused on my paddling. Each time I extended my arm too far forward or down, sharp, piercing pain shot into the side of my wrist. The pain was so quick it was shocking, and it quickly had my nerves on edge, waiting for the next debilitating attack.

There was virtually no wind all the way to Mamainse Point, and then the wind came up from behind and pushed me all the way to Pancake Bay. It felt as though the lake had tried to help me all day.

The beaches at Pancake Bay looked so perfect, they seemed man-made. A wide band of white-gold coloured sand spread out along the shore, ready for a mob of kids and their families with Frisbees, kites, and buckets with sand shovels. When I arrived on the beach there was no one there.

I set up my tent in the campground and then hiked to find a pay phone. When my dad answered the phone, there wasn't much he could say. I just needed moral support and the comfort of his voice. My dad suggested I tape a crystal stone he had given me to my sore wrist. I didn't know how that would help me, but later that night before going to bed, I taped the stone anyway. I decided it couldn't hurt. Remembering the shove from the mysterious hand when I was stuck on the rock face, I accepted there were some things I couldn't explain.

The pain in my wrist was still present when I went to bed, but I felt calmer about my injury. It was as though I had lost my fear and I believed everything would work out for the best. *Have faith, Michael. You must have faith,* I told myself.

When I woke in the morning and the lake was calm, I knew someone was looking after me. My wrist was still very sore, but I packed and left anyway. I kayaked from Pancake Bay to Corbeil Point and then across to Rudderhead Point.

Paddling close to shore, I saw a woman working in her yard, and when I got closer we both waved, and then she called out a warm greeting. I paddled closer, and we talked for a while until she invited me for a cold drink. Her name was Lysanne Chenier. She told me that she worked as a family counselor in small northern communities. While we talked, her fiancé Rene came home, and soon after, I was invited to stay for dinner and the night.

Over drinks, I learned that Rene and Lysanne had bought five lots along the shoreline four years earlier. Their log home had running water from April to November, a sauna, and vegetable garden. Conscious of a desire to live in peace and harmony with nature, they had left the shoreline just as nature designed it.

They both made me feel so comfortable and welcome it was like being in the company of old friends. Rene helped me move my kayak onto shore and lit the sauna so I could clean up. While I enjoyed a fabulous hot sauna and wash, my hosts prepared dinner. Afterward, we sat by the water and ate an assortment of fruit and cheese with a salad and drank cold beer. Everything tasted fresh and delicious.

Lysanne and Rene told me how the wind often pushed huge slabs of thick ice from Lake Superior on top of each other, creating ice caves near their shore. The ice caves, Rene explained, were opaque blue, and they often gathered inside with friends for wine and cheese parties. That night I went to bed feeling clean and content from an evening of great company.

I slept later than usual the next day. When my hosts got up, we ate brunch together—bacon and eggs, homemade bread, and freshly brewed coffee. During brunch, Rene and Lysanne convinced me to stay and rest my wrist. The two had plans to work in the yard and asked me to drive their truck to Goulais River for groceries and supplies.

Driving a truck again felt strange, as though I shouldn't be on the highway driving when I had told everyone I was kayaking. Even the speed felt bizarre. I had become so used to the speed of my kayak, it felt as though I had jumped into a spacecraft and was travelling at the speed of light.

For dinner that night, Rene barbecued a whole chicken on a rotisserie and served baked potatoes, salad, and chocolate with almonds. During dinner, my hosts told me funny stories about their first experiences with the local wildlife after they had built their house.

My favourite story involved Rene and a red fox that wanted to make it very clear who owned the property. Each time that Rene went outside to go pee, the fox would go over to the same spot and pee too. If Rene took a bucket to get water from the lake, the fox would stand in the way and look at him as if to say, "You can't come down here." And if Rene tried to take a step to one side to go around, the fox would move over and glare at him until Rene retreated back to the house. Slowly, over time, the fox eventually let Rene pass to get water and from then on the fox stayed close and even lay nearby in the sun while Rene worked in the yard or on his truck. The fox had decided they could stay.

I woke before seven the following morning feeling well rested. The sky threatened rain and there was already a stiff wind out of the south. It was difficult to say goodbye to my new friends. I felt we had become close in a very short time, and I sensed they felt the same.

I paddled into the wind for most of the day. Despite my wrist, I pushed hard to Goulais Point and then started the crossing to North Gros Cap. Half way across I had to go pee, but I was too far from shore and struggled to hold it. An hour later, my body refused to go on until I had emptied my bladder. I was barely able to move without triggering a release.

Reluctantly, I decided to try to pee in a bottle, but I knew it wouldn't be easy. Nervously, I took off my lifejacket, unzipped my dry suit, and pulled my head through the rubber neck gasket. Careful not to upset the kayak, I pulled my arms through the sleeves and pushed the suit down toward my waist. Meanwhile, I kept thinking how precarious the situation was for me. If anything happened right then, I was going into the icy water without any protection. I tried to shove a water bottle inside my pants but it wouldn't fit. With the angle I was sitting, it was too awkward. Desperate, I squirmed, wiggled, and bent my body until I could pee in the bottle. It was an uncomfortable and dangerous exercise that I did not want to repeat.

I arrived in the small hamlet of Gros Cap late in the day and camped near the Bluewater Inn. It was the second day in a row that I had not seen snow or ice, and I hoped that spring had arrived.

It rained hard the next day as I paddled from Gros Cap to Sault Ste. Marie. All morning my feelings had been mixed and confused. I felt exhilarated at the fact I had paddled safely across Lake Superior and was arriving in Sault Ste. Marie on schedule. I had completed something that many people had told me was impossible, or too dangerous to attempt alone. But I also felt sad and melancholy. I had known for days that I would eventually leave Lake Superior, but I hadn't anticipated the strong sense of loss that I felt then.

For thirty days, Lake Superior had been my companion, teacher, and confidant. Everything I saw or experienced was connected to the lake in some way. When I needed to talk, Superior listened quietly, patiently. When I needed to slow down and take more notice of life around me, Superior would hold me back, helping me stay focused on what was important *in the moment*. Our connection was subtle, yet it was very real to me. I felt as though I was leaving a close friend, uncertain if our lives would ever meet as perfectly again.

After seeing endless space between the shores of Lake Superior, I suddenly felt confined on the St. Mary's River. The only shipping channel that joins Lake Superior with Lake Huron, the St. Mary's River was busy with Canadian and international freighters passing every half hour. Although I was uneasy with the transition, I could not escape from the reality that my trip was quickly changing. Soon I would relinquish control in an effort to include the Canadian Cancer Society with my trip: a goal I had set in the beginning, but had forgotten during my quiet isolation on Lake Superior.

Rendezvous in Sault Ste. Marie

I reached Pointe Aux Pins by mid-morning as thick fog closed in around me. Wary of being run over by a freighter, I tried to follow the shipping lane markers down the river. It was similar to a game of blind man's bluff; I wandered on and off course in an effort to follow the river that often swelled to lake-sized proportions. Using my compass to guide my direction between marker buoys, I paddled steadily toward the Sault. After more than two hours of fumbling blindly through the fog, I saw the vague silhouette of the Rainbow Bridge that joins Ontario and the State of Michigan.

My next challenge was deciding which part of the bridge to paddle toward. I knew there was a Canadian water lock, but I had no idea where it was located. After studying the bridge for a few minutes, I noticed that all the boat and ship traffic entered and exited the fog from one location. Confused on where to go I decided to follow the ships. My course eventually led me between two high cement walls in the middle of the river. Hopeful that I was headed in the right direction, I continued along until suddenly a man came running out of a telephone booth-sized building wearing a lifejacket and waving his arms.

"You can't bring that rowboat down here," he ordered excitedly.

Anxious to know where I was, I asked him if I was on the Canadian or American side of the river.

"This is the U.S. side. You can't bring that rowboat down here," the man repeated emphatically. "Where did you come from?"

"Thunder Bay."

"You rowed that thing all the way from Thunder Bay?" the man asked in disbelief.

"No, I paddled all the way from Thunder Bay," I corrected cheekily.

Annoyed that I wasn't taking him seriously, the man told me he didn't care how I got there, but that I couldn't come through the locks. When I asked him where the Canadian locks were, he told me they had been broken for three years and that everyone used the U.S. locks. Worried that I wasn't going to leave before another freighter came through, the man ordered me to leave his canal immediately.

I paddled toward the Canadian shore, looking for a place to get off the river. As I got closer, I recognized the Canadian locks by the high cement walls like the ones I had seen on the American side. Cautious of the strong river current, I paddled into a calm bay and tied the kayak to a raft of floating logs that were chained to shore. Uncertain how long the canal was, I decided to scout ahead on foot.

I walked to the end of the locks and didn't see any staff from Parks Canada. It was probably close to a kilometre long, too far to portage my kayak and supplies. Uncertain what to do, I found a pay phone and called the cancer society in Toronto to let them know I had arrived safely. I spoke with Sara and she promised to call staff at the cancer society in Sault Ste. Marie to let them know I was there.

When I got back to my kayak, I called the coast guard and told them I had arrived. When I finished the call, Terry O'Neil from the cancer society pulled up in his truck. He told me he had the media waiting for me at the city marina, so I quickly unloaded my kayak, and we loaded it and my supplies on his truck and portaged past the locks.

When I went to climb into the kayak, I realized I didn't have my lifejacket. In a panic, I looked everywhere until a park employee who was working late found it and returned it to me. In the confusion after arriving, I had left it in a bathroom at the end of the locks.

I paddled the short distance from the locks to the city marina. When the small group of cancer society staff and supporters saw me coming, they began to clap loudly, and I raced to meet them. An MCTV camera man and a photographer from the *Sault Star* were among the crowd when I climbed out of my kayak. Erin, an employee from the Old Ski House, handed me a $100 cheque for the cancer society. It was a collection from the staff at the outdoor store in town, and my first visible donation towards Kayaking for Cancer. I was ecstatic from the experience of holding the cheque and then passing it over to Terry.

When the media and crowd had disappeared, I was left to figure out what to do with my kayak and where to stay the night. A junior staff at the marina told me I could store my kayak on the dock and talk to his supervisor in the morning. Recognizing there were no city campgrounds, Terry offered me his motorhome parked in his driveway outside of town.

Terry had to be up early the next morning, so once I had settled into his motorhome, we said good night. Fleur had sent a bundle of letters for me to Terry's address. Most of the letters were weeks old, but they were my only connection to her. After a hot shower, I carefully read and re-read each one late into the night.

I got up at 5:00 a.m. to catch a ride with Terry into town. I wanted to get back to the marina and settle matters over the storage of my kayak for the night. The marina charged $22 a night for docking, so I was hoping I wouldn't have a bill waiting for me when I arrived.

I called my parents before my dad left for work and told them I was in Sault Ste. Marie. I could sense they were relieved that I was off Lake Superior. After we said goodbye, I quickly called Mark and Cathy in Parry Sound, and then Cindy and Jim in Thunder Bay. Cindy called Fred Jones at CBC, and he called me for our last interview. When the interview was over, I was sorry to say goodbye. I enjoyed my interview conversations with Fred, and it made me feel personally connected to the city of Thunder Bay.

By the time I had finished the phone calls, the marina manager had arrived and offered me free storage for my kayak and unlimited use of their shower and laundry facilities. It was the break I was hoping for since I didn't have much money.

Later that morning, I walked twenty minutes to the hospital to have my wrist examined. The doctor confirmed my suspicion that I had tendonitis. She told me to rest my wrist for a week or two. When I told her I didn't have time to rest, she suggested I buy some ibuprofen to help reduce the swelling.

In the afternoon, I called and spoke with Mark Climie at the Canadian Cancer Society office in Toronto and experienced my first personal attack. Joyce had called Mark soon after I had left her home in

Marathon. She complained that she thought my reasons for doing the trip were disingenuous and that my only reason was to get a free kayak. When Mark questioned her, she told him that I had mentioned on the radio that the kayak company would let me keep the kayak if I finished the trip. Mark's first words to me felt like an inquisition.

"Did you say anything during a radio interview about the kayak company giving you the kayak?" The question took me completely by surprise.

"I don't know, I might have," I answered shakily, not understanding the meaning of the question.

After Mark told me about the phone call he had received from Joyce, I felt my integrity had been attacked. Mark had explained to Joyce, in my defense, about the work I had done to raise funds, but her accusation stung. I had been invited into her home and treated like family. It was hurtful to hear that she questioned my motives.

Mark cautioned me to be more vague about the kayak in the future. At the time of the interview, the question about where I got the kayak seemed innocent and benign. I didn't think anything about it. I needed a kayak for the trip, and the company wanted to advertise in Ontario. I paid to have the kayak shipped from British Columbia. If I finished the trip the cost of the boat was cheap publicity for them. Letting me keep it was as much sentimentality as it was business.

"Look, Michael, there's nothing wrong with you keeping the kayak," Mark told me as we talked about it over the phone. "You just don't need to be so open about the arrangement." I didn't know how to be anything but myself. I didn't offer the information about the kayak, it just came out in the interview. By the time I got off the phone, I was feeling angry, defensive, and confused. I knew I needed the media to help me get the public's attention and raise donations, but suddenly I felt unprepared to speak to the public or give an interview.

In the afternoon, Fleur called Terry's house and left a message that she was flying in from Sioux Lookout at eleven thirty that night. Wow! I was so excited to see her. Terry brought me back to his house and I called the Days Inn and made a reservation. My friend Cheryl, who had moved to Sault Ste. Marie to work for Forestry Canada, came and picked me up. We hadn't seen each other since our friends Kelly and Rick were married the previous September, so it was a nice visit. We went for coffee and caught up on life, work, and family news, while we waited for Fleur's plane to arrive.

When Fleur walked through the arrival gate, she looked radiant. Six weeks of tree planting had produced a lean and fit goddess with curves. Her hair was bleached blonde from the sun, and her face and arms were tanned. When I wrapped my arms around her middle, I could feel her strength and vitality. We kissed hungrily, without any concern for the other people around us.

The three of us went for coffee and a donut and talked for a while at a local Tim Horton's. It would have been rude to ask Cheryl to simply drive us to the hotel, but all I could think about was being alone with Fleur. Cheryl was great about the whole thing. She knew how much we wanted to be alone and soon whisked us off to the hotel.

It was one thirty in the morning by the time we checked in to our room. We had spent so much time apart since September that it felt a bit strange at first. We sat on the bed and talked and stared at each other, happy to be together. We took turns recounting our days since we had last been together. So much had happened to each of us, we both were eager to know every small detail. By early morning, we had become *one* again. Our hearts and bodies had come together and joined in that special union called love.

With no better place to be, we slept, came together as a couple, and lay in each other's arms until midday, when we decided to get up. We took a shower together and were enjoying the hotel's endless supply of hot water when we heard a loud knock at the door.

"Hotel guest services, do you have a flood in your room?" the voice called calmly through the door.

"No, we're okay here," I called back.

"Well, sir, we have water coming through the ceiling in our lobby below your room," the voice continued.

In a panic, I pulled the shower curtain back and gasped to see an ankle deep puddle of water on the floor.

"Oh my God, you're right, we do have a flood! Oh, I'm terribly sorry," I stammered back.

"It's okay, sir, we're used to it. The shower curtains are a bit short in that room. Can you make sure the curtain is inside the tub?" the voice asked before disappearing. It was an embarrassing moment, but once we were alone we laughed hysterically like two teenagers caught by our parents. We were together again, and nothing else mattered.

In the afternoon we went to the local shopping mall. Fleur bought me a pair of sport sandals for my trip, and we searched for a summer dress for her. She didn't find a dress that she liked, so we ate ice cream and went back to the hotel. The weather was unbelievably hot and sticky. Someone told us it was thirty-four degrees Celsius, but the humidity was stifling.

We swam in the pool, used the sauna and hot tub, and acted like a young honeymoon couple. In the evening, we went to dinner at a southwestern style restaurant called Kiva. I ordered smoked salmon sausages with rice and green beans. The food was delicious. For dessert, we bought a tub of Ben and Jerry's chocolate chip cookie dough ice cream and shared it in bed.

The next morning I woke early to call CBC radio in Sudbury for a live interview. After the call, Fleur agreed to walk with me to the coast guard and The Old Ski House to thank them for their help and donation. It was a long walk and the heat and humidity wore us down, so we stopped first for Popsicles and then for lunch in an air-conditioned restaurant called Giovani's. On the walk back, we went looking for ice cream in a shopping mall and Fleur found a dress she liked. She looked gorgeous and was really happy because the dress was on sale. Conscious of our money, we bought wine and groceries at the local market and cooked dinner on the balcony of our hotel room.

The next day, we woke up before seven. I had to get out of bed and back to my routine. It was our last morning together, and it had been a wonderful time. I was amazed at how I felt about Fleur. It seemed as though I was falling in love with her for the first time all over again. I couldn't touch, hold, or be close enough to her, and the feeling made me happy.

I called my mom that morning, and asked her if she would pick Fleur up at the airport in Toronto. The morning went by too quickly. After I made one trip to the marina with my kayak gear, I was forced to say goodbye to Fleur. A limo had arrived to pick her up and take her to the airport. To our astonishment, the limo was cheaper than a taxi. The scene of her climbing into a limo and waving goodbye was like something out of a movie. Guy and girl enjoy a romantic rendezvous in a hotel. Beautiful girl drives away in a limousine, leaving guy all alone.

Breakfast at the Green Lantern

Fleur's flight to Toronto left shortly after lunch. I spent the afternoon repacking the kayak with my new supplies, eventually leaving at three thirty. The heat and humidity continued, and I could feel the hot air travel across the water and rush over me as I paddled. I melted inside my dry suit and debated whether I needed to wear it now that I was off Superior.

I felt no connection to the St. Mary's River. After the isolation and beauty of Superior, I didn't like the feel of the river. Speedboats, fishing boats, yachts, and Sea-Doos all buzzed noisily past or around me. There were too many people and no moments of quiet. I paddled uneventfully through the St. Mary's River system past Little Lake George and Squirrel Island and into Lake George.

The St. Mary's River system was dirty with litter and looked polluted. I decided that I wouldn't eat any fish that came from the river, let alone swim in the water. I had spoken with a commercial scuba diver at the marina in Sault Ste. Marie who told me he had seen what the cities of Sault Saint Marie, Michigan, and Sault Ste. Marie, Ontario, had dumped into the river. He had advised me not to drink even filtered water until I reached St. Joseph Island, and I saw for myself why. While I paddled, I passed large clumps of floating algae and the water had a strong odor of raw sewage.

That night, I camped on Baschine Island on George Lake. I landed on a sand beach in front of an old, abandoned cottage. While I cooked dinner, I watched a porcupine five metres away swimming to shore.

It made sense that porcupines could swim, but I had never heard of a porcupine swimming before, and the sight of the prickly swimmer body surfing to shore made me chuckle

The evening was hot and muggy, with pesky mosquitoes and black flies. I wished I was back on the cool shores of Superior. I missed the lake deeply. As consolation, I promised myself that I would be happier once I reached Lake Huron. The change in temperature from Lake Superior was extreme. That night, I slept on top of my sleeping bag for the first time.

In the morning, the fog was so thick I couldn't see more than a few metres from shore. Birds sang beautifully while I prepared breakfast, which raised my spirits, until I noticed a sign on the dilapidated boathouse near my tent. The sign, written in faded red paint, said, *This is Indian Land—Trespassers will be charged.*

"Oh great," I mumbled. "Half a day from Sault Ste. Marie and I'm already attracting trouble."

I ate my breakfast quickly and left, hoping no one saw me. George Lake was very big but with the same dirty water as the river. The water didn't start to clear until I reached the St. Joseph Channel. Once I passed the bridge that linked St. Joseph Island to the mainland, the shoreline began to look more like the eastern shores of Georgian Bay: rock islands, windswept white pines, and sculpted rock. I camped in a grassy clearing on the north side of Campement d'Ours Island, situated in the middle of St. Joseph Channel on the St. Mary's River.

When I crawled out of the tent the next morning, a young, cinnamon-coloured deer jumped up from its bed in the tall grass. It had slept only thirty metres from my tent, seeking safety in my company. I made no attempt to be quiet while I made my breakfast, and the more noise I made, the more interest the deer showed toward me. The yearling was so inquisitive, it walked closer and closer until I thought it was going to join me for breakfast. Then the wind changed direction and it caught my scent, and the deer let out a loud snort, turned sharply, and leaped into the bushes.

I kayaked thirty kilometres that day, stopping on the beach in Thessalon. It was Father's Day, so I phoned my dad to say hi and wish him well. My dad told me his mom was still in the Newmarket hospital and that everyone was very worried. When my dad hung up, I called

117

my grandpa to wish him an early happy birthday and ask him about grandma. In my entire memory, she had always been the one that had taken care of him through one form of health problem after another—heart attack, gall stones, cancer. My grandpa wasn't used to being left alone to worry if someone else was going to get better, and I could tell he would gladly have traded her places.

When I returned to the beach, I met Dan, a young guy from Sault Ste. Marie. After a quick chat, he offered me a place to camp beside his family cottage, but by the time we had moved my kayak from the beach, he insisted I stay in their spare room. He had come to his family cottage in Thessalon to cut the grass and do some spring chores.

Dan told me later that his mom had died of cancer in February, and that was why he felt an instant connection with me. I found Dan friendly and easy-going, and we talked and played cards late into the evening.

The family cottage had an interesting history. Dan's grandpa had built the main room of the cottage at the turn of the century. When the Dionne Quintuplets were born in 1934, people started driving to North Bay to see them. The old Trans-Canada Highway went through Thessalon back then before the bypass. Cars were lined bumper to bumper going through town, and everyone was looking for a place to eat or sleep.

Dan's grandfather opened the cottage as a restaurant called the Green Lantern. Dan directed my eyes to a business card posted on the wall that said *Green Lantern—Meals—We guarantee our coffee—Lunches*. Dan explained that, as the demand for more tables increased, Dan's grandpa expanded the cottage. When the crowds stopped coming, the family was left with the cottage they enjoy now.

I found the history, and the fact that the Dionne Quintuplets were partly responsible for the construction of a family cottage fascinating. With the television and Internet culture we have now, I couldn't imagine people driving across the province to see five babies.

The next morning, I got up and made Dan and myself breakfast. Dan confessed that he wasn't a cook, and I took the opportunity to show my appreciation by making each of us a western omelet. Over coffee, I wrote out some information about my trip for Dan to take to the Thessalon newspaper. By the time Dan and I shook hands goodbye, he was a new recruit for the Kayaking for Cancer campaign, lending his support by taking a media release I had written to the Thessalon newspaper.

For the rest of the day, I never left the kayak. I paddled, ate and even peed while seated inside the *Mai Fleur*, eventually stopping around six o'clock near De Roberval Point. I made camp, cooked dinner, called the coast guard and eventually went to bed after writing only a short note in my journal.

I woke in the middle of the night to the sound of a deer snorting outside my tent. I suspected I had inadvertently blocked the deer's trail to the lake with my tent. The snorting went on for five minutes, until I started to snicker and the deer ran away.

"Maybe the wind changed direction and he got a whiff of my dirty socks," I joked before going back to sleep.

I woke again at 4:00 a.m., to the sound of big waves crashing on shore. I got up and checked on the kayak. There was thick fog, and I couldn't see beyond the shoreline. The kayak was okay, so I went back to bed.

When I got up later, the fog had cleared, and the sky had started to turn from grey to blue. The wind had been building all night, and by the time I was ready to leave, large breaking waves were crashing onto shore. Launching into big waves by yourself is difficult. I had to get into the kayak and close the spray skirt over the cockpit before the waves filled the kayak with water. Once the cockpit was sealed, I had to paddle away from shore before the waves could push me backward onto the beach. It took a couple of attempts, but eventually I made a successful dry launch and was on my way.

I struggled against strong headwinds and two-metre breaking waves all day. Some waves crashed on top of me and one ripped away a water bottle that was fastened under bungee cords on the kayak deck. It had been awhile since I had lost any gear, and I cursed the wave as it swept the plastic bottle out of sight. My first gift to Lake Huron.

I made slow progress that day. My right wrist was still very sore, and it tired more quickly than usual. I wanted to stop at least a half dozen times but pushed on despite the pain. When I checked my progress on the map and realized how slow I was paddling, my spirits sank. Never before had I felt more tired, sore, or emotionally drained. To combat the desire to stop, I forced myself to keep going.

Just to the next point, I told myself. *A little farther. Okay, just to the next island.* I pushed myself further by playing this mind game of focusing on landmarks and singing to myself to help distract the pain.

When my wrist became too sore to take another stroke, I started looking for a place to camp. Much of the shoreline had steep rock blocking my way to shore, and I was forced to keep paddling until I was desperate to stop. Then, as though some divine force was working in my favour, I found the perfect site—an island with a small sand beach, sheltered from the wind and waves.

Later that night, I sat on a rocky point at the end of the beach and watched the sun set while sipping a mug of hot chocolate. All my struggles melted away for the moment with the setting sun. I had paddled one more day closer to Toronto, and for that, I was truly thankful.

DOCTOR'S ADVICE

M Y STRUGGLES CONTINUED the next day. It rained on and off until the afternoon, and headwinds and two-metre waves forced me to work harder than I wanted. I didn't feel well. I skipped lunch but ate a Mars bar for energy. I noticed that I was tiring earlier each day and that I had to push myself to keep paddling. To stay motivated, I hummed the theme song to the movie *Rocky*.

I found it difficult to map my progress. I had purchased a few larger scale maps to save money, but now I regretted my decision. The scale was too large. Not all of the islands I was seeing were on my map.

When I felt I had passed my daily goal of Spanish Mills, I began to look for a campsite but saw nothing that was suitable. I had passed plenty of nice campsites hours ago, and this fact was an irritant. Island after island I searched for a place to camp, but I couldn't find a place to safely go to shore. My arms were like Jell-O, and I simply wanted some place to stop. As I approached the next island, I visualized a beach around the approaching point. To my delight, there was a beach surrounded by high rock hills. I had found paradise.

When I climbed out of the kayak, my legs buckled. I had spent ten hours in the kayak without a break. My body ached all over, and I walked bent over like a crippled old man. After I had finished my daily chores of cleaning the kayak and setting out clothes and gear to dry, I hiked to the top of the hill to set up my tent. The beach was nestled in a valley between two rocky hills. The sun was dropping and there wasn't much daylight on the beach, so I decided to make camp on the hill where there was more light and fewer bugs.

The view from my tent site was incredible. I felt so blessed to have found the site. I had been thinking during the day how much I missed Superior, but this site renewed my love for Huron, with its unique beauty of sculpted rock and windswept pines.

While I set up my bed, six gulls came to the beach looking for food. They were very persistent. While I was on top of the hill, they poked at my belongings aggressively. I ignored them, thinking they were just doing their thing, trying to scratch out an existence, until one of them shit on my kayak. After that, I didn't have any patience for them, and I chased them away or threw pine cones until they left my site.

That night, a glowing moon rose up and shone through the trees, bathing everything in its soft white light. The moment felt magical, and I wished someone was there with me to share the beauty. Far in the distance, I saw a lighthouse beacon flashing and decided I must be camped on Croker Island.

The next day, paddling was much the same routine, including my poor health. My stomach felt queasy, and I had lost the voracious appetite that usually fuelled my body. I found it difficult to decipher where I was much of the time. There were so many islands that my map didn't show.

After a long day, I arrived in Little Current at six in the evening. Unsure where to go, I paddled straight to the marina. On my last broadcast with the Sault Ste. Marie coast guard, the operator had told me to start contacting the Wiarton office once I reached the town of Little Current. I tried calling the Wiarton coast guard but had no luck making contact. Next to me was a large boat called the Malibu II, so I asked the couple on board if they would call the coast guard for me. Their radio barely got through, but they were able to make contact long enough to confirm my location and that I was safe.

After notifying the coast guard, I walked into town and called my parents, Mark and Cathy, and my uncle Greg in Nobleton. My grandma was still in the hospital but had started to show signs of improvement. That was good news.

For dinner, I treated myself to a homemade burger and fries from a food stand. The food tasted good going down, but afterward it didn't sit well. My stomach was still unsettled, and for a short time I wasn't sure if my meal was going to stay down.

I chose a campsite in the tall grass near the edge of the marina. While I was setting up the tent, I managed to crack one of my aluminum tent poles and had to repair it with duct tape. I went to bed feeling miserable but hopeful that I would feel better in the morning.

I woke early the next day feeling like I might throw up. Still tired, I went back to sleep and woke again at six. I got up, packed my tent, and walked for fifteen minutes back into town. I called my parents and asked them to call the Mountain Equipment Co-op store and order a new tent pole.

I walked back to the marina and waited until eight to use the washroom. It cost me a dollar fifty for a hot shower. Actually, they should have called it a "hot dribble" because they had a fancy Ontario Hydro nozzle on the shower head, so the water just dribbled out. While I showered, I saw a spider the size of a silver dollar crawl up the wall. It seemed funny to me that I was bothered by the bathroom conditions. I told myself to be happy it was hot water and not the ice water back on Lake Superior. I was aware how quickly my expectations had changed with my environment. When I was alone camping, I was happy with a flat spot to lay my head each night, but here I was complaining because there was low water pressure.

After my shower, I walked to Dunn's Food Mart and bought orange juice, muffins, and a banana for breakfast. I still had the desire to eat, but nothing sat well for very long.

The cancer society had given me the name of someone who lived in Little Current that was willing to store my food. That person was Beth Bond, and when I showed up at her house, she greeted me warmly. Beth was a few years older than me, attractive, and held herself with a strong sense of independence. She had stored the food and camp fuel that I had mailed to her in the garage, and the boxes were stacked neatly in a corner.

Beth wanted to help, so she introduced me to a news reporter with the *Manitoulin Expositor* newspaper. The reporter and I had an interview, and in the process I learned there was a doctor in town who was a kayaker.

After the interview, I went to the hospital to see Dr. Dieter Poenn about my tendonitis and flu symptoms. Dr. Poenn had been on the national whitewater kayaking team for ten years, so I was hopeful he would have some good advice. After examining me, he told me my tendonitis was caused by gripping my paddle too tightly during the forward push stage of my paddle stroke. He suggested that I loosen my grip, watch for symptoms, and take the ibuprofen to control the inflammation when it hurt. As for my stomach, he said I might have the flu but that it was hard to tell.

By the time I arrived back at Beth's house, I was feeling so ill I decided to stay another night. Beth told me I was welcome to set up my tent in her backyard. It rained all afternoon, and when she came home from work, she told me to move my tent into her garage. Beth treated me to dinner at the Old English Pantry, and then to ice cream at the local dairy. The dinner and ice cream tasted good, but I felt ill afterward and wished I hadn't eaten such a big meal.

During dinner, Beth told me that she had to leave for a family gathering at her parents' home. She had seemed distracted, as though she really didn't want to be with me, which made me feel awkward. As we talked more, she explained that her sister had died of bone marrow cancer and that her brother-in-law was visiting from Edmonton for the anniversary of her burial. After learning the significance of the day, I felt guilty for being there and keeping her from her family. Beth's willingness to be with me said a lot about who she was as a person, and I appreciated her kindness even more.

After we went for ice cream, Beth dropped me off at her house and left to join her family. I crawled into my dry tent inside Beth's garage. It was still raining, and although my tent site seemed odd, I was thankful to be there. I wrote in my journal and went to bed with an uneasy stomach for a second night.

No Time to Rest

It was still raining the next morning when I sat up in my sleeping bag. Looking through the garage door, I knew from the look of the clouds that it was going to rain all day. I ate breakfast with Beth, had a shower, and then packed my tent. Beth had bought me some oranges, apples, and cucumbers as a parting gift. It was another sign of her thoughtfulness, remembering an earlier comment about foods I had missed. I left Beth some dry food that I didn't need and some camp fuel she said she could use the next time she went car camping. It wasn't much to show my appreciation, but it was all I had to give.

At noon, Beth drove me to the marina. Huddled under an umbrella, she watched patiently while I packed my kayak. My body ached, I had a throbbing headache, and I felt as though I would vomit at any moment. The last place I wanted to be that day was paddling in the rain. But my friend Mark in Parry Sound had organized some kind of fundraising event on July 1 for Canada Day, and I had promised him that I would be there. I felt miserable, but I was determined not to be late. I had already taken a day and a half off from paddling and had only five days to paddle the roughly two hundred kilometres.

It was 12:30 when I finally left, and by the time I reached the island's swing bridge, I felt exhausted. A few minutes later the fog rolled in and a voice in my head whined, *I want to go to bed.*

A strong northeast wind pushed at the bow of the kayak as I struggled to stay on my compass bearing. Blinded once again by the weather, I searched for islands through the fog to check my progress. Trapped in the endless white tunnel, I felt like the day dragged on forever. The wind and rain never let up, and I had to force myself to keep paddling despite the nausea, headache, and cold chills.

I paddled all day and never left the kayak. Sometime late in the afternoon I started to look for a place to camp. The nausea and pain in my stomach had become too much to bear and efforts to induce myself to vomit had failed repeatedly. I paddled along the south shore of an unnamed island and part of Centre Island in search of a place to land, without success. The shore was blocked by large, jagged rocks that threatened to rip and tear at the *Mai Fleur* if I attempted to go to shore in the rough waves.

Anxious to make camp, I crossed over to Badgeley Island and followed its eastern shoreline. Strong prevailing winds swept down the east side of Badgeley Island and rolled over a shallow rock shelf that made landing look impossible. Judging from the breaking waves, I knew if I tried to paddle onto shore, the waves would bounce the kayak off the shallow rock shelf and damage the hull. Expecting the rest of the shoreline to be similar, I left Badgeley Island and paddled toward George Island three kilometres away.

When I eventually reached George Island, it was almost dusk. I had paddled thirty-three kilometres and was desperate to make camp. I had reached the point that I didn't care about the kayak anymore. I would have dragged the boat over a jagged rock wall if it meant that I could crawl into my sleeping bag.

I paddled into shore and bumped off beachball sized rocks. My hands and feet were numb with cold, and when I stood up, I had to jump up and down and swing my arms to help get the blood to flow. I unpacked my tent and sleeping bag and searched for a tent site. I spent twenty minutes searching in the rain, but I couldn't find any spot suitable to set up my tent. Not one. Not even a bad tent site. The ground had either jagged or pillow-shaped rock in every direction.

Frustrated, I gave up and repacked the kayak. The first stages of hypothermia had started, and I shivered uncontrollably. Since breakfast, I had only eaten an apple, and my stomach was too queasy to think of food. I knew that I needed to start paddling quickly to get warm.

Back on the water, I studied my map with a small flashlight. The village of Killarney looked like it was only five kilometres away, and it was probably the best place to search for a campsite in the dark. As I started to paddle, the rain changed to a fine mist and a bright full moon shone through the thick cloud cover, helping me find my way. Forty-five minutes later, I rounded the entrance into the channel between George Island and the mainland near Killarney. Immediately, my eyes were drawn to a faint light off in the distance. Spurred with hope that there was somewhere to camp, I paddled faster towards the light. It was ten o'clock when I stopped beside a dock filled with boats of different sizes. Loud voices and music bellowed from one boat that glowed like a giant jack-o-lantern.

The moon had disappeared and it was pitch black, so I couldn't see if there was any place to land. In need of direction, I called out a greeting to the men in the boat. The men were not expecting anyone outside their boat on a rainy night, and my call caused some commotion.

"Did you hear that? Turn off the radio," I heard one man say in a panic voice. When it was quiet, I called again.

"Hello in the boat."

After a few seconds a voice answered. "Who's out there?"

"A lone kayaker, is there a beach around where I can come ashore?"

In a flash, three men were standing on the dock shining flashlights in my face. After I had explained that I was looking for a place to come ashore, the men used their flashlights to guide me along the shoreline to a small gravel beach.

I had arrived at Killarney Mountain Lodge. When the men learned where I had come from, one of them went and fetched John Solomon, the night watchman. John was very sympathetic and found a place for me to set up my tent and offered me a hot shower. When my tent was up, the men returned to their cards and whiskey and John led me to the resort washrooms near the outdoor pool. After handing me fresh towels and a face cloth, John told me that I was welcome to use the sauna too, and then said good night.

Cold to the core, I relished the idea of a sauna and was thankful the room was still warm. I climbed the tiered cedar benches and sat down with my back against the block wall close to the ceiling. My pores sucked in the warmth like a sponge while my body slowly relaxed.

Exhausted from the day, I sat half asleep until suddenly I felt that I was going to vomit. Running out of the sauna, I got as far as the bathroom sink before I threw up. When it seemed like my stomach was empty, my bowels erupted, and I spent the next hour glued to the toilet. When my body was completely empty, I showered and walked back to my tent. It was 1:00 a.m. when I crawled into my sleeping bag.

I slept until nine the next morning. I would have liked to have slept longer, but my body was used to getting up early and I was eager to leave. I still felt sick and I wondered what was wrong with me. I had no interest in food, which was not normal for me. I had a shower, and then went looking for the owners of the lodge to offer my appreciation.

John Solomon had checked with Mrs. East, one of the owners, for permission for me to stay the night. I didn't know that Mr. East hadn't heard about my arrival, and when I met him in his office to say thank you, he was completely taken back. When I explained the purpose of my trip, he was unimpressed and coolly informed me that there was a fee for camping at the lodge and using the washroom facilities. Worried that I wouldn't have enough money with me to pay, I said that I would be sure to mention his wonderful hospitality during my next CBC radio interview. Mr. East seemed pleased with this suggestion, and I made a quick exit before he could change his mind.

Packing my tent was exhausting work. I felt like throwing up again, and I moved slowly to complete the simplest task. I left Killarney Mountain Lodge only minutes before noon. I had little energy to paddle and stopped early in the afternoon on a tiny island that fronted the larger Philip Edward Island.

Too ill to cook dinner, I spread my sleeping bag on the floor of the tent and slipped inside. When I opened my journal, I discovered that my dad had left another note at the top of page June 26. It said, *Hope you have a nice camp site!* The comment hit me funny because I hadn't noticed what my surroundings looked like. I set up my tent out of necessity and went to bed without eating or writing in my journal.

The sky was sunny the next morning, with only a few small white clouds. I felt better, but not a hundred percent. During breakfast, I psyched myself up for a long, hard day of paddling. I wanted to make up for the few kilometres I had paddled the day before. I paddled against the wind all day. For an area noted for its prevailing west winds, I had run into some bad luck with the weather.

To make better time, I paddled two to three kilometres from

shore. Out in the open, there was no shelter and no breaks. If I stopped paddling, the wind pushed me back twenty metres a second, so I pushed myself hard all day and didn't stop to pee, eat, or stretch my legs. My body complained regularly to stop and rest, but I was driven to reach Parry Sound on time. At that moment it meant everything to me not to let Mark down.

I arrived at the Bustard Islands at 4:45. Despite the wind and my poor health, I was pleased with the progress I had made. I meandered through the maze of islands and marveled at the scenes of sculpted rock and windswept white pines. It was my fourth visit to the Bustards, and yet I still had not explored every passageway through the cluster of islands.

Later that night, I wrote in my journal, *What a beautiful place! I must come back again.* I camped on the southwest end of the group of islands and enjoyed a red sky sunset. My stomach felt much better that evening, and I ate a full dinner for the first time since my meal with Beth, two days ago.

FINAL PUSH TO PARRY SOUND

I woke to the sound of birds singing. The sound was happy and cheerful, and it reflected how I felt. My body was finally back to normal, and I felt great. I was ready for another long hard day of paddling. I left the Bustard Islands and decided to paddle blindly on a southeast compass bearing of one hundred and thirty degrees. It was the shortest distance from the Bustard Islands to Byng Inlet and would take me beyond sight of land until I was near the Champlain Islands, fourteen kilometres away.

It felt weird paddling and not seeing land in the distance. It looked as though I was headed across an ocean. I paddled for two hours until eventually the grey outline of the Champlain islands materialized off in the distance to my left. From there, islands were visible the rest of the ten kilometres to Byng Inlet.

While I paddled, I saw a lot of boat traffic, and I missed the solitude and reflection time that came from being away from people. The trip had started to take on a new feel, and I wasn't sure I liked it as much. I looked forward to arriving in Parry Sound, though, and the prospect of seeing friends and family and eating food I had missed. Thinking about food was a common distraction from the routine of paddling, and I entertained myself by making a list of all the treats I would buy when I found a store: chocolate milkshakes, cold juice, cold beer, watermelon, garden salads, red meat, ice cream, coffee …

When I reached the mouth of the Magnetawan River at Byng Inlet, I chose to push on. The weather was good, and I decided that it was too early to camp. To be able to paddle in good health felt like a gift, so I paddled to the outer islands opposite Bayfield Inlet. When I stopped, I had paddled forty kilometres and still felt strong.

I had a new problem though. I had developed a painful rash under my armpits. For some unknown reason, my shirt had started to chafe the skin raw while I paddled. I couldn't see the skin, but the area was very tender to the touch and made paddling painful. Pain had become routine to me, just another obstacle to overcome. I had bought some powder in Sault Ste. Marie for my feet, and I used some on my armpits. I knew that if the skin didn't heal overnight, paddling was going to be unbearable in the morning.

Before going to bed, I called the Wiarton coast guard and they told me a storm was approaching. I had noticed the signs during the day. A giant ring around the sun often meant rain within the next day or two, and I took extra care that night to secure my tent and kayak.

Even though I was tired, I slept poorly that night. The rash under my armpits was very sore, and the skin wept clear fluid. As I slept curled up in my sleeping bag, the folds of skin stuck together and dried and then tore apart when I moved. To avoid the pain, I slept with my arms behind my head to let the air flow over the skin. It was not a comfortable way to sleep.

It started to rain hard early in the morning and continued off and on as I prepared to get up. Each time the rain stopped and I got ready to go, the rain would start pouring again even harder. I found it amusing because it seemed like "the gods" were watching me and playing with a giant garden hose. Eventually it stopped raining long enough for me to pack and get away, but I had only paddled a few minutes before it started pouring again.

I paddled all day in the rain, thick fog, and headwinds. The conditions were rough, but I felt like a machine. "Kayak Man is back!" I announced. I paddled past the lighthouse at the entrance into Pointe au Baril, past Shawanaga Island and Hertzberg Island on my way to Dillon Cove. I was in familiar territory, and the feeling was similar to coming home after a long absence.

I lost my lunch bag sometime during the day. It was one of the nylon bags Cindy had made me the night before I left Thunder Bay. I thought maybe I had left it on the back of the kayak when I stopped to go pee, and it had fallen into the water. I lost three chocolate bars, a quarter jar of peanut butter, and a small container of jam. I was sick of Mars bars anyway, but I hated losing the bag Cindy had made for me. I hoped someone would find it floating in the water and bring it home to use.

I arrived at Dillon Cove Marina at six thirty. I bought an ice-cream bar, called Peter in Powassan, and then called my parents. My dad was relieved to hear my voice. The Ontario Provincial Police had contacted him that morning at breakfast and told him that the coast guard hadn't heard from me.

While he related the story to me, I could tell he was still rattled by the false alarm. Getting a call from the O.P.P. that his son was missing had been one of his worst fears since I started the trip. Learning that the coast guard had screwed up and caused my mom and dad to worry was frustrating for me, but there was little I could do except to say that I was okay.

My dad had good news for me too. My grandma was feeling better and had started to eat again. Her breathing problems had cleared up, and it looked like she was on the mend. I had worried she might die while I was kayaking, and the news was a huge relief.

I camped that night on a sand beach on Franklin Island. The rash under my right armpit had become worse, and I flinched with pain each time I moved my arm. I didn't know what had suddenly caused the skin to chafe, but I suspected it had something to do with me sweating in my dry suit. For the time being, I saw no solution to the problem. The water on Georgian Bay was still very cold, and I wore the dry suit every day even though the air temperature was warm. Most of my paddle route along the north shore of Lake Huron and the eastern shore of Georgian Bay were in isolated, cold water, and I was determined to wear the dry suit until I reached Parry Sound.

Otter Island Lighthouse, Lake Superior

Rough water, leaving Port Burwell, Lake Erie

Historic wreck in Windfield Bay, Georgian Bay

Camping on the dock in Tobermory

Flower Pot Island, Lake Huron

Lake Huron shoreline near Bayfield, Ontario.

Ambassador Bridge, Detroit River

Ocean vessel on Thames River

Arriving in Toronto

Rejoicing in Parry Sound

It was cloudy and threatened rain when I left Franklin Island the next morning. I enjoyed paddling in the familiar territory, but it also felt strange to be around so many cottages. It seemed as though I had been away for a very long time, and now the area looked different than I had remembered. I paddled the twenty-five kilometres from Franklin Island to Kilcoursie Bay easily, arriving at Killbear Provincial Park at two that afternoon.

Anxious to tell my friends I had arrived, I walked to the park office and called Mark and Cathy in Parry Sound. On my walk back to my kayak, Peggy Murphy saw me and stopped. Peggy worked at Killbear Provincial Park as a naturalist, and we knew each other from when I worked in Parry Sound. Mark couldn't come and get me for a few hours, so I drove around the park with Peggy and caught up on life and gossip about mutual friends.

Mark arrived at four o'clock to pick me up. We loaded my kayak and gear into his truck and drove back to Parry Sound for a welcome home barbecue. We carried my kayak into his backyard and then joined Cathy and our friend Heather on the sun deck. I felt jubilant and I sensed my friends shared my feelings. Mark and Heather were especially interested in the kayak and how it had performed. When Heather noticed that I hadn't fastened the straps that were part of a self-rescue system, she was quick to comment.

"This isn't going to help you like this," Heather chided me gently. "You'll never get this set up in an emergency if these straps aren't attached ahead of time," she added with enough bite in her voice to emphasize her horror. I knew she was right, and I was embarrassed that she had noticed my oversight. I had carried the inflatable air bags on the back deck of the kayak without taking the time to learn properly how they worked.

Eager to help, Heather attached the straps to the kayak's hull in case I had an emergency later on my trip. The system was designed so a kayaker could quickly clip two inflatable air bags on either side of the hull. Once the air bags were clipped on and inflated, the kayak became more stable for paddling in rough water or to allow someone to climb back into the cockpit after they had capsized. I appreciated Heather's help, but I hated looking foolish to my friends, and I hoped the story wouldn't spread too far beyond our circle.

The evening passed easily in the company of my friends, and the beer, wine, and Sambuca flowed late into the night as I recounted stories about my trip. Everyone was curious about Superior, and I loved telling them how I had paddled among huge chunks of ice after I had left Thunder Bay.

No one really wanted the night to end, but we all knew that I had to go back to Killarney in the morning, so we called it quits shortly after 1:00 a.m. It felt as though I had just fallen asleep when I woke up and it was 7:00 a.m. My body had a routine that I couldn't ignore. Peter arrived from Powassan after breakfast and announced that he would like to join me for the paddle from Killbear Park to Parry Sound. The idea hadn't even occurred to me, but Heather had offered Peter her kayak and he had jumped at the chance.

Mark and Cathy had work to do organizing my arrival and fundraising, so Heather drove Peter and me to Killbear, where Mark had picked me up. We started paddling shortly past ten, setting an easy pace so we could paddle side by side and talk. We followed the shoreline along Killbear Point and then crossed Parry Sound over to Three Mile Point on Parry Island.

In my recent past, I had made the five kilometre crossing to Three Mile Point many times in an eighteen-foot aluminum boat. For three years I had worked alongside Eric McIntyre, setting and checking trap nets as part of an annual study of the local lake trout population. Most of my memories were of us driving the boat home on cold November days in rain or snowstorms and crashing up and down rolling waves while I peered into the icy black water. Thankfully, the day Peter and I paddled together it was warm and sunny, and we had the help of a friendly tailwind all the way to town.

Peter and I kayaked onto Waubuno Beach at twelve fifteen on July 1, for the Canada Day celebration, as planned. As we approached the sandy shore, a young man with a megaphone announced my arrival, detailing my start from Thunder Bay on May 14 and my entire route all the way to Parry Sound. When Peter and I touched shore, a large crowd clapped and cheered while kids waved Canada flags on sticks.

Some of my family were the first people to greet me on the beach with warm hugs and handshakes. My mom and sister Crystal, grandma and grandpa Hill, uncle Greg and his boys Andrew and Rob, aunt Carol and uncle Joe with their daughters, Carrie and Jessica, and Joe's mom, grandma T. all swarmed around me.

I stayed on the beach and talked with people and collected donations until the crowds disappeared. It was difficult to tell my mom and family that I couldn't go back with them to our cottage on Windfall Lake. Mark had planned a fundraising event for that evening, and so my family would have to wait to see me.

At three o'clock, I went back with Mark and Cathy to their house for drinks before heading to the town dock. Mark had worked really hard to organize publicity for me. At his own expense, he had made signs and banners to draw attention in hopes that people would donate money to Kayaking for Cancer. We displayed my kayak on two sawhorses at the town dock, and I spoke with a lot of people who were in town for the Canada Day celebration. Some people quietly walked up and put money in the jar and left, but there were others who made a point to make a donation and stay to chat.

It was my first real public display, and the experience helped to galvanize my understanding of how people felt about cancer. One man walked up to me wearing his Canadian Legion outfit. Without a word, he approached me as I stood beside the *Mai Fleur* and put a large cash donation in the jar. He turned and hugged me warmly, and then silently walked away. The experience touched me deeply, and I floated above my body for the rest of the night.

The town started the fireworks at ten o'clock, but it began to rain, so we packed up and went home. Seated around the kitchen table we counted the paper bills and loose change people had given us during the day. When the final total was added, we had three hundred and seventy-five dollars. Cathy didn't like the sound of the uneven amount, so she added twenty-five dollars to make it an even four hundred. I only wrote a few words in my journal that night, but what I scribbled expressed succinctly how I felt: *It feels so great to have friends who care so much.*

Layover on Windfall Lake

T HE FOLLOWING MORNING I organized my gear and packed everything that I didn't need to send home with my mom. I had a phone interview with the Parry Sound radio station CKLP to talk about my trip, cancer, and the fundraising efforts. After lunch, Peter, Mark, Cathy, and I went to my family cottage on Windfall Lake. It was time for me to be with my family, and it felt wonderful that they (including my aunt Deanna, who missed my arrival but joined us at the cottage) had made the trip to Parry Sound.

We enjoyed a relaxing day, swimming, playing Frisbee, and simply enjoying our time together. At first glance, it looked like any summer weekend at the cottage until you overheard the conversations about frozen feet, tired muscles, or long days fighting the wind. After supper, my friends went home so I could be alone with my family. I enjoyed simply being there with them, surrounded by their love and support for what I was doing.

My dad called after supper to say hi and told me that he was sorry he couldn't be there. Earlier that day, my mom had told me that there had been a sewage problem at Bolton Camp where he worked as the property manager, and that my dad had to stay behind. I sensed that he was upset that he couldn't be there. It was the first time I could remember my dad sounding truly disappointed. He rarely said much about how he felt, but that night I knew it had been important to him to be there and that he felt sad he had missed the celebration. Ironically, the fact that he was upset made me feel proud.

The next morning I slept in for the first time, getting up at ten thirty. I swam, ate too much pie and ice cream, and enjoyed a lazy day without any demands. I was conscious that I had to say goodbye because my visit would soon be over. Everyone but my grandparents left in the afternoon for the long drive and anticipated "long weekend" delay through Barrie.

At five o'clock, my grandma and grandpa Hill drove me to Parry Sound. My grandma gave me twenty-five dollars and a warm hug and promised to see me again in Goderich. I arrived back at Mark and Cathy's house, exhausted. So much had happened it felt like I had been in Parry Sound for a week. I spent some time alone and wrote Fleur a letter and then made a list of things I needed to buy.

In the evening, Mark took me for a long ride on his motorcycle outside of town. Somehow the speed of the bike and the sudden jump back into my life with friends and family felt weird and almost dreamlike. On the way back, we stopped for ice cream at the Creamery. Exhausted, we all went to bed early that night.

In the morning, I ate breakfast with Mark and Cathy before they left for work. When I was alone, I packed and then walked to the North Star newspaper for an interview. When I returned to the house, I called CBC radio in Sudbury and CKVR television in Barrie and told them I would arrive in Penetanguishene on Wednesday at four o'clock. Afterward, I realized two days wasn't a lot of time to reach the town of Penetanguishene from Parry Sound.

Cathy drove me and my kayak to Waubuno Beach after lunch, and then she napped in the truck while I repacked the *Mai Fleur*. I had a fresh supply of summer clothes, stove fuel, and more fresh and dried food. It took me two hours to organize and repack my supplies so I could easily find what I wanted. I didn't feel very motivated to leave. In some ways it felt like I had come home and the trip was over.

I knew, however, that I had to prepare myself mentally for the trip ahead. While I packed, I told myself that there was still a lot of big, empty water; I needed to stay alert in order to reach my goal of Toronto.

A Lesson in Media Relations

W HEN I FINISHED packing, I woke Cathy from her nap, and together we gently half-lifted, half-slid the boat into the water. It was four o'clock when we hugged goodbye, and I headed off in the direction of Penetanguishene.

Paddling through the South Channel in Parry Sound was a unique experience. I was passed by two dozen boats of different sizes, including the gigantic Island Queen cruise ship, which managed to sneak up behind me and scare me with its loud air horn. I camped on a small island near the historic fishing community of Sans Souci.

For dinner, I cooked a wonderful chicken stir fry and ended with a large serving of lemon cake, thankful to be finished with dehydrated food. I had thoroughly enjoyed my stop in Parry Sound, but I was once again drawn into the adventure of the unknown. It was day fifty-two of my trip, and I was grateful and excited to be back in my kayak.

It rained all that night and was still threatening rain in the morning when I got up. I packed and left as quickly as I could. I didn't mind paddling in the rain, but I hated to pack during a storm. I paddled against a strong headwind, but after an hour, it switched to a crosswind which I found even more difficult. The wind that day was stronger than anything I had seen on my trip. It blasted violently across the open water, and I fought to gain only inches with each paddle stroke.

As the day went on, the waves grew bigger until I was bracing against the impact of three-metre waves. Watching a wall of water come toward me was intimidating and reminded me of the start of the '70s television

148

show *Hawaii Five-O*. The *Mai Fleur* handled the big waves easily, and I found the experience of paddling in the rough waves challenging, but fun.

I paddled all day and arrived at the mouth of the Penetang Harbour at seven thirty in the evening. I stopped at a house and called my dad's friend Bob Wilkes, who lived somewhere in Penetang Harbour. My dad was already there waiting for me, so they jumped into Bob's boat and came out to find me as I paddled into the long bay. Somehow they missed me on their way out of the harbor, and I had almost made it to Bob's house before they found me.

My dad was beaming by the time we met and hugged on Bob's dock. I had kayaked more than fifteen hundred kilometres since we had said goodbye in Thunder Bay, each of us uncertain when we would see each other again. Although we had spoken a number of times on the phone, he seemed overjoyed to see with his own eyes that I was well. I had never felt more honoured by my dad than on that night.

I had accomplished what must have seemed impossible to him, and yet it was what came naturally to me. I was never the mechanical motor and wheels type, like my dad, and this had always been a barrier to our relationship. That evening, I filled up on pizza and recounted some of my adventures, always cautious not to be too graphic about any of the real dangers I had encountered.

The next day, I met with the media to raise awareness for the cancer society and make a plea for donations. I organized two formal receptions to be held at one and three o'clock at the town dock with the local radio station, *The Observer* and *Free Press* newspapers, and CKVR television. As usual, I found the public relations work the most difficult. Although I had already kayaked into Penetanguishene, the television cameraman wanted to film me kayaking as though I had just arrived. This request seemed innocent enough, and Bob had arranged for Don Parker of the Midland legion to pipe me in as I paddled to the docks. However, the cameraman kept asking me to go back and paddle to the dock over and over again, so he could film me coming at different angles. By the third request, it started to feel too staged and unnatural.

When I got out of the kayak, I shook hands with Jim Malcom, the regional manager for the Canadian Cancer Society. Suddenly, a Royal Bank representative was there shaking my hand and squeezing beside me so the newspaper photographer could take his picture as he handed me a Royal Bank T-shirt. The whole episode happened so fast I didn't have time to react. When it was over, all I could think about was who invited the banker, and where was his cheque for the cancer society? When the media crew left, I felt that I had been used to promote someone else's agenda, and I promised myself that it wouldn't happen again.

Later that day, my dad and I drove to the IGA stores in Penetanguishene and Midland to thank the managers for using the donation cans and collecting money on behalf of Kayaking for Cancer. When we got back, Bob took my dad and me to dinner with his wife, Diane, and their sons, Trevor and Robert. Uncle Bob, as he was known in my family, had always been generous, and that night he treated me like a conquering king, insisting that I not look at any of the prices on the menu.

When we got back from the restaurant, my dad took me aside and told me some very sad news. My uncle Greg and his wife had decided to separate after being married for seven years. Although Greg was my uncle, he was only one year older, and he felt more like a brother to me. I knew his marriage had been suffering, but the news shocked me and I didn't know how he would cope with living away from his kids.

When I asked my dad why Greg hadn't said anything in Parry Sound, he explained that Greg hadn't wanted to ruin the excitement of my arrival. I was stunned by the news, and my heart ached when I thought about the pain he had hidden for my benefit. The reality of the situation made me realize that *my* life was on hold while I focused on kayaking, but everyone I cared about was busy living the lives that I had stepped away from for the summer. I would have liked to talk with Greg in Parry Sound. I hoped he knew he was in my thoughts and prayers.

My dad's alarm woke me the next morning at six, and we chatted a bit before he had to drive back to work in Bolton. He was nervous and reluctant to say goodbye. As good as our visit had been, I sensed that he found it difficult that I would be kayaking alone again. When we hugged, there wasn't the same feeling of fear and dread I had felt from him in Thunder Bay, but the heavy weight of parental worry was still detectable.

As soon as my dad left, CBC radio called me for an interview, and then Bob got up and made me a mushroom omelet for breakfast. I spent the morning talking with Bob about my trip and making a run into town for fresh groceries. By the time we got back to Bob's house it was noon, so I agreed to stay for lunch.

I was dragging my feet, but I knew I had to leave at some point. Being with friends and family in Parry Sound and then Penetang with my dad had left me feeling pulled toward two very different worlds. After lunch, I packed my kayak and then had a short nap. I had let myself relax enough to notice that my body was tired and in need of rest. I forced myself to leave at three o'clock. I said goodbye to Bob, thanking him for his hospitality, and then quickly raced directly across the Penetanguishene Harbour and headed north along the coast.

The Kindness of Strangers

I PADDLED NON-STOP, checking my progress on my map as I cruised past Pinery Point, Adams Point, and Sawlog Point. At eight thirty I reached Cedar Point and looked across to Christian Island, marked on my map as Indian Reserve number thirty. I was pleased with my progress and ready to find a campsite. Most of the shoreline since leaving Penetang had been over developed with large homes and cottages, unwelcoming to a kayaker seeking a place to "come ashore."

I paddled past a log cottage, and two guys shouted something like "nice kayak" to me as I glided past their private beach. Hooked by their friendly manner, I stopped, and met Bill Johnston and Bob Korstanje. The men were staying at the cottage with their families, who had gone for an evening paddle in canoes. Bob and Bill asked me curiously where I had come from and when I told them Thunder Bay, they shook their heads in disbelief and then offered me a beer. Concerned about the time, I asked them if I could camp on their beach, and they said, "Sure." I hadn't been there long when their families came back, and I was instantly peppered with questions from the kids about my trip.

"What made you want to do this? Do you ever get lonely? What do you eat? Where do you sleep? Don't you get bored?" The questions were honest and interesting, and I enjoyed answering all of them much more than the usual questions reporters seemed to ask. When the mosquitoes came out, I was invited to join them inside the cottage. Bill and Marg had rented the log cottage and invited Bob and Lori to join them for a few days. We sat on cozy couches and chairs, and Marg put out a platter of fresh fruit to snack on while we talked. I learned that Bob and Lori had lived in Japan for six months teaching English, so I got to ask them lots of questions too.

Lori told me that the experience had changed their lives. "We never thought of ourselves as materialistic, but before we went to Japan, there were lots of things we thought we had to have. After we saw how people in Japan got by happily with a lot less, we started to simplify and shorten our list of material wants. It was a wonderful experience," Lori explained with a smile.

As I listened to her share her insights, some things she said resonated with me. Travelling by kayak was an exercise in living a minimalist lifestyle. I lived with all of my possessions in a tiny boat, which made me feel more appreciative of what I had, and less focused on what I didn't have. I think many people would be surprised how liberating having less can be. Much of what we think we need is only a perception of wealth. Right then, no one seemed wealthier than I felt. I had my health, plenty of food, and a safe shelter. By comparison to others around the world, I was very rich.

Around midnight, I mentioned that I should go and set up my tent, but my hosts wouldn't hear of it. Bob and Lori offered to make room for me in the guest bunkie where they were staying. I felt a wonderful warmth from Bob, Lori, and their daughter, Georgia. They willingly shared one room and offered me the other.

The bunkie cabin had thin walls that didn't go to the ceiling, so it felt like we were camping indoors together. When everyone was settled into bed and the lights were out, Bob played the part of the dad in the television show *The Waltons*, calling out, "Good night, John Boy," and we all shared a laugh. Moments later it started to thunder and lightning, and rain fell hard on the cabin roof. Thankful to be indoors, I fell asleep, happy and content in the company of new friends.

I woke up the next morning with the Korstanje family. They had invited me to join them for breakfast the night before, so I sat down and enjoyed a meal of bacon and eggs, toast, fresh fruit, and coffee. I had a hot shower, said my goodbyes, and left at ten o'clock under cloudy skies.

It started to rain early in the afternoon, but I paddled non-stop to Balm Beach and called the cancer society office in Toronto from a pay phone. I asked if they had arranged for anyone to meet me in

Wasaga Beach to raise funds, but was told that no one was available. This news really annoyed me. Mark Climie had told me he would coordinate volunteers and staff from the cancer society to help me raise funds, but at that point, I felt that the cancer society had done very little to help. It felt to me that I was working all alone.

The Nottawasaga Bay shoreline that stretched south toward Wasaga Beach was over developed and busy with people. It felt like I had arrived in the big city. People were everywhere. I paddled from Balm Beach to Woodland Beach and stopped to look for a phone.

I knocked on the door at the first house I saw, to ask if I could use their phone. A young girl came to the door, but before I could speak, her mother ran and intercepted with a look as though I was an escaped criminal. The woman flatly told me that she didn't have a phone and didn't know if anyone had a phone in the area. Minutes later, I found a pay phone across the street from her house. It was a sad contrast from my experience with the Korstanje and Johnston families, and I wondered what it was going to be like relying on the generosity of strangers for the rest of my trip.

I camped on a public beach not far from the home of the woman who told me she didn't have a phone. It was probably illegal for me to camp there, but I didn't care. I was tired, and there was nowhere else to go.

I woke the next day around 7:00 a.m., and started to pack up my tent before anyone noticed I was there. When I got the tent down, a fit looking middle-aged couple who were walking on the beach stopped briefly to chat about where I had come from. They walked down the beach a short distance and then came back, introduced themselves as John and Mary, and asked me if I would like some coffee. They had a cottage close by and returned a short time later with a picnic bag filled with a large carafe of coffee, bottled water, fresh strawberries, apple turnovers, and apple bread from a bakery where they lived in Hamilton.

We enjoyed our breakfast together, talking about paddling. John and Mary were new canoeists, so I told them the Wilderness Canoe Association was a great organization for meeting new friends that are passionate about canoeing. My surprise breakfast guests were a nice reminder that most people everywhere are kind-hearted.

WASAGA BEACH BLUES

A FTER BREAKFAST, I launched my kayak into a very big surf. The wind was driving big crashing waves onto the shallow beach, and a lot of water dumped into my open cockpit. Launching into big crashing waves took practice. Sometimes I was too far from the water's edge and was left stranded on dry land, or I was too far out in the water and was pummeled by the crashing waves before I could seal my cockpit and start paddling.

I arrived at Wasaga Beach at eleven in the morning. The main beach area had already started to fill with people and the rock song "Get Over It," by the Eagles, was blasting across the water. A volleyball tournament was under way, and bikini-clad women were everywhere. I paddled to shore and pulled my kayak onto the beach beside the nearest lifeguard tower. I spoke with Phil, a muscled lifeguard who nicely told me that I wasn't supposed to kayak inside the roped-off beach area. He explained that he didn't really care, but that his boss would give him heat if he saw my kayak. Phil had heard of my trip and wanted to help, so he offered to watch my kayak while I walked to the local IGA store.

Radio stations Rock 95 and Q107 community events mobile units were at the beach, so I left news releases with each of them and then walked for thirty minutes to the local IGA store. When I arrived, I didn't see any of the donation cans, so I spoke with one of the owners. The woman said she didn't know anything about the Kayaking for Cancer fundraising that IGA was sponsoring, but she told me her husband would be back in forty-five minutes. This news shocked me, because a picture of me and my kayak would have been in their weekly price flyer at least twice by then, explaining my trip and fundraising in the stores.

I waited at the store, and when the owner returned, he told me he had decided not to participate in the fundraising for cancer. When I asked him why, he told me it was too much work during the summer. Remembering the late nights my grandma Pat and cousins Owen and Jennifer had spent taping labels on cans, I asked him if he would send the cans back to Oshawa Foods so other stores could use them.

By the time I walked back to my kayak, I was feeling very grumpy. I saw my stop at Wasaga Beach as a missed opportunity for the cancer society to raise money and talk about the importance of using sunscreen. The walk back from the IGA store in the blazing sun had been the final straw for the day. I couldn't wait to get back into my kayak and paddle away.

A Short Visit

T FOUR O'CLOCK, I launched my kayak into more big crashing waves and set my sights for the town of Collingwood. Collingwood was fifteen kilometres away as the crow flies, but I could distinguish the grain elevators in the distant horizon as I left Wasaga Beach.

The wind pushed metre-and-a-half-high waves toward me as I used my kayak paddles to burn off my frustration. Three hours later, I arrived at the grain elevators. I had an open invitation to stay with Louanne and Gerry Murphy, friends who lived in a condo community somewhere along the shoreline.

I missed the entrance into the condo's marina, so I stopped and asked for directions from a fisherman named Don, who was fishing from the concrete pier. Don happened to live in the same condo beside Louanne and Gerry and was able to tell me where to go. Gerry was fishing from another pier while waiting for me, and he started waving and shouting as I approached. Louanne was my uncle Greg's soon-to-be ex-sister-in-law, but his failed marriage didn't affect their hospitality for me. Gerry led me home and fed me beer and barbecued pork chops, while I talked their ears off about my trip. I had spent enough time with Louanne and Gerry over the years for them to feel like family, and it was easy to feel at home in their company.

It was cloudy when I woke up the next morning, so I stayed in bed and enjoyed a lazy sleep-in. When I finally got up, I ate breakfast and then talked with Louanne and Gerry over coffee. At noon, my mom and dad arrived with my sister Crystal and my other sister Angela and her husband, Maurice, who were visiting from Truro, Nova Scotia. I hadn't seen Angela and Maurice since Christmas, and the fact that Angela was pregnant made the family gathering even more special. Angela had had a series of miscarriages in the past few years, but now she was in her last trimester and looked great. My mom beamed with glee every time she looked at her daughter, excited for her first grandchild.

Uncle Greg arrived with his kids an hour later and we spent the day outside in the sun, catching up on family news. Louanne prepared a wonderful meal reminiscent of special holiday dinners, complete with two kinds of pie and ice cream for dessert.

Sadly, everyone left around eight that evening. It was difficult to say goodbye to Angela and Maurice after such a short visit, but I reasoned that it was better than no visit. I was happy that Angela's pregnancy was going well. She had waited a long time to start a family, and she was ready. I kissed her goodbye, hopeful to meet my new niece at Christmas.

I didn't have any time to speak with Greg alone, but I hugged him extra hard when we said goodbye, and I whispered in his ear that he was in my thoughts and prayers. Like me, he was on a journey he had to make alone. I could only pray that he would find his way safely through the turbulent waters of divorce.

TOAST AND MILK

THANKFULLY, THE NEXT day was warm and sunny with very little wind. I called the cancer society and asked if they had a contact for me in Tobermory. I met with two Collingwood newspaper reporters and had a phone interview with the Collingwood radio station CKBB before lunch.

Once again, I felt reluctant to leave the comfort of friends. I enjoyed my time with Louanne and Gerry, and it always felt strange to stop in familiar places. I got away around one thirty and followed the western edge of Nottawasaga Bay north toward Tobermory. I stopped after thirty kilometres at what I thought was Boucher Point, exhausted. The first day after a rest stop with family or friends was always the toughest mentally. It seemed to take a day to psyche myself back into the physical grind required to put my head down and keep paddling. Too tired to make a real meal, I ate a meagre dinner from my leftover lunch, set up my tent, and crawled into bed.

The sky was clouding up quickly the next morning, so I ate a hurried breakfast and left. I paddled a couple of hours before I realized that I hadn't camped at Boucher Point, but had bypassed the town of Meaford and camped on the border of the Canadian Military Meaford Tank Range. I had seen *No Trespassing* signs and an army jeep on a road beside the lake, but I hadn't believed that I could have come forty-five kilometres in an afternoon. Knowing how far I had paddled the day before, I realized why I felt so tired. I wasn't out of shape from visiting family, I was in the best shape of my life.

I paddled all day against strong headwinds. Headwinds were my curse, and I was forced to eat my lunch in the kayak so I wouldn't lose ground. I was lonely for Fleur. It felt like a long time since I had seen her.

Later in the day the sky cleared, and it turned sunny and hot. I pushed on so I would be close to Owen Sound the next day. I stopped and camped at Hibou Conservation Area. The signs said no overnight camping, so I waited until the people left in the evening before I set up my tent.

I felt little twinges of guilt and excitement at breaking the rules, but I rationalized my decision to camp illegally as necessary. Finding legal, reliable campsites would prove to be an even bigger problem later.

It was cool and cloudy the next day when I finished the short paddle into Owen Sound. I called Anne-Marie McCleach at the local cancer society office. She arranged for the media to meet me on the beach at three, so I went for an exploratory paddle up the Sydenham River.

I arrived back at the beach at three and was greeted by a small crowd which included the *Owen Sound Sun* newspaper and a CKNX television crew. When I had finished the media interviews, I met with Anne-Marie, Bert and Lenora Morrison, Betty Hendricks, and Lou Burns, all high ranking members of the local cancer society. Everyone was very nice and encouraging of my efforts.

When the media left, Bert drove me to the local radio station, FM 106.5, in Owen Sound to record an interview. I don't remember the name of the person who interviewed me, but I do remember thinking the interview was better than most, aside from the CBC. I don't know why, but there was a distinct difference in the type of questions and how CBC radio hosts interviewed. Every CBC interview felt more like a conversation than a questionnaire, and this interview was like that too.

After the interview, Bert and Lenora invited me to have dinner with them and stay over at their home in Owen Sound. Lou Burns joined us for a nice meal at a local restaurant and came back with us to Bert and Lenora's house. We sat in their living room and talked late into the evening. Each of my hosts was a fascinating individual who lived an interesting and exciting life, and I enjoyed listening to them recount stories about places they had been.

By eleven, Lou had gone home and Lenora had gone to bed, so Bert invited me to join him for his evening ritual of toast with raspberry jam and cold milk. It was simple pleasures such as this that I remember most.

The next day was July 14, day sixty-two of my trip. I woke early, as usual, and ate breakfast with Bert and Lenora. Lou picked me up at eight fifteen, and we started a whirlwind day. First we went to the Owen Sound IGA store and met Ben Vollering, the store manager. Ben was very supportive of my Kayaking for Cancer campaign, and had donation cans at each of the checkout aisles. He even insisted on giving me my groceries for free. Lou took me to the cancer society office so I could confirm my schedule with dates and towns I planned to visit in hopes of receiving help to raise funds.

I didn't leave Owen Sound until two in the afternoon. I hadn't planned on a late start, but the day just rushed past. I paddled out of the bay with sunny skies and strong winds that pushed metre-high waves towards me. The shoreline is very rocky and overdeveloped near Owen Sound. Every inch of the shoreline had a home or cottage and a man-made breakwater of steel or concrete.

LESSONS IN KINDNESS

I PADDLED ALL afternoon and into the early evening, hoping to camp at Commodore Point, but I couldn't find a safe place to land the kayak. Large waves were rolling and crashing against a boulder shoreline. I pushed on, a bit unnerved about my chances of finding a safe place to beach the kayak. When I looked ahead for as far as I could see, the shoreline was blocked by rock, steel, and concrete. Every cottage had barricaded the shore from the assaulting waves that stole precious inches of their property.

I pulled my map out to see if there was any conservation land nearby where I could camp. Immediately the wind and waves turned the kayak and pushed it back in the direction I had just come. The sun had already set, and I was growing anxious to make camp. I had just acknowledged my need for help when a shout drew my attention to a man standing on shore, waving his arms wildly to attract my attention. I stuffed my map away and paddled closer so I could hear what he was saying.

"Do you want to come ashore and stay the night?" the man shouted over the sound of the crashing waves. Flabbergasted at the timing of his offer, I turned and quickly paddled my kayak into the shelter of his boat ramp out of the building swells. There I met Dave Grim, who was quick to welcome me into his cottage. Dave explained that he had been sitting in his living room chair and reading about me in the local newspaper, when he looked out his window and saw me paddling past.

Eager to play host, Dave made me a sandwich and handed me a cold beer. We instantly made a connection, and the conversation started and never stopped. We talked about life and shared our ideas on goal-setting and the power of thought. Dave told me a little about his life. His dad had died when he was sixteen, and he dropped out of school to help his mom pay the bills. Fifteen years later he started studying to get his grade twelve equivalent diploma, and then went on to study business courses and accounting. He credited a book his mom had given him, called *The Power of Positive Thinking*, with changing his life.

"Before I read that book, I had an inferiority complex," explained Dave. "I was afraid of my own shadow."

You would never know it today. Dave was warm and friendly, looking me in the eye while we talked. He was the father of two married daughters, owned a twenty-four foot "Bluenose" styled sailboat which he loved to sail on Georgian Bay, drove a Honda Goldwing motorcycle, and tutored illiterate adults who had been in trouble with the law. Dave was an incredible example of living life big.

We stayed up and talked until midnight, when Dave suggested that I was probably tired. The truth was that, beyond my physical fatigue, I felt energized by Dave's spirit and likeminded ideas that anything is possible. Dave set me up in a guest room with a cozy bed, and it wasn't long before I fell asleep.

BECOMING A REBEL CAMPER

I WOKE AROUND six thirty and stayed in bed writing in my journal until Dave got up at seven. For breakfast, Dave served cereal, toast, and eggs, a real day-starter meal. By the time we had finished breakfast, it was raining with occasional flashes of lightning, so we sat and talked in the living room until the storm passed.

I left Dave's cottage shortly past ten o'clock. The rain had stopped, but a thick fog had rolled in and hidden the lake. The shoreline was very rocky along the eastern coast of the peninsula, not very welcoming to a fiberglass kayak. I paddled all day, hidden from view in the quiet curtain of fog.

I arrived in the town of Wiarton around three, wet and cold from a damp day paddling in the fog. I called Mark Climie to update him on my progress and inquired about future fundraising plans. Afterward, I called my mom and dad at their cottage and then stopped at the Wiarton newspaper, the *Echo*. At four thirty on a Friday afternoon, everyone was gone, so I left some press release information for the editor.

I tried to get in touch with Lillian Thompson, my contact with the cancer society in Wiarton, but had no luck. Reluctantly, I set up my tent on the town beach. *Another illegal campsite*, I cautioned myself. There was a designated campground away from the lake, but I didn't want to be separated from my kayak and belongings for the night. Even though I had an optimistic trust in people, I worried about leaving the boat alone.

In the morning, I packed my tent, placed an information sheet about my trip on my kayak, and walked to the main street. I called the local newspaper and asked to speak to one of the reporters or the editor, but neither was available. I tried contacting Lillian Thompson again, and this time she was home and most willing to help with fundraising. Lillian met me at the town beach to see me off and promised to meet me in Lion's Head in two days.

I left Wiarton at eleven and paddled all the way to Barrow Bay. I had heard about a protected cove where small boats anchored during storms or rough waves. Anxious to find its whereabouts, I paddled up a short river passage that led away from the lake and discovered the small cove.

It was not, however, a secret oasis. As the western sky filled with a blush of crimson and orange, cottage lights, and glowing campfires linked its edges in a moving dot to dot picture show. Eager to make camp, I found a quiet area near the entrance where I had arrived, away from any visible cottages.

The stony ground was very low, and there was no vegetation other than some grass and the occasional daisy. It was not an ideal campsite; however, the daylight was fading, and I just needed a place to set up my tent. I ate a quick pasta dinner, washed my dishes, and crawled into bed. Some days were simply routine: wake, eat, paddle, set up camp, eat, and sleep.

I woke the next morning to mourning doves singing. It was a song I associated with *home*, and it made me feel melancholy for family and friends. While I was eating breakfast, the property owner came to see me. He had seen my tent from his house and told me I was camped on private property. I tried to explain why I was there and thanked him for the use of a tent site, but he rather coldly expressed his desire that I leave as soon as possible. A half hour later, the man returned with a friendlier demeanor.

"Hi. My name is Fred. My wife and I were wondering if you would like to come for breakfast and a hot shower?"

His turnabout took me by surprise. I had just finished my breakfast and was feeling full, but I didn't have the heart to decline his invitation. I imagined that he had gone home and talked things over with his wife, and had come to a different conclusion. I packed up my tent and met him and his wife, Naomi, at their cottage. After a luxurious hot shower, we sat down to a glorious meal of eggs, fresh tomatoes, toast, and coffee.

By the end of my stay, the two of them couldn't do enough for me. Fred wanted to give me everything he had, thermal coffee mug, jacket, sweatshirt. I refused their gifts with gratitude. I already had everything that I needed, and no extra room to spare.

I left Fred and Naomi at 1:00 p.m. and paddled toward Lion's Head. I took my time, sightseeing and exploring the shoreline. I found a small water cave that fit half of the kayak. It would have been fun to swim into the cave, but there was no place to leave the kayak. The shoreline coming into Lion's Head was very rocky, with steep cliffs that you would expect to attract rock climbers.

When I arrived at the Lion's Head beach, I met three young pre-teens: a boy and two girls from Lansing, Michigan, who were there boating with their families. They told me they had seen much of Georgian Bay in the past few years, Snug Harbour, Byng Inlet, Bad River, and Killarney. I found it funny listening to these young Americans speak intimately about these places that many people in Ontario had never seen.

The kids told me that Lion's Head was given its name because someone saw the head of a lion resting on its front paws in the rock cliffs. I couldn't see the lion's head, but I think it's like many of these places with sake names. You have to look with creative eyes to see something. I was still trying to see the woman's face at Old Woman Bay on Lake Superior, so maybe I just didn't have enough imagination.

When the kids left, I sat on the beach and read a newspaper Fred had given me. The kayak worked like a magnet to attract people who came to look it over and speak with me. I camped in a public park area near the beach, in sight of the *Mai Fleur*.

Before bed, I called my parents and talked to Angela and Maurice for the last time before they went home to Nova Scotia. It was a difficult call for me, wishing I could have been there for the goodbye dinner.

The next morning I got up as the sun was rising and photographed the beach and boats in the marina. The sun was warm and painted the early morning in a wash of orange and golden light.

While putting my breakfast dishes back in the kayak, I met a man who was walking the beach. He was short, in his mid-sixties, and possessed a noticeable grin that seemed to advertise that he had a secret to share. Interested in my kayak, he came over and as we began talking, I quickly learned that his secret was the fact that he had recently retired.

"I'm learning to rediscover my life," he explained proudly. "I feel as though a heavy weight has been lifted off my shoulders. It still hasn't fully hit me that I'm free," he confessed. "Isn't it nice to do what you want?" I couldn't help but feel a little sad for him that he had waited so long to experience these feelings. *How do people get trapped into lives they don't enjoy?* I wondered. *He's one of the lucky ones who is still healthy enough to start living,* I thought. How many people wait until they retire to start living their life, only to discover that their health has failed? He went on to explain that he and his wife planned to travel and camp like gypsies without a schedule across Canada. I felt excited for them that they were making a positive change to start enjoying themselves. I believe life should be fun. Each day should be a celebration of life. As my mom would say, "We only have today, Michael."

In Good Hands

I WAS SITTING in the shade of a maple tree near the Lion's Head marina when Lillian Thompson arrived in the afternoon to help me fund raise for the cancer society. A retired school teacher, Lillian was a breath of fresh air. Interest and enthusiasm for life radiated outward from her tiny form, giving her the energy and spark of a teenager. Instantly, I liked her. She was warm, bright, and seemingly unbridled by her age.

I had been given Lillian's name as a cancer society volunteer, and I had called her from a pay phone in Wiarton two days ago to ask if she would help. Now here she was, carrying two homemade banners that read *Kayaking for Cancer, Thunder Bay to Toronto*.

There weren't many people at the Lion's Head beach that day, but my kayak and banners did attract some attention. By the end of the day, we had collected a modest twenty dollars in donations for the cancer society. Most donations were two dollar bills or 'Loonie' dollar coins, but Lillian did write one or two receipts for people who asked.

I had decided long before I started the trip that I wouldn't be responsible for collecting any money unless a cancer society representative was there, so I was glad Lillian had come. Before she arrived that day, I'd had to turn down a twenty dollar donation because of the concern I had about accepting money. If there were people that would accuse me of doing the trip to gain a kayak, I didn't want anyone to have the opportunity to accuse me of pocketing cancer society donations.

When the beach emptied late in the afternoon, Lillian invited me to dinner at a local diner. It wasn't a great meal, but the raisin pie and Lillian's company were outstanding. The conversation flowed easily, and it wasn't long before I learned that just a few years ago, Lillian had spent several months on the African continent as a school teacher, her second teaching assignment since "retiring." She was a role model for any age, and she inspired me with her keen observations and philosophies on life.

When I expressed my disappointment about only collecting twenty dollars, Lillian tried to help me see things differently.

"Is the money all that matters to you, Michael? Is that why you are doing this?" Lillian asked. "You know, you will touch people on this trip even if they don't give you a donation." Her questions surprised me and forced me to think deeply on the matter.

After dinner, Lillian introduced me to her brother-in-law, Dave, who had offered to let me camp in his backyard near the town beach. Lillian had to go and help a friend, but first she promised to meet me in Tobermory in a couple of days to help with my fundraising efforts. Dave was very quick to explain that his wife had just died of cancer in June. Hearing this sad news, I thought it seemed as though no one I met was untouched by the disease. It also explained why Lillian was willing to help. She never mentioned her sister to me, so I kept the knowledge to myself.

Dave too had business to attend to, so once I had set up my tent, I walked back to the beach area beside the marina where I could watch my kayak.

I hadn't been there long when I met Sjak and his son, Justin, who had just returned from a short canoe paddle on the lake. Sjak had a refinished cedar canvas canoe, and he proudly offered to let me paddle it before dark.

Afterward, Sjak invited me to join his family for a campfire and a hot drink. I spent a pleasant evening talking with them, and it wasn't long before they felt like old friends. Sjak shared that he taught high school wood shop but sometimes that meant he was teaching "lessons about life" with a little bit of woodworking added in. I could tell he had found his niche, and I would bet his students were glad they had a teacher like him.

Two days later, I woke up in Winfield Bay at Cabot Head anxious to make the thirty-five kilometre trip to Tobermory. Opening the zipper door of my tent, I watched an orange sun rise above Georgian Bay and then disappear behind a grey curtain of cloud. Winfield Bay is a popular mooring site for both sailboats and pleasure craft. When I had arrived the day before, there had been seven yachts anchored in the bay, and by the time I had finished eating my dinner, there were eleven. People are lured there by a natural protected harbour with enough room to easily accommodate twice that number of boats.

A wooden shipwreck is permanently on display there, an added treat for visitors. Fifteen metres long and built from heavy wood timbers, the burned-out ship was beached in shallow water ten metres from shore. I paddled around the hull and took some photographs. One side of the ship's hull was burned away, giving me a look inside. The lower hull of the ship was divided into separate sections, each two-thirds full of water and fish. The ship's hull was acting as a giant aquarium. Attracted to the ship for cover and available food, the fish had been trapped inside the hull since the last time the water levels on Georgian Bay had dropped.

New Friends

O N July 20, shortly before 9:00 a.m., I paddled out of Winfield Bay into a strong westerly headwind. Pulling myself into the wind, I felt as though I were towing a second boat behind me. Each draw of the paddle was an effort, and it was a struggle to make the slightest progress forward. Winfield Bay was so well protected I hadn't realized how strong the wind was on the lake. I thought about turning back, but I disliked the idea of giving in and admitting defeat. I don't know if this was plain stubbornness or vanity, but I felt compelled to arrive in Tobermory that day.

The wind was always a big presence in my life. Some days it seemed the wind was my best friend, while at other times, my nemesis. Today the wind had a mean temperament. By far this was the toughest day yet. The waves were only a metre high, but the wind pushed back at me with unrelenting viciousness. The wind never let up, so I couldn't stop to rest, eat, drink, or go pee. Stopping would only allow the wind to steal away any progress I had made, and because of the waves, there was no easy place to go ashore.

I had become accustomed to paddling without food and water, but holding the urge to pee was still very difficult and painful. I held my bladder for two hours after the first sharp pains began. The pain consumed me, and I found it difficult to think of anything else. At some moments I thought I would pass out from the pain.

What happens if your bladder explodes? I mused to myself. *Would urine be released into my blood?* Kayaking with the pain was unbearable, yet I wouldn't allow myself to simply pee my pants.

As I focused on the pain, I remembered my grandpa describing to me his chemotherapy treatment for bladder cancer. I winced, recalling the image of a nurse sliding a catheter tube inside his private area. That image seemed truly unbearable to me, yet I remembered him relating the experience as though he was speaking about something routine, like getting a needle or a tooth filling. He had explained how the chemo was released through the catheter and flooded into his bladder, burning as it moved through his body. The worst part, he had confided, was being told by the nurses to hold the burning chemo in his bladder with the aching desire to pee. Remembering my grandpa's cancer treatment gave me new strength, and I pushed on, blocking out my own suffering.

There were no great distractions that day while I struggled against the wind. All that I could do was put my head down and paddle. Stroke, stroke, stroke. If it hadn't been my own choice, it could easily have been described as torture. Muscles ached under the strain, but the feeling was now familiar and, perversely, almost enjoyable, as though the pain was a sign of my physical and mental strength. Having never been a marathon runner, I wondered if this was the same pain that runners become addicted to and what drives them out of bed to run early in the morning.

Halfway to Tobermory, I realized I hadn't seen a single boat all day. On Lake Superior I had never expected to see a boat, but on Georgian Bay it seemed inevitable. The lack of other boaters emphasized the feeling of isolation more than any other time since I had started my trip.

I arrived at Tobermory at five o'clock. Paddling into the "little tub" marina, I was filled with relief and elation. With my kayak sheltered from the wind, my arms suddenly felt light. Sailboats, pleasure craft, and cruise boats of every size and description from all over Canada and the U.S. filled the marina boat slips. Heading toward the first empty dock, my heart soared with excitement at the sight of so many visiting boaters.

I paddled over to an empty dock slip and was met immediately by Jim and Michelle Stokely from Sarnia. With a grin, Jim told me he was shocked to see me paddle into the harbour because most of the boaters had decided it was too rough and windy to leave the harbour that day. After I checked with the harbour master for permission to dock my kayak, Jim invited me to join them for a beer on their boat. Jim and Michelle were both easy to talk with, and I soon learned that they owned a restaurant on Sarnia Bay. When I explained my trip and fundraising efforts for cancer, Michelle eagerly jumped at the chance to get involved.

"I don't know what we can do," Michelle said, "but we'll think of something for when you arrive in Sarnia." Realizing there was no place in the harbour to pitch my tent, Michelle invited me to stay the night on their boat. They had only been married a week, so they had plans to go out for dinner but promised to meet me later that evening. Accustomed to finding my own way, I used the harbour showers and got dressed in my nicest camping clothes.

Tobermory is an exciting place to visit. There are shops, pubs, and restaurants built beside the water, attracting tourists and boaters from all over North America. As the sun set, the harbour adopted a carnival atmosphere. Strings of outdoor lights hung above the waterfront boardwalk, and people gathered and talked excitedly about port towns they had visited or were headed to next.

After my shower, I cooked my dinner on the dock, sandwiched between three large luxury cabin-cruisers equipped with microwaves, televisions, stereos, and fancy bathrooms. The contrast of lifestyles was a bit overwhelming, but I decided that I was content with my simple life. *I'm living more freely than they could ever dream to be,* I told myself. *I have no engine or pump problems, no gas bills, just me and my kayak.*

I walked around Tobermory harbour, acting like a tourist on vacation, before meeting Jim and Michelle for a beer at a local pub. While we sat talking around a table that overlooked the water, a thunder and lightning storm quickly unleashed a torrent of heavy rain outside. Worried about open windows and canopy covers on their boat, we ran back through the rain and were immediately soaked to the skin.

When we arrived, we discovered that their dock neighbours were already on board, closing windows and zippers to keep the rain water out. It was this sense of community that often drew people into the world of boating, and I liked what I saw. Once the storm was closed out, Jim and Michelle retired to their "honeymoon suite," while I fell asleep on a pullout bed, thankful for their generosity.

173

I woke early the next day, my body trained by routine. Jim and Michelle had decided to attempt to go home. The weather was overcast and unsettled, with more rain in the forecast. I helped them shove off. We hugged, said goodbye, and promised to see each other in three weeks when I arrived in Sarnia. After breakfast, I went and started my laundry. Later, I went back to my kayak and discovered that Jim and Michelle had returned. "Too rough," they announced with frowns. They decided to wait and try later.

I ran around town completing errands and talking to the local newspaper reporter. I met Lillian Thompson after lunch to hold our fundraiser for the cancer society. I really enjoyed this part of the trip. I found the people I met very interesting. Vince Kerrio, the former provincial Minister of Natural Resources, came over to speak with me and made a donation.

Lillian and I stopped fundraising around 6:00 p.m. After we had packed up, she insisted on treating me to a special dinner at the Grandview Restaurant. The restaurant sat perched high up on a rock overlooking the harbour. We ate a delicious meal of broiled whitefish. Lillian told me it was the restaurant's specialty, which draws in people all summer.

Our waitress noticed me as "the guy with the kayak" and asked lots of questions about my trip. I could tell she was genuinely interested, not just "acting" as the friendly server. When I told her my personal reasons for doing the trip, she told me her name was Michelle and that her mom had a rare form of cancer that the doctors had no treatment for. She said her mom had an excellent attitude and that her family was very positive, but I could sense that Michelle was worried. At the end of the meal Michelle handed Lillian back her four-dollar tip as a donation to the cancer society. Knowing that Michelle was a student earning money for school made her donation seem bigger and more significant to me.

It was moments like this that moved me and gave me extra strength on my tougher days. People had been skeptical whether my fundraising could be effective because I didn't have cancer myself. Moments like this proved to me that it wasn't me that people were connecting to cancer, but themselves and everyone they knew that cancer had touched.

Lillian wasn't sure if we would see each other again, so we said our goodbyes that evening. I really liked Lillian. She was full of spirit and an unstoppable zest for life. Over the past two meetings, I had heard and seen pictures of her experiences in West Africa, where she had taught in Gambia for eight months, and of a trip to the Arctic Circle. I loved and admired her sense of adventure. So many people lose their spark, but here she was, shining brightly in her senior years. When I didn't notice her wrinkled features, she seemed more my age than some of my friends. I hugged her goodbye. I really hoped I would see her again.

After Lillian left, I went back to the harbour facilities and had a hot shower. The harbour showers were available for travelling boaters who pay to dock in the marina. Hot water was a luxury I loved and appreciated. When I was alone on Superior and Lake Huron it hadn't mattered that I wasn't showering. Now that I was around people again, I couldn't go a day without feeling clean.

That night, I followed a crowd to the Crow's Nest Pub. Inside a crowded room, people were gathered around small tables listening to a singer named Jeremy Greenhouse perform on stage. A songwriter who played the guitar, fiddle, and harmonica, Greenhouse entertained the crowd with his folk-style songs, including an encore finale of Stan Roger's song, "Barrett's Privateer." After being away from music for what had seemed like years, watching a live performance was marvelous.

At the end of the show, some guy I didn't know offered me a place to sleep on a couch at the back of his boat. Someone else I had met had introduced him to me the night before, and now I couldn't remember his name. Forgetting names was a common problem because I was often meeting so many people during short introductions. The man kept talking to me like we were longtime friends, and I felt embarrassed to ask him his name after he had invited me to stay with him.

I fell asleep, curled up in my sleeping bag on the strangers' boat. It seemed oddly comfortable and strange to be welcomed and cared for by complete strangers. I liked the experience, though, and slept with the peace that comes from knowing that someone was taking care of me.

A Swift Awakening

I WOKE UP at five thirty to the sound of the sailboat beside me starting its engine. I felt it was time to leave Tobermory and head south along the western shoreline of the Bruce Peninsula. While I packed, my host, who I had learned was named John, got up and made us breakfast. I left the "big tub" harbour at eight thirty, excited to be back on the water. The breaks from paddling to meet people and fundraise were enjoyable, but the lure of being on the water heading somewhere new was constant for me.

When I paddled outside the protection of the harbour, I faced strong headwinds and waves. I paddled steadily, glad to feel the strain against my muscles. The coastline from Cape Hurd and south presented some rough water. Shallow shoals created metre-and-a-half-high breaking waves that had to be navigated around.

When the worst seemed to be over, I stopped paddling to eat my lunch in the kayak. While I sat eating, strong winds were pushing me towards shore. At first I wasn't terribly concerned. I felt that I had plenty of time to paddle away from the rocks when I got too close, but suddenly I realized that I *was* too close. The waves were getting bigger, and the shoals were just off my bow and close to shore. Quickly, I threw down my lunch, sealed the spray skirt over the cockpit, and grabbed my paddle.

Just as I had finished closing the cockpit, a silent wave a metre high rose up out of the water without warning and slammed down on top of me. Unprepared, the kayak flipped over on top of the rock shoal. Instantly, I tried to roll up, but the paddle broke in two pieces from the strain of force against the rock shoal. Still in the kayak, upside down and on top of a rock, I let go of the paddle and pulled myself from the kayak.

My first thought was my camera inside my lunch bag. I hadn't had time to seal the dry bag before closing the cockpit, and I feared the camera would be swimming in water. Standing on a rock shoal, I held onto the kayak while powerful breaking waves pulled at the kayak, trying to push the boat towards the rocky shore. Timing my efforts with the rhythm of each new wave, I quickly closed the dry bag, hoping that the camera was okay, but thinking it would be a miracle if it was dry.

At that moment, I realized I wasn't wearing my Tilley hat. Scanning the water, I saw my hat floating toward shore on a wave, closely followed by my broken paddle. Trying to steady the kayak against the breaking waves beating down on top of me was very difficult. All the water inside the cockpit was heavy and made the kayak unwilling to stay perpendicular to the waves without constant struggle. Everything I had in the cockpit was now floating in the lake—water bottles, maps, toothbrush bag, trip itinerary, and my list of contacts were missing or floating away from me. Looking up and down the coast, I saw that the shoal extended in each direction as far as I could see, without a haven from the breaking waves. I decided that walking the boat to shore was impossible. The waves were stronger than me, and if I ever slipped and let go of the boat, it would be gone. I knew that I had to climb back into the kayak and paddle to shore.

I tried to bail some of the water out of the cockpit, but it was hopeless; water was pouring in more quickly than I could bail it out. I grabbed my spare paddle and climbed back into the cockpit, being careful not to tip. There was no time to seal the cockpit; the waves were constantly beating down on top of me, and I had to steady the kayak for each assault. Wave after wave rose up over the shoal and crashed down on top of me, yet I slowly managed to paddle away to deeper water.

Finally free from the crashing waves, I paddled south along the coast to the first bay. The wind and waves followed me into the bay, so I paddled until I found a sheltered spot where the wind and waves could not reach me. The shoreline was guarded by sharp, jagged rocks, so I climbed out of the kayak and began to bail water out of the cockpit.

When I had finished bailing water, I was set on finding my missing gear that I hoped was being washed up against the shoreline. The distance along the rocky shore was too far to walk, and there was no place to leave the kayak, so I started paddling back. I was forced to backtrack north to an island to find a place to leave the kayak. As it was, I had to moor the kayak in a shallow channel between the island and the mainland. Eagerly, I walked the rocky shore in search of my belongings. Every item was crucial to me, and I didn't want to lose anything.

The first thing I found was half of a paddle. As I examined the shaft, I discovered that the shaft had cracked, so the joiner plug that connects both ends separated from the broken shaft. I slowly searched the shoreline and shoals. I wanted my hat back. I had come to depend on that hat each day for protection from the sun, but it was more than that to me. The hat was a gift from Tilley Endurables that I didn't want to lose. Luckily, I did find my map case that contained my trip itinerary and contact information floating and bobbing against the rocky shore. Twenty-five metres away, I found the other end of my paddle. I searched the shoreline for an hour, but I could not find my hat, water bottle, or toothbrush bag. *Another payment to the gods for safe passage,* I told myself.

I went back to the kayak and ate my lunch. When I examined my camera, I was pleasantly surprised to find it mostly dry, except for a little moisture. Looking up toward the heavens, I offered a simple thank-you prayer. It was a quick reminder not to be careless or cavalier with the lake; the price could have been far more severe.

I left the island and paddled for a couple more hours. I had lost four hours due to my carelessness, and I was angry with myself. The kayak could have been broken on the shoal. My maps were soaked. The well-used plastic map cases were obviously not "drown-proof." With nowhere to go but south, I pointed the *Mai Fleur* in the direction of Sarnia and paddled. When I reached Eagle Point, I decided to stop for the day.

The ground was covered in small stones, not the most pleasant campsite. I decided it would do for one night. With the practice of routine, I set out my maps to dry and put up the tent. Afterward, I cooked a spaghetti and tomato sauce dinner. While I packed the kayak for the night, I saw the orange glow of the moon peeking over and through the tree tops. A few moments later it emerged above the trees, a beautiful orange ball glowing in the sky. After a day of struggle, it was the perfect way to end the day.

As I admired the beauty of the moon, I thought back to Lake Superior and the evening that I had crossed to Otter Island against two-metre swells, unable to find a campsite and watching a red sun slip into the lake. *You are only a visitor here*, I reminded myself. *You may come or go, live or die, but the sun will continue to rise and set each day.* I went to bed, still angry with myself for being so careless.

No Camping in Oliphant

===

THE FOLLOWING MORNING, I met a couple who lived in a cottage nearby. They were out for a walk and stopped to talk. When I had finished packing, I walked to their cottage and asked to use their phone. I called my mom and dad and, after assuring them that I was okay, I asked them to phone Nimbus Paddles and Tilley Endurables for a new paddle and hat. Immediately, my dad wanted to know what had happened, but I didn't want to admit my carelessness or cause him to worry, so I brushed the losses off to bad weather. I could tell my dad was in a mood to talk, so we chatted about my last few days and family news before saying goodbye.

I started paddling late in the day, determined to get back on schedule. The sun was bright and hot. I wore a ball cap for shade, but I missed the wide brim of my Tilley hat. I paddled steadily without a break until the sun was low and bled an orange blush across the western sky. Lake Huron sunsets, as I wrote in my journal, are the most beautiful I have seen anywhere on earth.

The next day, I pushed myself to paddle hard all day and arrived at the town of Oliphant late in the afternoon. Unfamiliar with the town, I landed in what appeared to be a waterfront park equipped with picnic tables and a washroom facility. The park was empty except for an older couple from Hope Bay. We talked about my trip, and then they asked if they could take my picture, which felt odd, but I graciously agreed. When the couple left, I found a pay phone and called my parents to inquire if they had succeeded in arranging replacement items from Nimbus

Paddles and Tilley Endurables. My dad had phoned both companies, and promised me that the paddle and hat would be shipped that week. When I returned to my kayak, I saw that a rainstorm was moving toward me from across the bay. I had just enough time to set up my tent before the rain started to fall.

While I set up the tent, a man came over from his house across the street and told me I couldn't camp there overnight. I tried to explain that, because of the lightning, I didn't want to go back on the water. Unmoved, he told me that if I didn't move, the bylaw officer would come and give me a seventy-five dollar fine. A half hour later a town parks employee came to lock the washrooms. He too told me that I couldn't camp there overnight. When I tried to explain my situation to him, he wasn't sympathetic either. In a matter of fact manner, he explained that if I didn't move, someone would move me.

Feeling both perturbed and vulnerable, I went and phoned Lillian Thompson to ask if she knew anyone at the OPP detachment in Wiarton who might be able to help. Lillian promised to do what she could, but warned me that she didn't know anyone with the local OPP.

While I sat in my tent sheltered from the rain a car pulled up and shone its headlights on my tent. The lights shone on the tent for ten minutes, but no one came to my tent, and I didn't go out in the rain to investigate. After ten more minutes, the lights went out, but the person left the car engine running. Soon after, Lillian arrived and called my name from outside the tent. By the time I had put my rain coat on and crawled out of the tent, the bylaw officer was outside speaking with Lillian. Lillian was trying to explain to the woman who I was, and that I was fundraising for cancer, but the woman wasn't interested.

The bylaw officer demanded to see some identification. I refused, explaining that I didn't have any proper identification except for my credit card. Hostile and unwilling to make an exception for my circumstances with the weather, the bylaw officer told me that I would be removed when the police arrived. She then promptly returned to her car and waited. Prepared for a showdown, Lillian and I sat in her car and waited for the police. A half hour later, the police arrived and within minutes I was told that I had to leave.

At first, I agreed without any debate. I started packing my soggy tent in the rain while three officers stood watching. Suddenly, a growing anger welled up in my throat. Halfway through packing, I stopped and confronted the officers. Short of swearing, I expressed my outrage, citing a boater's right to take refuge from a stormy lake.

"What would I do," I demanded, "if I didn't have someone to come and help me? Were you prepared to arrest me and put me in jail if I didn't agree to leave?" Glancing at the bylaw officer, I continued my rant. "I've paddled from Thunder Bay, and I have never been treated like this until now." Taken aback by my sudden boldness in the face of authority, the officers looked at each other and then pulled me gently aside.

"Look," they started, "we understand you're upset, but unfortunately our hands are tied. We've been asked to enforce a municipal bylaw, and when asked we have to respond."

For a moment their explanation softened my anger. But as the bylaw officer drove away and I realized that I would have to leave my kayak and most of my belongings there overnight, my anger resurfaced. Neither Lillian nor the police were equipped to transport my boat somewhere safe. I was forced to secure my kayak with a wire cable to a wooden sign post.

My heart ached as I left the *Mai Fleur* behind. I knew it was only a kayak, but after seventy-three days together, we had shared a lot, and I couldn't bear the idea of someone taking her. I said a silent prayer before we drove the ten kilometres across the peninsula to Wiarton.

Lillian brought me home for the night. There was no limit to her kindness toward me. I went to sleep thinking about the *Mai Fleur* and woke at 6:00 a.m. anxious to return. Lillian made me scrambled eggs for breakfast, but my thoughts were in Oliphant. I arrived back in the town at seven thirty-five. Seeing the *Mai Fleur* parked safely where I had left it was a wonderful relief. I repacked the kayak and said goodbye to Lillian. She told me she was going to try to meet me in Sauble Beach at one o'clock.

As I paddled away, my mind kept returning to the image when the bylaw officer told me that I had to pack up my tent and leave. It was easy to stay stuck feeling angry, but I was determined to focus on the positive. *You know, Michael,* I reminded myself, *you were breaking the town's bylaw. Besides, the situation allowed you to spend more time with Lillian, and that was a good thing. Don't let the bylaw officer's actions get to you. Think of yesterday as a dream. Today is a new dream. Let it go, Michael, it's for the best.*

A New Point of View

AFTER A COUPLE of hours paddling, I arrived at Sauble Beach North at ten o'clock. I tied my kayak to a post in front of a restaurant beside the Sauble River. I was hours ahead of my scheduled arrival time at Sauble Beach, so I enjoyed a cup of coffee and wrote in my journal. I must have looked like every other tourist that visits Sauble Beach because I sat quietly by myself the entire time.

I started paddling at twelve forty-five, confident that I could reach the waiting group of cancer society volunteers by one o'clock. I didn't know exactly where the group was waiting, but someone had told me they would be at an archway on the beach. As I paddled closer and saw the archway, my eyes focused on Lillian's face. Her familiar smile was a beacon. When my kayak touched the beach, I was greeted by Lillian, Betty Hendricks, Lou Burns, Ross Ireland, and some of his friends from the Amabel men's club.

I stayed on the beach talking with people and fundraising until four o'clock. When it was time to go, Ross invited me to stay at his home and join him and his wife, Marj, and friends Garth and Pat Walker for dinner. This created the daily dilemma of what to do with the kayak at night. Luckily, I was surrounded by resourceful people, and soon we had loaded my kayak in the back of someone's pick-up truck. With three metres of my kayak sticking out the end of the truck box, we escorted my kayak down the road with me and two of Ross's friends supporting one end of the kayak.

After dinner we went back to the Chesely Lake campground where

Garth and Pat were staying. There I met their daughter, Brenda; her husband, Nathan; and their three kids. They were all really kind and friendly people. We stayed until dark, enjoying pleasant conversation while the kids cooked hot dogs over a campfire.

I stayed for another day at Sauble Beach to fundraise. Over breakfast with Marj and Ross, we made plans to find help moving my kayak back to the beach. I had noticed earlier in the trip that the kayak was a natural attraction. Many people had never seen a sea kayak before and were curious about its design. Once they were close enough to the kayak, they noticed me and my fundraising signs.

After lunch, Harry Little, Ivan Walter, and Bill Blacklock helped me transport the kayak. We arrived at the beach at one. Betty was there waiting for me and willing to do anything to help raise funds. I felt rejuvenated and inspired by the commitment of the volunteers. Later that day Lou arrived, and together we spoke with people and collected donations.

Back at Marj and Ross's home at the end of the day, I fell into bed exhausted. Fundraising had become a major role in my day and although it was enjoyable, it was almost as tiring as paddling. Lying awake, I relived the events of the past few days. Special people who started as strangers had opened their hearts, homes, and lives to me. The feeling of being connected to these people was joyous, like the magic at Christmas when strangers share their humanity freely. I felt blessed by the experience.

An alarm clock woke me from my dreams at 5:00 a.m. After a quick breakfast and warm goodbye to my hosts, Ross and his friends helped me transport the kayak to the beach. Once again, I was being "seen off" on my journey. I felt comfort knowing that as I left Sauble Beach, I had a new group of well-wishers on my team.

At six thirty, I paddled away from Sauble Beach. The sun was rising to meet a bright baby blue sky, and the water was calm. It was a good day to paddle. Confident in the safety of the conditions, I paddled a kilometre offshore, enjoying the rhythm of paddling. Stroke, stroke, stroke … kayaking had become a physical addiction that my muscles craved each day. Accustomed to the physical demands, my body and mind simply wanted to keep paddling and never stop, just as cyclists or runners *do it* simply for the pleasure.

With time to spare, I raced down the western shoreline past

Frenchman Point, Southampton, and Port Elgin, where I was scheduled to stop and meet fundraisers at one. Paddling simply for pleasure, I followed the coast all the way to the Bruce Nuclear Power Station. In less than five hours I had paddled approximately forty kilometres. I thought back to my start on Lake Superior, when this kind of speed had been inconceivable.

I ate my lunch in the kayak, regarding the oddity of the nuclear station. Friends had jokingly warned me not to paddle too close. "I don't know, Michael," Mark had joked. "You don't want to get any of that water on you. Never know what might fall off or start glowing in the dark."

Once I had finished eating, I turned around and paddled the twenty kilometres back to Port Elgin. When I reached the Port Elgin beach, I was greeted by cancer society volunteers, the mayor of Southampton, a representative for the mayor of Port Elgin, plus two local newspapers. After a small ceremony with the town representatives and interviews with the local newspapers, I met with cancer society members. Jean Meisenhimer and Elaine Palmer from the cancer society stayed and raised funds with me on the beach until four thirty. Afterward, the two women treated me to a wonderful dinner at a local restaurant.

Bored of cooking trip food, I found the meal in a restaurant was a nice change, and I appreciated the generosity immensely. During dinner we discussed our mutual feelings of frustration with the lack of organization around fundraising. To my surprise, I learned that no one from the cancer society's head office in Toronto had told the Port Elgin staff about my fundraising trip until just a day ago.

After dinner, Elaine produced a brand new kayak paddle and Tilley hat from her car trunk that my dad had arranged to be shipped to her. I didn't know how he had coordinated the replacements so quickly, but it felt great to have him working on my behalf.

One of the reasons I had started this expedition was because of my feelings of low self-worth. Planning the expedition gave me a purpose that I needed. When my mom and dad had expressed anger with me for not asking for their help, I hadn't understood. In truth, maybe I didn't want their help because I was afraid it would show that I couldn't do it on my own. Now that it was clear that I could use some help, I felt no shame in asking. Instead, it simply felt like family caring enough to want to help.

Later that evening, Jean and I went back to the town harbour and fundraised on the pier. In a couple of hours we collected a hundred and eighty dollars. When it seemed as though everyone had gone home, we drove to Jean's house and discussed fundraising plans for Kincardine, Goderich, and Grand Bend. Determined to help, Jean promised to call the cancer society offices on my route and ask them to work with me when I arrived.

I stayed at Jean's house that night and woke early the next morning, ate a quick breakfast, and was on the water before 7:00 a.m., feeling enriched by the care and generosity of another stranger turned friend.

I paddled while the sun came up, warming the start to a beautiful day. Paddling past the Bruce Nuclear Power Plant was a bit unnerving. The strong current from the effluent discharge of the power plant met the incoming waves from the lake and created turbulence and large standing waves. Remembering the teasing of friends, I cautiously paddled through the rough water, telling myself, *Don't tip, don't tip.* I enjoyed a leisurely paddle down the coast and arrived as planned in Kincardine at three thirty, met by the mayor, people from town, and cancer society volunteers. The crowd was very welcoming and congratulatory on my success, but nothing was planned for fundraising. I stayed on the dock for a couple of hours collecting donations with little success. Despite Jean's phone calls, with little time to organize, nothing had been planned until that day.

A small group of volunteers with the cancer society took me out for dinner. Even with their warm generosity, I felt both discouraged and frustrated at the lack of organization. Although I appreciated their moral support, I would have preferred to forgo dinner and work on fundraising somewhere in town.

I don't know how the conversation started, but it wasn't long before organization politics was out on the table, and I soon learned that there was a divide between grassroots volunteers and the head office in Toronto. From my early meeting with Mark Climie, I had been led to believe that I would have the help of staff and volunteers in the towns along my route. It was now clear that the Toronto office had not informed the staff of my fundraising trip. The realization was upsetting, and each of us expressed disappointment that an opportunity had been missed.

"Michael, we are really sorry," Molly offered. "If we had been given more notice from Toronto, we could have built a fundraising campaign around your arrival." Despite the heaviness of the conversation, spirits remained high from the success of my trip. With help from a cold pint of beer and some encouragement, I quickly shed away a coat of despair and began sharing stories about my trip and the wonderful people I had met.

Two days after my stop in Kincardine, I was back in my kayak and headed for the town of Goderich. I had camped the night before beside the lake near the town of Kintail Beach. The shoreline was all sand beaches and busy with people enjoying the sun and water. I passed kilometres of shoreline from Boogies Beach to Point Farm Provincial Park and watched countless families playing games like Frisbee, football, and tag in the water. One family in particular captured my attention, as three young children, a boy and his two sisters, and their mom and dad each floated past on air mattresses or floating animals tied together end to end like a train. It was a happy summer scene.

Morning Coffee Getaway

L ATER THE SAME day, July 31, I arrived at the town of Goderich. I didn't know where to go, so I paddled until I saw a group of people near the town's main dock. As I approached, Mel Farnsworth and his wife, Beth, waved at me with a cancer society banner.

There was a huge surf blowing onto the exposed beach. The breaking waves were big and numerous, which made landing a kayak dangerous business. There was always the chance of being tipped or having a large wave collapse overhead. I waited a few minutes and studied the wave patterns. I didn't want to make a spectacle of myself. When I felt confident that I could beach myself safely, I waited for the right moment, and then rode a pushy wave onto the sand and gravel beach. Instantly, a group of strangers were grabbing parts of my kayak and dragging me higher onto shore before the next wave could collapse on top of me.

After I had climbed out of my kayak and was speaking with Mel and Beth, my mom and dad showed up with my grandma and grandpa Hill and my uncle Greg with his kids, Kelsey and Andrew. After I met the mayor and the local newspaper reporter, Mel introduced me to Jim Bridle, the owner of the North End Marina, who had offered to store my kayak. Jim was a cancer survivor who had lost his larynx to the disease. He had to speak through a small device implanted near his Adam's apple. Jim smiled warmly at me as we shook hands. Without any words, he conveyed his appreciation for my effort, and instantly my spirit soared.

In the evening, my family and I gathered at my cousin Amber's farm outside Goderich. Everyone wanted to hear about my adventures since leaving Parry Sound, and we stayed awake talking, drinking, and laughing late into the night. Before going to bed, I wrote a single line in my journal: *To be surrounded by the loving embrace of family is a wonderful feeling.*

I woke early the next morning while most of the other guests slept. Eager for some private time alone, my dad and I slipped away to town for a morning coffee at Tim Horton's. I don't recall what we talked about, just the feelings that passed between us and the pleasure of having the time to simply be in each other's company. Sometimes there are no words to share between a father and son. I knew my mom and dad worried about me while I was kayaking, and I didn't know how to ease their fears. When we got back to the house, everyone was up and sitting down to breakfast. I loved the feeling of being around a large family; there is no greater sense of comfort or security.

After breakfast, my day was filled with media interviews. First I spoke with a reporter from CKNX radio in Wingham. When I hung up the phone, I had to race to town for an interview with the Goderich newspaper. Then, when that interview was finished, I had just enough time to climb into my kayak and make an appearance kayaking to the town dock for the CKNX television station. After a short interview on camera, I fundraised on the beach with Mel Farnsworth. During the course of the afternoon, we collected seventy dollars, plus a promise of a hundred dollars from a woman who attends church with Mel. I had a grand time meeting and speaking with many well-wishers and people who stopped to make a donation.

Sometime in the afternoon my family went home, and I was left alone again on my solo journey. It was then that I realized that my favourite paddle was missing. Somehow in the confusion of coming ashore the day before, many hands had helped by grabbing things from me while I spoke to different people, and the paddle had disappeared. With the paddle missing, I was left with the paddle I'd broken near Tobermory and the replacement, which I didn't like. I couldn't explain why I didn't like the new paddle. It felt heavier and uncomfortable to paddle with, even though it looked the same as the one I'd broken. Regardless, I wouldn't use the new paddle, so I was forced to fix the one I had broken. There was no way I was going to ask my paddle sponsor for another replacement.

When we had finished fundraising, Mel brought me back to Amber and Rob's for the night and promised to pick me up in the morning. That evening, Amber's husband, Rob, helped me glue together my broken paddle. Afterward, we sat and talked about my trip. He asked if I had any stories of mishaps and adventures, but I was cautious about what I was ready to share, worried the stories might reach my parents.

The next morning, I spoke with Jason Chenier from CHOK radio in Sarnia. Before I left town, Mel and I stopped to see Jim Bridle and thank him for storing my kayak, but he wasn't there. I took his business card with plans to send him a postcard. I finally left Goderich around one in the afternoon, under a heavy northwest wind. I battled my way to Bayfield, arriving in the harbour at five o'clock, exhausted. No one was expecting me in the small town, so I had a quiet night curled up in my sleeping bag on a patch of grass, a stone's throw from the marina.

After two uneventful days, I camped in Pinery Provincial Point, where I enjoyed a quiet evening exploring the park's famous sand dunes. I had been missing solitude and time alone to reflect on the past few days. My evening at Pinery Park was exactly that, peaceful and quiet. The area was new to me. Never before had I seen anything like the sand dunes, and it would have been nice to stay longer. I often felt that I wasn't on a personal trip, and I focused my sights on reaching the next destination with hopes of raising donations.

The morning was overcast, threatening rain, but I loaded the kayak regardless of the gloomy skies, determined to paddle. I hadn't paddled more than ten minutes when it started to rain—hard. Sheets of rain pushed by the wind looked like a wall of white coming toward me. The wind increased, building bigger waves. I enjoyed the feeling of paddling in harsh weather. I felt more alive in the throes of a storm. I decided to keep paddling as long as I didn't see lightning. The rain never stopped. It slowed to a drizzle for a while and then pounded down on top of me with more vigor.

I stopped in the afternoon on a small deserted beach in the middle of nowhere. The rain did not stop. There were very few trees on shore, as though over time the wind had forced them all to move inland. Tall grass that stood two metres high guarded the landscape past the sand beach. It was still early in the day, but I felt that I needed more time away from people asking me questions or the demands of fundraising. I wanted time to be alone, yet I also felt a sense of duty to 'push on' and act the role as a cancer society ambassador. The two needs were in conflict. I set up my tent and slept for a couple of hours.

I woke later to the sound of a heavy surf crashing on shore. I peeked outside my tent and noticed that my kayak had moved. I went outside and discovered that the water had risen two metres on the beach. Heavy winds and waves had pushed my kayak higher up on shore, and waves were crashing against the hull. I pulled the kayak to higher ground away from the water and tied it to a tree. When I felt confident that the boat was secure, I went back to my tent.

Inside the tent, all I could hear was the sound of crashing waves. The wind shook my tent, making my candle lantern swing from the ceiling. I don't know why, but I have always loved weather like this when I am inside a tent. I felt safe, as though my tent was a giant womb where nothing could touch me.

When I woke the next morning, the wind was still pushing big waves up on to shore. Although I was eager to reach Sarnia, I decided to take another rest day, which I convinced myself that I deserved. The trip had taken on a new feeling of *being a job*, and I didn't feel ready for the busy activity of a city like Sarnia.

I stayed in my tent all day and read, ate, and slept when I wanted. At times during the day I felt guilty for not paddling and debated whether I should leave. In the end, I stayed.

The sunset that evening was beautiful. An orange and red sun slipped slowly down from the sky, as though the gods were lowering it down by invisible strings. When it had disappeared into the lake, the western horizon was awash in a blush of orange, red, and pink. *Moments like these are pure magic,* I wrote in my journal, *Oh, how I wish Fleur was here to share this sunset with me.*

Too Sick to Go On

I WOKE TO the sound of birds singing the next morning. The wind and waves were gone. It took me a long time to pack my tent and belongings. Since breakfast, I had started to show signs of diarrhea and was forced to stop packing regularly to relieve myself.

I paddled slowly toward Sarnia, not sure what was wrong with me, but knowing something wasn't right. I was still fifteen kilometres away from Sarnia when I could make out the Blue Water Bridge from the distant shore. The bridge that joined Sarnia, Ontario, with Port Huron, Michigan, was gargantuan in size, a beacon that was impossible to miss.

As I paddled closer, I stopped and counted the masts of sixty-five sailboats. Their white sails filled my view of the water and sky as they sailed across the bay toward me. Later, I learned it had been a race. For a while it seemed we were on a collision course, when suddenly the lead boat quickly turned and cut sharply around a large buoy marker and began sailing away in the opposite direction. When I was close enough, I watched in awe as the crew members from each of the sailboats worked together to master their sails and turn their boats around. Within a few short minutes, all of the sailboats were moving away from me and heading back toward the St. Clair River.

I arrived in Sarnia at 2:00 p.m. on August 6. The short voyage down the St. Clair River was both hectic and exhilarating. The river was abuzz with large boats. As I was funneled into the river, I was quickly sharing space with sailboats, jet skis, small boats, and private yachts the size of post-war houses. The wake from all of the boat traffic created unnatural waves that tossed my kayak about recklessly.

I made my way down the river, darting around the traffic, careful to avoid a collision. I eventually landed my kayak safely on the sand beach across from Jim and Michelle's restaurant, McGuiniss on the Bay. Thinking back to my encounter with Jim and Michele on their boat in Tobermory, I hoped their enthusiasm for helping me raise funds was still alive.

When I found the restaurant manager, I learned that Jim and Michelle were not there, but had left instructions for their staff to feed me lunch and take care of me until they returned.

My god, I thought to myself, *it's like being hosted by royalty.*

Thankful for the hospitality, I sat outside on the patio and read a newspaper while I waited for my lunch. It was then that I learned for the first time about the genocide happening in Rwanda. The graphic words leaped off the page as I read about the mass murders taking place on the other side of the globe. The story left me feeling shocked and saddened.

During the time I was kayaking, my trip had come to represent all things good in the world, like caring for others, generosity, and celebrating life. Reading about the horrors unfolding on the African continent brought me out of my bubble and face to face with the fact that life could be harsh and unfair. The news about the inhumanity was too much for me to absorb all at once. I turned the paper to baseball and the Toronto Blue Jays for distraction. *I wonder if the Jays will win the World Series for a third time?*

Since I had awakened that morning with diarrhea, my stomach had felt unsettled. I had hoped that a nice lunch would help me feel better. Instead, the nausea grew worse. During lunch, Jim called me on the phone. Any concerns I had about his enthusiasm for my arrival vanished as soon as we spoke. Excitedly, Jim flipped back and forth from asking me about my trip to relating their plans to help me fundraise for cancer.

As we spoke, gas pains started to balloon inside my stomach and erupted in what I had hoped would be a silent fart. To my horror, I shit my pants. Barely able to contain myself, I hurried to get off the phone, worried that my khaki shorts had become brown. Frantic, I pulled my long shirt tail over my shorts and quickly walked to the nearest washroom.

For the next twenty minutes my body drained everything I had inside me. Remembering my experience in Killarney, I wished I had the luxury of a private washroom. When it seemed safe to get off the toilet, I washed my shorts in the washroom sink. Thankfully, no one walked into the washroom while I was in there. The room didn't have a hot air hand dryer, so I was forced to wear my wet shorts out of the washroom. Self-conscious, I sat near my kayak away from people and wrote postcards until Jim and Michelle arrived.

It was awkward for me to have to explain that I was ill and experiencing diarrhea, but Jim and Michelle treated me like family. Immediately, they helped to make me feel comfortable and cared for me like longtime friends. After arranging to store my kayak at the town marina, they took me to their house in the country. Situated on sixty-six acres, their property consisted of a remodeled farmhouse, two barns, and a baseball park for hosting tournaments. The home was like something shown on the cover of *Better Homes and Gardens* and had an equal blend of style and comfort. After they had given me time to shower and clean up, we sat and talked in their kitchen until it was time to go for dinner.

Back at their restaurant, we met their boating friends John and Judy, who I had met in Tobermory. After the usual handshakes and hugs, John and Judy presented me with a laminated map of Lake St. Clair and the St. Clair River. It was a thoughtful gift that I knew I would cherish long after my trip.

During dinner I learned that, like me, they had all met on the water. Drawn together by the excitement of boating, they met on Lake Huron and quickly became friends. Surprisingly, the reunion felt natural, as though we had known each other forever.

John insisted that I meet them the following Saturday for their second annual cardboard boat race on Wadpole Island. They were making a fourteen-foot canoe out of cardboard treated with Thompson's WaterSeal.

"Last year," John explained, "our boat was good enough not to sink, but this year I've improved the design and construction techniques." With a slight smirk, Judy added, "John's an engineer, so he takes this pretty seriously."

Intrigued by the expected fun, I told them that I would love to come but wasn't sure if it would fit into my schedule. When I shared that I had read a book about a guy who had built a paper kayak and paddled it from Montreal to Florida, they thought that was unbelievable.

Although I enjoyed the company, my health deteriorated over dinner and limited my full enjoyment of the night. I didn't have to visit the bathroom, but everything that I consumed caused an uncomfortable stir in my stomach. To my disappointment, I declined dessert, the true litmus test to show how badly I was feeling.

We arrived back at Jim and Michele's after one a.m. Tired and feeling *not quite right*, I said good night with the invitation to sleep as late as I wanted. Jim and Michelle had planned an afternoon of fundraising and media attention for the next day. I wanted to be well rested and in good health by then.

The diarrhea started early the next morning. I stayed in bed and only left to visit the toilet. My body ached constantly. The only good thing about the situation was that Fleur had sent two letters to Jim and Michelle's address, hoping they would arrive while I was there. Curled up with my knees against my chest, I re-read her letters between frequent visits to the toilet. It was the first news I had received from her since Parry Sound, and I was hungry to hear about her summer.

The letters were recent and exceptionally long. One letter was twenty handwritten pages describing her experiences leading canoe trips in northern Ontario and hiking trips in the Adirondack Mountains in New York State. When she described a beautiful mountain view or lake sunset and shared how much she wished that I had been there, my heart soared.

Unwilling to cancel my fundraising appearance, I forced myself to get out of bed and dress. When Michele returned to pick me up at two thirty, I was dressed and ready. I don't know where I found the strength, but I managed to kayak from the town marina to the public beach near the restaurant. A small crowd, including cancer society volunteers and newspaper reporters, met me on the beach. We fundraised for an hour, and then Jim and Michelle announced that they would donate fifty cents from each drink ordered at the restaurant for the next hour.

Jim and Michele had to go home and prepare dinner for their friend's birthday, so they left me at the restaurant talking with cancer society volunteers. Later that evening, after the birthday dinner, I was invited to join the group of friends for an evening cruise on the St. Clair River.

"We've rented a boat," explained Michelle, "and you're more than welcome to join us." I knew that I shouldn't. The little voice in my head warned me to stay behind and sleep. The problem was that most of my summer had been spent either in isolation or meeting people to raise funds. I had enjoyed the company of all the people I had met, but I missed socializing with people my own age. The chance of going to a party was too much for me to turn down. Against my better judgment, I went, and I paid the price. Even though the people were nice and there was a live band playing, I felt miserable. The thought of drinking alcohol didn't appeal to me, so I was surrounded by strangers who were there to party hard and have a good time. There are few experiences more alienating than being surrounded by people drinking when you are sober. I spent the night wandering the boat, silently wishing that I was alone in bed sleeping.

When I finally went to bed, I couldn't sleep. Painful stomach cramps had suddenly returned and forced me into a continuous relay between my bed and the toilet. Angry with my decision to go to the party, I berated myself for being so stupid. I stayed in bed the next morning until 9:00 a.m. Tired and still experiencing stomach cramps, I got up to inquire what Michelle had planned for her day. She was on her way to work, but when she realized how bad I looked, she suggested one of her staff at the restaurant drive me to the hospital.

After waiting a couple of hours at the local hospital emergency room, an impatient nurse took my pulse, temperature, and blood pressure and then told me to wait for a doctor. Twenty minutes later, a doctor arrived and informed me it could be a viral infection or simply the flu. In either case, he wrote me a prescription for a bacterial infection and suggested that I take something for the diarrhea.

After a short stop at the drug store, I was back in bed at Michelle and Jim's house for the remainder of the day. My needs were modest: solitude, a bed, and a toilet. Food was the last thing I wanted.

Time slipped away, with me drifting in and out of sleep. Sometime in the early evening, Jim and Michelle came home and checked in on me. If they had any concerns or reservations about becoming a shelter for a sick, wayward kayaker, they kindly hid their feelings.

After I told them what the doctor had said, they shared what news they had picked up in town. The day before I arrived in Sarnia, the municipal officials had closed all of the beaches from Grand Bend to Sarnia due to health concerns. After the recent rainstorm that I had kayaked through, agricultural runoff had contaminated the lake. Someone told Michelle that the acceptable fecal count is one hundred units, but before they closed the beaches it measured more than two thousand.

As the news registered with me, I had a vision of me kayaking through the lake water contaminated with animal manure. Although I never drank water straight from the lake, water often sprayed or splashed on my face and lips from waves. I was experiencing *Montezuma's revenge* without the exotic Mexican vacation.

The next day was a repeat of the past twenty-four hours. My stomach was still in knots, and food would not stay down. The only difference was that I had moved from my bed to the downstairs couch. Lacking my usual energy, it was all I could do to push the buttons on the television remote. As I sat on the couch watching sleazy talk shows or '70s reruns, I felt guilty. Even though Jim and Michelle made me feel welcome under the circumstances, I didn't feel that I belonged there. When I had first arrived at Jim and Michelle's, I took one step inside their front door and said, "This place is gorgeous, that's it, I'm never leaving." It was now three days later and I *was* still there, and my words haunted me. The last thing I wanted to be was a guest who overstayed his welcome. When Michelle came back from the restaurant to check on me, I awkwardly blurted, "I was only kidding about not leaving." Michelle smiled and assured me that it was okay for me to stay, and that I should focus on getting better.

Feeling miserable can nurture and encourage negative thoughts and emotions. Desperate to speak with Fleur, I dialed her friend's house where she had planned to stay during her day off work. My heart raced with excitement at the possibility of hearing her voice. When her friend Neta answered the phone and told me that Fleur wasn't there, my heart sank. Neta told me to call the next day around six in the evening, but I barely heard her speak before I hung up the phone.

STRUGGLING ON

I WOKE IN the morning determined to leave Jim and Michelle's home. I wasn't feeling much better, but I wouldn't allow myself another day on the couch. Jim kindly drove me around town so I could pick up some groceries. I said goodbye at the Sarnia Bay marina. My new friends wished me well and promised to see me when I arrived in Toronto. I departed at twelve fifteen under grey skies. My stomach felt queasy, with the occasional sharp stabs of pain. This was one of those times when I didn't want to be kayaking.

Fortunately, the fast river current compensated for my lack of motivation to paddle. The grey sky and endless development along the water did little to help lift my spirits. "Man's idea of what *nature* should look like," I scoffed as I paddled past steel breakwaters and rising skyscrapers.

I arrived in Port Lampton at four forty-five. I had fifteen minutes to find a phone and call Bill Steele at the Windsor CBC radio station. By grace, I found a pay phone in front of the Cook-E-Tree Bakery, across the road from the river. After the interview, I went into the bakery and met the owner's daughter. I hoped she had a public washroom because the sign said, "coffee and donuts." When I asked about a bathroom, the girl told me the bakery was take-out only, and they didn't have a public washroom for customers. Desperate and slightly frustrated that she didn't allow me to use her bathroom, I bought an apple turnover and went looking for a public washroom.

After a short walk down the road, I found the Toad's Place Restaurant, a public washroom, and a quiet booth where I could sip hot tea and wait to call Fleur. Just before six p.m., I walked back to the phone booth and met Tim Papps, the owner of the Cook-E-Tree Bakery. He had heard me say on CBC radio that I was outside his bakery and learned later that I had been in his bake shop. For good luck, he gave me a bag of his bakery cookies and wished me a safe journey.

At exactly six o'clock, I phoned Fleur at her friend's house in Kingston. It had been so long since I had talked with her, I desperately needed to hear her comforting words of encouragement. When her friend's mom told me they were out water skiing, my heart sank. It took some coaxing from her mom to convince me to call back in ten minutes. Hanging up the phone, I was filled with questions. Why wasn't she waiting for my call? Neta told me to call at six, so why wasn't she there?

Poisoned by sickness, fatigue, and the strain of being separated, I jumped to irrational conclusions. *She doesn't miss me. She doesn't care about talking with me. She's more interested in water-skiing than hearing that I'm sick. She probably met some guy in Kingston,* I tortured myself.

By the time ten minutes had passed, I'd convinced myself there was no need to call, but I had to. Fleur answered the phone on the second ring. My heart raced from the excitement of hearing her voice. Convinced our relationship was over, and feeling angry and hurt, my first words were rough and filled with accusations.

"Why weren't you waiting for my call?" I demanded.

Startled by my harsh first words Fleur stammered back, "What? What are you talking about?"

Still on the offensive, I repeated my attack with short, punctuated stabs, "Why, weren't, you, waiting, for, my, call, at, six, o'clock?"

Fleur's answer was brief, gentle, and to the point.

"Michael, what are you talking about? I miss you, and this isn't how I want to waste this call."

Unable to switch from my offensive, I continued, "Then why weren't you waiting for my call? Neta told me to call you at six, and you weren't around."

"Neta didn't tell me you were going to call me at six," Fleur responded softly. "If I had known you were going to call, I would have been near the phone." As she began to feel the sting of my attack, Fleur's words lost their softness and took on an impatient edge. It took me a few more minutes to cool down and change my attitude. We hadn't spoken since July, and I had been looking forward to this call every day. The call wasn't going as I had dreamed. The silence through the phone line warned me that I had to do something quick to repair the damage.

"I'm sorry," I offered softly. "I miss you, and I really needed to hear your voice right now." Thankfully, I chose the right words. In an instant, we were talking freely once again. For the moment, we forgot that we were apart and caressed each other with words through the phone lines, briefly sharing our adventures and desire to be in each other's arms. We hated to say goodbye, but eventually we ended the call. When I left the phone booth, I was close to tears. I missed my friend, and I was upset with myself for wasting part of the call.

Outside the phone booth I was met by Jim Goodman. He too had heard my interview on CBC and when he saw me standing near my kayak, he figured I had to be the same guy. We talked about my trip for a few minutes and then Jim invited me to stay with him and his family. He lived down river another half kilometre with his wife, Donna, and daughter, Carrie.

Excited over the prospect of not camping along the polluted river, I raced my kayak to his house. Jim was a canoeist, so we sat and talked into the evening about different rivers we had paddled or wanted to explore. It had been awhile since I had met someone who paddled and was interested in talking about canoeing or kayaking.

It was raining heavy drops the next day when Jim helped me carry my kayak across the road from his house to the edge of the river. Over breakfast he had told me that it takes him three hours to paddle to Wallaceburg from his house. From that news, I figured I had an easy day ahead of me.

Instead of heading off in the rain, I walked to the Toad Restaurant. Seated in a quiet corner booth, I sat out the rain drinking coffee and writing letters and postcards to family and friends until late in the morning.

When I started paddling, I only travelled a few more kilometres down the St. Clair River before detouring east on the Snye Channel. My original route would have kept me on the South Channel, avoiding the Snye, Johnston, Chemastogan, Middle, and North Channels of the St.

Clair River, but when I was invited to Wallaceburg by a group of cancer society volunteers, I eagerly jumped at the chance.

The Snye Channel proved to be a fortuitous opportunity for me to regain a feeling of connectedness with nature after the crowded urban life surrounding Sarnia and Port Huron. The water in the Snye Channel was the colour of spring leaves. Unmarred by wind or waves, the water reflected green mirror images of me and my kayak as we sped silently past.

The channel was a watery road that zigzagged between Walpole Island and the mainland. The marshy habitat along the water's edge was a sanctuary for all types of birds. Mallard ducks, great blue herons, belted kingfishers, and ducks with names I didn't know all waited cautiously along the shore until I rounded a corner. Then, seeing me and the long nose of my kayak, they would lift up in flight and fly ahead or behind me, out of sight. The trip down the Snye was a wonderful change from paddling on the big lakes. Relatively narrow, quiet, and protected from the wind, it was like paddling in a fairyland.

It was long past 1:00 p.m. when I turned off the Snye and began paddling up the Sydenham River toward the town of Wallaceburg. I had been travelling slower than usual. This was partly due to taking my time to notice the surroundings, and partly because I was still not feeling my best. Realizing that I was running late, I picked up my pace and sprinted up the Sydenham.

As I paddled closer to Wallaceburg, I started to see boats again, small aluminum fishing boats and larger custom cruisers with their passengers waving warmly. I arrived in Wallaceburg a little late, but I was warmly greeted by a group of cancer society volunteers, supporters, and three local newspapers, including the *Chatham Daily News*.

After my long interview with the newspaper reporters, Ted Oliver introduced himself and invited me to stay with him and his wife, Molly. Molly was a cancer society volunteer and both were eager to help in any way. By this point, I had become accustomed to being taken in and cared for by strangers, so I eagerly accepted, thankful for the opportunity to relax and not worry about where I was camping or what to prepare for dinner. It was a wonderful gift to be embraced by strangers. I always felt grateful and blessed to have the opportunity to meet so many kind and sharing people.

As was customary, I repaid Ted and Molly's kindness by recounting stories from my adventures on the water. It seemed to me that folks that live near lakes and rivers all seem to take pleasure in hearing about places they were connected to by water. Whether they knew a town intimately, or hoped to visit someday, Lake Superior, St. Mary's River, Lake Huron, Georgian Bay, and the St. Clair River all had their admirers and dreamers.

The next day, I still felt ill and fatigued, and I had a growing concern that maybe my sickness was more serious than I had originally thought. I was accustomed to fighting off any illness easily. I began to think that maybe I needed some different medication.

Four years earlier my friend Steve and I had gone to Acapulco, Mexico, on a winter vacation. We drank recklessly, ate food from outside vendors, and foolheartedly enjoyed ourselves until the diarrhea started. We never left our hotel beds until we found a doctor that gave us a needle in the ass and directed us to drink four liters of electrolytes in sugar water.

Hopeful for a similarly easy solution, I walked to a medical clinic in town. When the doctor and nurse had finished their usual questions and tests, the doctor informed me that my illness simply had to run its course, which I took to mean that he didn't know what was wrong with me. I walked back to Ted and Molly's home, resigned to *let things run their course*, even though I knew it would not be easy.

With an invitation to stay another night, I used the rest of the day to call cancer society volunteers in the Lake Erie region and schedule dates and times to meet. Later that evening, I called Mark and Cathy and was ecstatic to learn that they planned to meet me in the Port Stanley or Port Burwell area along Lake Erie. I had not seen my friends since Parry Sound, and I relished the idea of seeing them again soon.

No Land in Sight

It was raining heavily the next morning when I said goodbye to Ted and Molly and a few supporters at the town docks. Huddled under their colourful umbrellas, they watched with fascination and interest as I quickly packed and then sealed myself inside my boat. Before a chorus of shouts and cheers of "good luck!" I was back on the water and racing down the Sydenham River.

When I reached the Snye Channel, I was disappointed to see that the river was no longer green. Discoloured from silt runoff from neighbouring tributaries, the water was a dirty chocolate brown and lacked the mystical allure I once felt. I paddled all the way to the lake in a blur of motion, without noticing a single feature or landmark.

I reached Lake St. Clair at ten past one. Thirty kilometres wide, the lake was so vast I couldn't see land across it. Unlike Lake Superior, with its rugged shoreline and high hills that could be seen thirty kilometres away, Lake St. Clair's shoreline was flat and featureless.

As I looked across the water, I understood how it might feel to cross an ocean in a small boat. Your eyes deceptively tell you there is no end in sight. Only your map and logic can convince you that a shore is out there. Excited about the opportunity to experience an open crossing where I would not be able to see land in any direction, I made my decision to paddle across Lake St. Clair. I used my map and pocket compass to determine a bearing to take me to Stoney Point. Confident in my decision, I pointed the nose of my kayak toward the invisible shore and began to paddle. The rain had stopped and half-metre waves pushed toward me. The weather conditions were perfect for a lake crossing.

After an hour of paddling, I could not see land in any direction. I was lost in the immense size of the lake. The only way out was to keep paddling. Crossing a large lake felt different to me than paddling in dense fog. Fog only hid reality from your view, but once you accepted the fact that you couldn't *see* shore, it was still comforting to know it was there. Paddling across what seemed like an endless expanse of water without a shore for a lifeline was a different mind game. Although my crossing was truly nothing compared to an ocean, it did give me a small glimpse into how it might feel to leave the safety of shore.

A short time into my crossing, the wind picked up and the waves grew bigger. As the waves grew to one and a half metres, the wind gained in strength. Once again, I found myself trapped in a pushing match with the wind. Despite my weakened state, I loved the challenge and the demands on my muscles. After four hours, I still could not see land, and I started to feel a bit concerned. I thought by then that I should have been able to see a vague outline of the shore. On Lake Superior, I had become very skilled at judging distance by the shade of grey in the distant tree line. Each variation in shade between the black and light grey shoreline was a measurable distance gauged by experience. Without a shore, it was easy to start worrying.

It took five and a half hours before I saw the first grey outline of trees in the distance. Seeing land again was a great relief. Battling the wind and waves, uncertain when I would see land, had been both physically and mentally draining.

I arrived near Stoney Point at 6:30 p.m., exhausted but jubilant at my success. I found an open section of shoreline and set up my tent. The beach was covered thirty centimetres deep with zebra mussel shells that crunched under my feet. As soon as I got the tent set up, it started to rain again. Remembering my experience on the southern end of Lake Huron, I secured my kayak on shore before taking shelter from the rain. Moments like that made it easier to believe in the Greek gods of wind, water, and sun. How else can I explain why the rain waited until I was safely ashore? Inside the safety of my tent, the sky opened up and thunder bellowed and rain fell hard. The rain, thunder, and lightning lasted all night. I couldn't sleep through the storm. My tent had started to leak for the first time, and I woke regularly to check on the water seeping in.

I fell asleep sometime in the early morning and woke after only a few good hours of sleep. My body complained when I forced it to get up. I had made plans to meet volunteers in Windsor, and I didn't want to be late. I anticipated that I had a forty-kilometre paddle ahead of me. Physically, my body was in great shape, but since my illness in Sarnia, I wasn't able to kayak as fast as before. Grudgingly, I knew I would need more time to get there.

I left my camp at 9:00 a.m. under clear blue skies with no wind. Once I started to paddle, I felt better, energized by the warmth of the rising sun. It didn't take me long to get into a rhythmic meditation. After I had been paddling for an hour, the wind picked up, creating waves. In a few minutes, the calm lake was transformed into an endless expanse of metre-high waves. The west wind blew into my face and pushed the waves violently toward me. It was hard work to move the kayak, and I tired quickly. The wind was ruthless and seemed as though it had something against me. After ninety-three days on the water, I was beginning to believe in the possibility that the sun, wind, and rain were ruled by gods of mercy and cruelty. As the hours passed, the waves grew to two metres in height. Intent on making it to Windsor, I stubbornly refused to quit, paddling even harder, face first into the wind and waves. Each paddle stroke was literally a fight to move forward even a few small centimetres. Requests to rest, eat, drink, or go for a pee were refused.

Waves are too big to open the cockpit cover, I told myself. *The kayak would get swamped with water. Keep paddling.*

But I'm hungry, I responded in protest.

We can't stop, keep paddling! I commanded.

This dialogue would seem outrageous if anyone could have heard me, but it kept be moving. I continued to paddle while I fought a two-way battle, one with the wind, the other with myself. One side wanted to quit and go to shore, the other was determined to make it to Windsor at any cost. My muscles ached with fatigue from each paddle stroke. I glanced sideways toward land. By guess it looked to be two kilometres to the nearest shore. For a moment I contemplated giving up for the day. I imagined the volunteers waiting for me on the beach in Windsor, wondering where I was and if I was coming. That image was enough to keep me paddling forward.

After hours of steady paddling, the city of Windsor skyline remained an elusive prize in the distance and out of reach. The illusion that I was not making any progress was demoralizing. When I realized that I couldn't reach Windsor by two thirty as scheduled, I accepted defeat, but I never stopped paddling. I arrived at Windsor's beach at five fifteen. The beach was empty except for two lifeguards who were packing up for the day. Ready to go home, the lifeguards told me that the cancer society volunteers had left thirty minutes earlier. I felt terrible for keeping them waiting.

I phoned Cheryl Henshaw, my cancer society contact, and apologized for being late. Cheryl answered the phone warmly and quickly offered for me to stay with her family. Her husband, Paul, picked me up and brought me back to their home. Paul was a student working on his PhD in environmental engineering. Cheryl was a lawyer who practiced civil law. Along with their two daughters, they lived in a comfortable, but modest, residential home in Windsor.

We ate pizza for supper and shared stories about our families and lives. Paul and Cheryl made it feel easy to be a stranger in their home. It had been a long time since I had been around a young family. Most of my experiences on the trip had been with retirement-aged volunteers. The energy and silliness of the young girls was a joy and delight to be around.

I spent the next day speaking with the media in Windsor. Cheryl had arranged for me to meet CKCO and CHWI TV crews at the marina in the morning. I also contacted Bill Steele at CBC radio so he could tell his listeners where I was headed next. In addition to the radio and television, I called the *Windsor Star* newspaper and arranged an interview for later that day. Each time I spoke with a reporter, I got better at selling my message. My goal was to talk about cancer, the role of the cancer society, and the need for donations. Spouting statistics given to me from the cancer society, I emphasized the need for sun protection and the likelihood of knowing someone touched by the disease.

Before meeting the reporter with the *Windsor Star,* I wrote my own press release. I had become fed up with all of the errors the newspapers were writing, like, my grandfather had died of cancer or that my mom had cancer. It didn't seem to matter what I said, someone either misquoted me or stretched the truth to make the story more dramatic. It wasn't enough that I was simply doing the trip, the newspapers were always looking for the hidden *angle* to the story. Almost every time, the reporter would ask, "So are you doing this because you have cancer?" It felt as though they thought that if they simply asked me, I would suddenly confess to having the disease.

I arrived at the marina that evening ready to speak with the reporter from the *Windsor Star*. To my astonishment, Judy, whom I first met in Tobermory and again with Jim and Michelle in Sarnia, was at the marina waiting with a small group of kayakers. As I stepped out of the car, Judy raced over and hugged me, saying dramatically, "You're alive, you're alive." She hadn't heard that I'd arrived safely until minutes earlier, when some friends told her they were going to meet a kayaker who was travelling from Thunder Bay to Toronto.

Before the reporter had a chance to say anything, Judy told me that her friends had cancelled the Walpole Island cardboard boat races due to the threatening weather. Worried about me, she and John had spent the entire day looking for me on the lake. I was floored by this news. Aside from our meetings in Tobermory and again in Sarnia, Judy and John barely knew me. Their concern for me was very touching and reinforced my sense of being watched over by a new extended family.

When I finished my interview, Judy introduced me to some of her kayaking friends. One of them was Steve Lutsch, a former international kayak racer who had started a kayak store and instructional school in Windsor. Steve and a small group of kayakers from the area met regularly for evening paddles on Lake St. Clair and the Detroit River. They were about to go for a paddle that night when they heard rumors of my recent arrival and pending interview with the local paper. The meeting was short and sweet. After a few encouraging words, the kayakers left for the river and Judy hugged me goodbye and gave me her phone number in case I needed anything while I was in the area.

The next morning, I woke early to a warm day with clear blue skies. Paul and Cheryl had been unbelievably kind to me, offering to help in any way they could. After breakfast, I spoke with a Leamington radio station and WJR Radio Detroit, with hopes that some residents in Michigan would donate money to the local branch of the American Cancer Society.

Michael Herman

Afterward, Paul drove me to the marina. Before leaving, he gave me a spare watch to replace the one I had just lost and a large lunch he had packed himself. Paul's generosity made me feel overwhelmed with gratitude and the recognition that I lived a blessed life.

Falling From Grace

Ipaddled away from the Windsor beach at noon. I had expected an easy day drifting down the Detroit River. The river looked exactly as I had anticipated. The water was black and represented everything that I feared about cities—crime and pollution. Some people that I had met had joked that the water was so polluted, it would melt my kayak. I didn't believe them, but the idea did make me shudder at the possibility.

Similar to the St. Clair River, the Detroit was busy with boat traffic. For the most part, I stayed well out of the way of the other boats. When I stopped to take a picture, I was surprised by a large ocean freighter that snuck up from behind me. I sensed its looming presence before I heard it coming. When I turned around, its monster-like bulk was only eighty metres away. I had just enough time to put my camera on my lap and paddle out of its path. It shocked me that a large ship could be so quiet. When I paddled past Fighting Island, I saw ten white swans, a stark contrast to how I felt about the river.

I stopped briefly at Edgewater Beach at four thirty to call a local Windsor radio station. I was still hopeful I could generate more publicity and donations before reaching Lake Erie. It was six o'clock when I finally arrived in Amherstburg. I went ashore at Duff's Marina and Restaurant and made arrangements with the harbour master to store my kayak.

The shoreline along the Detroit River and mouth of Lake Erie was *overpopulated* and over developed. Judy had expressed concerns about me finding a place to camp and told me to call her at the end of the day.

Thankful for a friend, I called her from a pay phone, and she picked me up and drove me back to her home in Windsor. Judy felt like my guardian angel, ready when I needed her. Over dinner, we shared the personal details of our lives. Judy told me how she lived alone with her two twenty-something-year-old sons after her husband had left her for a younger woman.

"I had no idea. We were married for twenty-two years, and I didn't have a clue," she explained. Her voice hinted that she felt guilty, as though she thought she should have known. It was obvious that the pain was still close to the surface. Then her carefree smile returned and she added, "But then I met John, and things are looking better." I admired Judy's courage and strength not to give up. Optimism had always been an admirable virtue to me.

Rushing to make it to work the next morning, Judy drove me back to my kayak in Amherstburg at 7:00 a.m. It was too early to get my kayak from the marina, so I called my mom and dad and told them about the last few days. Afterward, I sat in a café and drank hot chocolate and wrote in my journal until the grocery store opened at nine. When I had stocked up on food supplies, I stopped and spoke with the editor of the *Amherstburg Echo* newspaper. The editor was very interested in my story, and he interviewed me as we walked back to my kayak.

Back on the water, I continued down the river of filth. Garbage of every description floated past me on my way to Lake Erie. By the time I reached the lake, I had seen enough of the Detroit River. Although I had read about the river's reputation growing up, words cannot help you to understand what pollution feels like. Staring into the water, I recalled a quote I'd read from Tanaka Shozo, a noted Japanese environmentalist: *The care of rivers is not a question of rivers, but of the human heart.* Pondering those words, I wondered where the people were who loved this river.

I left the Detroit River without a second glance, hopeful to find cleaner water ahead. Sadly, I was disappointed. When I arrived at Colchester Beach late in the afternoon, public sanitation workers were cleaning the beach. Armed with rubber gloves and garbage bags, men walked the beach and picked up plastic tampon applicators, syringes, toilet paper, and human waste. Even though staff were warning people that the water wasn't safe for swimming, teenagers and young toddlers with their parents continued to swim in the lake. When I spoke with a public worker, they informed me that all of the public beaches between Amherstburg and Kingsville had been closed due to raw sewage washing up on the shore.

"It happens a lot," he explained. As he told me this, I watched a parent walk over to a child, pick up a syringe from the beach, and deposit it into a nearby garbage can. I shook my head in disbelief.

"Any time we have a big storm, the Detroit sewage plant overflows and dumps raw sewage into the river," he added as a matter of fact.

When his words sunk in, I recalled seeing "stuff" floating in the lake during my paddle to Colchester. The brown chunks had looked like human waste, but I had dismissed the idea as impossible. Disgusted at the realization that I had paddled again through polluted water, I left the beach hoping that I wouldn't get any sicker.

A few kilometres away, I spotted two teenage boys sitting on a small beach drinking beer. As I kayaked toward them, they moved away from the water, trying to hide their beers. They told me later that they thought I was an undercover narcotics officer. When I called out to ask if it was okay if I camped there, they walked closer and invited me to stay. Their names were John and Joe, both seventeen. When I told them what I had heard about the water, they weren't surprised. John's family property backed onto the beach, and he told me that he often saw tampon applicators and twice had picked up used syringes.

The boys lived sad lives, reminiscent of the worst Geraldo Rivera or Jerry Springer talk shows about dysfunctional families. Sipping their beer, they told me stories about how their lives were tainted by drugs, teenage sex, and suicide. I don't know why they spoke so freely or honestly with a stranger they had just met. Maybe it was the beer, or maybe they just needed someone to talk to, and I was there.

"Our lives are so fucked up man, you can't believe it," explained Joe. "Some of the stuff we see is mind-bending ... drugs, girls having group sex in public ... it's all like something out of a movie."

Just two months earlier they had watched another kid shoot himself in the head at a house party. John shared with me how he threw up at seeing the blood fly everywhere. "It's not like television," he added solemnly. They both admitted that they suffered from nightmares every other night, and used drugs or alcohol to try to forget.

Their stories didn't have a bragging tone. I got the sense they knew that it wasn't right for them to be living through such adult experiences. John told me that his family was rich and that he could have anything he wanted, but his parents didn't care about him. "Fuck them," he swore softly into his beer. "I just take care of myself," he added bitterly.

I couldn't imagine living in their shoes, and their stories left me feeling lonely and wanting to go north where everything seemed "cleaner" and more innocent. When they finished their beer, John and Joe went home, and I was left to try and make sense of what I'd heard. I couldn't stop thinking about them. I fell asleep wondering if it was possible to fix their broken hearts.

The next day, I enjoyed an easy paddle to Kingsville and was greeted by a waiting crowd of cancer volunteers and a group of thirty kids and counselors from a day camp. They welcomed me warmly and asked me every conceivable question.

"Where do you go to the bathroom? Do you get lonely? Where do you sleep? Do you get scared?" The Kingsville newspaper was there to do an interview but the kids asked all of the fun questions. After the interview, a group of teenage camp staff came over to talk with me. To my surprise, one girl asked me for my autograph. No one had ever asked me before, and the request made me feel embarrassed. Autographs were for celebrities, and I didn't see myself as anyone special. Nervously, I wrote something about following your dreams and signed my name with the notation, "A Celebration of Life," underneath.

When the crowd disappeared, I started to look for a place to store my kayak for the night. It didn't take long for me to meet Darren, an employee with the town of Kingsville and a fellow kayaker. Almost immediately, Darren offered to host me for the night. We moved my kayak from the beach to the township's public works garage.

Darren then brought me home to meet his wife, Kim, and their daughter, Tessa, and son, Keean. Keean, I quickly learned, had leukemia and was missing his hair from receiving multiple chemotherapy treatments over the past ten months. Kim and Darren were warm and friendly people who made me feel comfortable from the moment I entered their home. When I asked them how they handled the strain of Keean's disease, Kim was quick with an honest answer.

"Michael, it's really hard when you watch him receive the chemotherapy. He is in so much pain. He looks up at me with eyes that say, 'Mom, why are you letting them do this to me?' As a parent, it hurts." Despite their family challenges, Darren and Kim were remarkably positive. It felt refreshing and uplifting to be in their company.

After dinner, Darren arranged for us to go back to Windsor and paddle with Steve Lutsch and members of his kayak club. We both had a laugh when I admitted to Darren that I had met Steve briefly when I was in Windsor.

It was too complicated to bring my oversized kayak, so we borrowed a river kayak from Darren's brother Greg. When we met at the beach, I was given a hero's welcome by the group for my accomplishment of kayaking solo from Thunder Bay. Buoyed by their admiration and respect, I joined them for a paddle around Peche Island Provincial Park. Later, as people were pulling their boats out of the water, someone asked me if I wanted to paddle his new sea kayak. I knew there was no greater honour among boaters, so I accepted willingly. An offer to paddle someone's new kayak could be compared to a guy asking another car lover, "Do you want to drive my new Porsche?"

When I slipped into the empty cockpit, the owner casually commented that the boat might be more tippy than my own kayak. Comfortable in boats, and maybe a bit too confident, I didn't pay much attention to the warning. I wished later that I had. I hadn't moved very far from the dock and was leaning over my paddle when the kayak suddenly flipped over without warning. It happened so quickly I wasn't prepared. In that instant my mind thought of all the rumors I had heard about the toxic Detroit River. Instead of calmly focusing on technique, I hastily tried to muscle the kayak upright. The kayak rolled halfway up, enough for my head and shoulders to rise above the surface before falling back down into the black water. Everyone I had spoken with since Sarnia had expressed the same sentiments about the Detroit River.

"Be careful. It's full of toxic waste; you don't want to swim in there." Panicked, I attempted to roll up again with the same rushed and sloppy technique. As my head and shoulders rose out of the water, it was apparent that I wasn't going to make it all the way up for the second time. At that moment, I was greeted by the nose of a kayaker's boat. Desperate to get out of the water, I abandoned my roll and used the kayakers bow as a platform so I could push myself up and out of the water. In a mere five seconds, I had fallen from grace. One moment a kayak guru, the next a novice beginner.

Sheepishly, I looked at my rescuer and then the rest of the group. No one said a word. The boat's owner broke the silence first. "It's a tricky boat to roll; it took me a bit to get used to it too." I was grateful for his excuse, but I knew it didn't let me off the hook. Although no one said anything, I imagined everyone was wondering how I had paddled all the way from Thunder Bay if I couldn't roll a kayak. The situation seemed too hopeless to try and make excuses: *Guys, I panicked, thinking about the toxic river. I can roll a kayak ... really.*

I didn't say anything. I decided to let it go. Off the river, Darren and I joined Steve for a post-paddling beer at Steve's apartment. Still shaken from my embarrassing performance, I was glad that no one said a word about my botched roll, but I thought about it all night.

DELIVER ME FROM TEMPTATION

THE FOLLOWING DAY, I was scheduled to arrive in Leamington for a fundraising event on the beach. The town was gearing up for its annual tomato festival, so my timing was perfect. Darren and Kim were planning to attend the festival that night. There was going to be a dance with a live band, and they invited me to join them and then come back to their place for the night. It felt so easy to go with the flow, I didn't even think about it. Beaming from the offer, I simply said, "Sounds great."

It took me just over two hours to make the trip across Pigeon Bay from Kingsville to Leamington. I was greeted by a small crowd which included the town mayor, a local member of parliament, and the Leamington radio station and newspaper. I collected donations on the beach with a cancer society volunteer until four thirty and collected fifty-five dollars. It was my first fundraising effort since Windsor, and I was disappointed by the meager results. Afterward, I paddled to the town marina to store my kayak and take a hot shower.

I really enjoyed arriving at a marina. There was something unique about the camaraderie found among boaters. Many of the boats came from somewhere else, so people shared an interest in travel and being on the water. It didn't seem to matter if they had a sailboat, power yacht, or a kayak, people were accepted as water travellers. Either by curiosity or politeness, people often asked me where I'd come from, and when I told them Thunder Bay, their eyebrows would often lift up in disbelief.

I ate my dinner alone at the marina and then walked to the festival grounds in search of Darren and Kim. We eventually met in the beer tent. Right away, it was obvious that Darren and Kim were in a mood to let loose and forget Keean's troubles for one day. The band was a local favourite that played Top Forty music, and they had the crowd dancing most of the night to songs like "Mr. Jones" by the Counting Crows or "Start Me Up" by the Rolling Stones. I danced with Kim and her friends, happy to be a part of the festival crowd. When Darren and Kim announced that they were ready to go home, I slumped into the backseat, thankful that I didn't have to drive. I fell asleep on their spare bed, exhausted but happy. It had been a wonderful day.

After a leisurely pancake breakfast the next morning, I said goodbye to Kim and Keean. Darren and his daughter, Tessa, drove me to the marina to see me off. I felt very close to each of them and found it difficult to leave. The timing and circumstances of my visit seemed to have forged deep feelings between us. Later that night in my tent I wrote, *I feel very close to Darren and Kim ... I hope we stay in touch.*

The water in the Leamington harbour was calm, but once I left the protection of the breakwater, I was blasted by heavy wind and metre-and-a-half-high waves. Fortunately, my destination was only a few kilometres away at Point Pelee National Park. As I paddled, the wind picked up and a storm started to build off in the distance behind me. Big, black clouds moved toward me quickly. When the first crack of thunder boomed overhead and echoed across the water, I immediately thought of lightning and raced toward shore.

Light rain fell as I approached the beach. I had been told someone from the local cancer society was going to meet me on the Point Pelee beach, but I didn't see anyone. Uncertain where to go, I surfed onto a quiet, deserted area with a sign that was marked *West Beach*. By the time I climbed out of my kayak, it was raining heavily.

There was a family eating their lunch in a gazebo back from the beach. When they got up to leave, I walked over and briefly introduced myself and asked them if they would stop at the visitor services building and tell the staff I had arrived. The park seemed large, and without a car I didn't want to spend much time walking in search of a park office.

It wasn't long after the family left that a park warden named Fred, showed up in a four-wheel drive SUV. Fred was very friendly, greeting me with a big smile while explaining that they had been expecting me.

When I admitted that I had never been to the park before, he took me on a guided tour. Fred was a great guide, and I quickly learned about the park's unique Carolinian forest. I also learned that Point Pelee was the most southern land mass of Canada, making it a favourite migration stop for millions of birds and butterflies.

"We're loved by birders and beach goers," Fred announced with a grin. "My time is spent dealing with people who are trudging into restricted, sensitive areas or young couples having sex under a blanket on the beach." Judging my look of disbelief, Fred nodded his head to confirm his point. "It's true. We deal with hundreds of thousands of visitors a year. You would be shocked at what we see happening on the beach."

After my tour, Fred dropped me off at the visitor services building so I could see some of their displays and learn more about the park. While I was there, I met Priska, a young woman who worked as a park naturalist for the summer. Priska was slender, with long hair and eyes that danced when she talked about things that she was passionate about. I liked her immediately and found it impossible not to find her attractive. When she finished work for the day, she invited me back to the park staff house for dinner. Over a meal of chicken stir fry, we talked endlessly, each sentence overlapped by the other. She had recently bicycled through Europe, and we found a common thread in adventure and a love for exploring new places. We also shared an affection for the people and culture of France, and we swapped stories about places we both had visited, such as the Pyrenees, Le Mont Saint Michel, and the Lascaux cave paintings. My meeting with Priska had been a complete surprise. She was the first woman I had met since Fleur who stirred my emotions, and my feelings for her startled me.

You're a pig, I scolded myself later in the privacy of my guest room. *A few days ago you were worried that Fleur had forgotten you, and now you're thinking about having sex with someone you just met.*

Priska and I said goodbye in the morning with our honour intact. I caught a ride back to my kayak with a park warden named Tom. By nine thirty I was on the water, heading for the tip of Point Pelee. Rolling waves were breaking over the shallow, sandy spit of land. During my guided tour with Fred, I had learned there was a dangerous undertow near the tip of the peninsula. And despite warning signs, people drowned there every year. Heeding his warning, I steered clear of the tip and set a course a safe distance away from the breaking waves.

A Visit with the Doctor

I FOUGHT A weak headwind all the way to Wheatley Provincial Park, arriving by mid-afternoon. The paddle had been uneventful. Compared to Superior and Huron, I found Lake Erie boring and lacking in character. When I arrived, I was greeted by a small group of cancer society volunteers, including Ron and Ruth Neily and Audrey and Murry Knox. While we talked on the beach, park visitors joined us, and I stayed and chatted with them for over an hour. Afterward, Ron and Ruth invited me to come to their house for supper.

I set up my tent and enjoyed a hot shower before Ron returned to pick me up and take me to their home in Wheatley. Their house was a solid brick bungalow nestled among beautiful mature hardwoods and surrounded by flowers. I enjoyed a wonderful meal with Ron and Ruth, engaged in conversation about almost everything under the sun. Ron chauffeured me back to my tent at ten. Completely exhausted, I fell asleep easily.

The next day, I woke at seven with plans to get an early start. The night before, Ron had explained to me that the shoreline from Wheatley to Erieau had high cliffs. My schedule had been to stop at Ouvry, but if Ron was correct, I worried that it would be impossible to stop, which meant that I would have to push all the way to Rondeau Provincial Park. On my map the distance measured more than fifty kilometres. Regardless of the weather, I anticipated a long day of paddling.

When I was packed and ready to leave, Audrey arrived to wish me luck with a care package of homemade muffins, tarts, and cookies. We

218

sat and talked in her car for twenty minutes, drinking coffee. There is a definite character trait among all of the cancer society volunteers. They are all busy people, involved in various personal and community projects, and all are *interested* in other people. Still focused on reaching Rondeau that day, I sadly had to cut our visit short and say goodbye.

The sky was clear, and there was a slight wind from the east when I left Wheatley Provincial Park. It was eight thirty, long past my planned departure time. Ron had been correct. I paddled past the high clay cliffs all day. By noon, I found the scenery dull and boring.

Sometime in the afternoon, I thought about the fact that I hadn't heard or seen a loon in such a long time. Possibly Georgian Bay, I pondered. For fun, I made a loon call and was shocked when the familiar cry was answered.

Wow, is that ever weird, I thought to myself. I called again and waited for a reply, hopeful of pinpointing the sound. When the call was returned a second time, I changed my direction and paddled toward the haunting call. Soon enough, I caught sight of two adult loons bobbing up and down on the waves. It was a marvelous treat. I had missed seeing loons on my trip. Lately, I had grown homesick for the wilderness and the quiet comfort that nature offered me.

I arrived at Erieau at five thirty. It had been a long day of paddling. From Erieau, I paddled around the tip of Rondeau and up the eastern shore of the peninsula. A pounding surf was crashing on the beach. Studying the shore, I noticed that most of the peninsula was developed with cottages. Rondeau was the second oldest provincial park in Ontario, and the cottages were part of an old ninety-nine year lease with the government. There were so many cottages, I couldn't tell where the park boundary started or ended. I sat in my kayak, away from shore and the crashing surf, and looked for a clue that would tell me where to go ashore. There was an area on the beach with eight picnic tables, and I decided that it must be part of the park, even though there were houses.

When I spotted a couple walking the beach, I yelled over the sound of crashing waves.

"Hello, is this the park?" When the couple confirmed my suspicion, I surfed my kayak to shore and quickly pulled the boat to safety. The couple kept walking, so I left my kayak on the beach and headed inland to see how far the campsites were from the lake. The campground was hidden behind a single row of cottages a few hundred metres from the water.

When I returned to my kayak, the same couple was walking back, and they stopped to say hello. Barb and Blair Pierce was a healthy looking couple in their mid-forties who owned a cottage that backed onto the beach. Blair asked me if I planned to camp in the campground and offered to store my kayak in their yard. Grateful for the offer, I launched myself back through the breaking waves and arrived on shore a few hundred metres away in front of their cottage. Blair helped me carry my loaded kayak into his yard. When the kayak was safely stored, I tramped off to make camp with an invitation to come back for a visit.

In the evening, I returned to a warm reception by Barb and Blair and their young daughters, Abby and Martha. Sipping drinks in their cozy cottage, we swapped stories about our lives and the joys of owning a family cottage. Barb and Blair hadn't heard about my kayak trip, and this fact made our meeting feel extra special. They had invited me into their home for no other reason than simple generosity.

When I walked back to my campsite, I marveled at how perfectly my experiences fit together. I couldn't remember a time in my life when everything *flowed* with as much ease. Every need or want materialized almost as soon as I acknowledge a desire. I met the right person, was at the right place, arrived at the right time, or simply had the experience that seemed right for me. I had been a student of the "laws of attraction" theory by writers such as Napoleon Hill and Norman Vincent Peale for many years, but I had never seen it work so clearly. For the most part, I was attracting or creating a dream experience.

Well, except for the lack of support from the cancer society, the skeptic in my head added. *Yet, if the idea that I attracted everything into my life with my thoughts was true, then I attracted those experiences too,* I warned myself. *Maybe it would be best to focus my thoughts on the help I am receiving.*

I fell asleep with a strong sense of feeling grateful for everything I had or experienced. *You may not have a job, but you are living a blessed life,* I told myself.

I walked back to the lake early in the morning and listened to the surf crash onto the beach. To me, the waves were a visible sign that the lake was alive, as though each wave was proof that the lake was breathing. I witnessed so much pollution in Lake Erie that I often wondered if the lake was dead. It was reassuring to me to hear the waves, even though my logic told me the waves had nothing to do with the health of the lake.

I met Susan Atkinson from the cancer society at my campsite at nine thirty. I wasn't expected to arrive officially at Rondeau Provincial Park until three that afternoon, so we discussed plans for my official arrival. Susan had contacted some local media outlets, but she wasn't sure who would show up.

"No one would commit to me," she explained disappointedly. "They said they had to wait and see what other news happened that day." I wasn't surprised. I had learned that bad news stories always trumped good news.

When Susan left, Blair arrived at my campsite with two mugs of coffee. We sat and talked at a picnic table beside my tent. I learned that Blair was a doctor with a family practice. When I asked him whether he enjoyed his profession, he shrugged his shoulders and gave me a smirk, which I took to mean yes, but ...

Blair must have felt that I was open to listening because without prompting he started to share the problems he faced trying to spend time with his patients.

"People expect to see a specialist even when they don't need to," he explained. "It makes it hard for me to offer the care that I'm trained for." Blair explained that there was no incentive for him to take the time with his patients. "The government pays me the same amount just to refer someone to a specialist," he complained. "Then there are prescriptions. Everyone wants you to prescribe something for a quick fix. After a while, you get tired of fighting with people. I could spend twenty minutes explaining to a patient why I'm not going to give them a prescription and the benefits of letting the symptoms run their course, and when I'm finished they'll ask me, 'Aren't you going to give me some penicillin?'" Throwing his arms up in the air, he added, "Eventually you say to yourself, *Why bother?*—and you just give them what they want."

Blair's words trailed off as he stopped to take a sip of coffee. I could feel the disappointment in his words and sensed that he wanted to be more of a *doctor*. When he put his coffee back down, he was smiling again. "I still love practicing medicine." Switching gears, Blair explained that he treated a lot of terminally ill patients. "Most are referrals," he told me proudly.

Blair confided that most of his rewards and job satisfaction came from caring for patients during their darkest moments. He shared that the thank-you letters he received from family members afterwards had the most meaning to him. "You know people appreciate what you do when they take the time to write a letter four months after someone they loved has passed over."

I really liked Blair. I found him to be a *real* person and easy to talk with. Any doctors I had ever met were always quick to let you know who they were and how much they knew: "Hi, I'm doctor so and so …" Blair wasn't like that, at least not on the beach with me. There were no airs about him, and I believed he would be the same in his office.

After our coffees, Blair suggested that we go for a bike ride to explore some of the park's interior trails through the Carolinian forest. Ready for a new experience, I eagerly agreed and was offered his older daughter's bike. We headed toward the tip of Rondeau, riding under the shady canopy of hardwood trees and talking endlessly like old friends. When we reached the trail, we stashed the bicycles in the bushes and, armed with a tree book from the cottage, we headed out like two budding young botanists. I had studied a few Carolinian forest tree species in school but had never seen any in the wild. Rediscovering species such as sassafras, tulip tree, spice bush, and a rare orchid called Orchis was exciting, and a bit exotic. The plants and trees were very different from any place I had ever lived.

We turned back at two thirty so I could make my meeting with Susan and whatever media she had wrangled to come along at three. We found Susan at the beach with her husband, Sheridan; Marie-Anne McCrae; and Molly and Ted Oliver from Wallaceburg, who had come to see me one last time. After a short greeting, I was interviewed by two local newspapers. Susan had arranged for us to meet at her house for a barbecue, so I reluctantly packed up my camp. I appreciated all of Susan's efforts to convince the newspapers to interview me, but I was also disappointed to leave Blair and his family. Barb, Blair, and Abby joined me on the beach to say goodbye. I felt like a kid saying goodbye on the last day of summer camp. We exchanged addresses, but I knew that it was unlikely we would meet again.

BIKERS HAVE DADS TOO

I T TOOK ME fifteen minutes to paddle to Susan and Sheridan's home further up the coast. We gathered in their backyard for a celebratory-style meal of burgers, summer salads, and cake. Before dinner, I had two phone interviews with local radio stations. Afterward, my companions and I spent a quiet evening talking mostly about where I had come from and where I was headed next.

Ted and Molly were especially interested in my adventures since I had left them in Wallaceburg. Sheridan was fascinated with my kayak and its ability to travel on the big lakes. Using his own Lake Erie map and mariner dividers, he calculated that I had travelled sixty-three kilometres from Wheatley Provincial Park to Blair's cottage at Rondeau.

"That's a good days travel, even for a sailboat," Sheridan remarked with astonishment. "That's some boat you have, Michael." I simply nodded my agreement. I did feel a great sense of pride in the *Mai Fleur*, and I had developed a special bond, as many mariners do toward their vessels.

The next day I got up early and walked down to the lake to watch the sunrise. It had become a morning ritual on Lake Erie that I tried not to miss. I was too late to see the sun rise out of the water, but it was still a red ball low in the horizon when I sat down on the beach. Sheridan met me there, and we talked for almost an hour before breakfast.

I waited most of the morning for a call from a local radio station. At noon the station still had not called, so Sheridan drove me to the IGA food store in Ridgetown. I met the store manager and thanked him for fundraising with my donation cans. After buying some groceries, we went back to Sheridan's house for a late lunch.

It was almost three o'clock when I said goodbye to Sheridan. On the water, the sun's heat was oppressive, and it drained my energy until I felt too tired to paddle. The lake was dead calm, with no sign of a breeze. Sweat soaked my shirt and hat. In an effort to fight the heat, I dipped my hat into the lake and then put it back on. This offered some relief, but the sun quickly baked my hat dry, and I was forced to repeat the process again and again.

The shoreline from the bottom of Rondeau to Port Glasgow was similar to my paddle from Wheatley to Erieau. High clay cliffs rose up toward the sky from a beach-free shore. I arrived at Port Glasgow at seven o'clock, exhausted and eager to find a place to camp. I found a municipal park near the town with a grassy area and enough trees to offer me some seclusion for the night.

While I sat in a sunny clearing, a young couple rode in on a Harley-Davidson motorcycle. They were both dressed in black leather pants and jackets and presented an image that suggested they lived a 'wild and free' lifestyle. I watched them walk the beach and stop at my kayak on their way back toward their bike. They walked straight toward me.

"Hey, man, is that your kayak?" the guy asked rhetorically. "Where did you come from?" When I told them that I was on a trip from Thunder Bay, the guy quickly expressed admiration. "That's great, too cool, man." When I added that I was doing the trip to raise money for cancer, the guy went instantly quiet and his face turned solemn. For a moment he stared at me as though he needed to figure something out. Then he shoved his meaty fist out toward me in a request to connect knuckles, saying, "Right on, man; my dad died of cancer."

After touching my fist, he pulled out a leather wallet on a chain and handed me a five dollar bill. I told him that I didn't personally accept donations but asked him to donate to his local chapter of the cancer society or IGA store. He told me that he wanted me to have the money to buy myself lunch or a special treat. At first I tried to give him back his money, but he was very insistent, and I could tell that it was important to him that I take the money. I never expected to make a connection like that with anyone on my trip, but the feeling was rewarding. Grateful for the gift, I accepted the money and smiled while I slipped the bill into my pocket. Satisfied, the motorcycle couple wished me luck, then jumped on their Harley and rode away.

That night in the tent, Fleur was all that I could think about. In my journal I wrote:

> *I haven't said much about my feelings lately … mostly just writing the who, what, where … but I miss Fleur very much and each time we are apart I wonder if it will be the same when we get back together. My love for her has grown into something stronger than I have ever known. I feel jealous of other men who spend time with her. Sometimes I think of her kissing someone else. Why? I don't know, maybe because I was attracted to Priska and thought of kissing her. I think Fleur is wild and adventurous and I am uncertain of how she would respond if a guy she liked started flirting with her. Fleur is the most independent woman I know and I hope she will be happy settling for me.*

When I finished writing, I fell asleep, thinking of Fleur and wondering what she was doing.

I woke sometime after seven the next morning. The sun was up, but the sky was black and a front was approaching. Thunder was off in the distance. I decided to wait and see what happened with the weather. I didn't want to launch during a lightning storm. Within an hour, the front had moved on with only a few drops of rain.

When I was ready to leave, a threatening surf was crashing onto shore. Judging the size of the waves, I knew it was going to be a challenging launch. I climbed into the kayak at the water's edge and then paddled through the shallow water toward the crashing waves. It was not easy. The breaking waves collapsed and fell toward shore with amazing force, and I had to paddle hard to get through. When I made it past them, I was soaked from my chest up. Fortunately, the sun was already hot so I didn't care too much.

After an hour of paddling, my face was covered in sweat that dripped into my eyes and made them sting from the salt. For the second day, the sun was unbearably hot and there was no breeze. I was amazed at how quiet the lake seemed. I had not seen a single boat since Wheatley.

The clay cliffs that started again past Wheatley were very dramatic. When the sun shone on them, they appeared as white rock in the distance, and they reminded me of England's White Cliffs of Dover. Curiously, I wondered if that was how Port Dover got its name, and I promised myself I'd ask someone when I arrived there.

I didn't see any sign of Port Talbot from the water, so I paddled straight to Port Stanley. The town's harbour was up Kettle Creek, so I paddled up the river in search of a place to dock. I met an old man fishing off the end of a pier. He asked me where I'd come from, and when I told him Thunder Bay he scoffed, "Oh, yeah," and turned away. When I didn't say anything else, he turned back around and looked at me and demanded, "But not in that," shaking his head in disbelief. When I affirmed that I had indeed paddled from Lake Superior he grinned and shook his head.

"That's a long way!"

I enjoyed reactions like that. It's not often you get to shock people with something you do. Further up the river, I spoke with two guys fishing from a small boat. They told me to dock at Stan's Marina. The folks at Stan's Marina were very friendly and let me tie up my kayak while I walked around town and ate an ice-cream cone. When I returned to the marina, a young employee told me that the town owned an empty lot across the river.

"You can camp over there," he said, pointing. "No one will bother you." Finding a place to camp had become a major concern for me since Oliphant, so I was grateful for the news. I set up my tent and went to bed as soon as it was dark.

I woke the next day, excited about my plans to see Mark and Cathy that evening. My friends had promised to make the trip from Parry Sound and spend the weekend at Port Burwell Provincial Park with me and our friend Peter. Although we had spoken a few times on the phone, much had happened since Parry Sound, and I looked forward to seeing their familiar faces.

A group of cancer society volunteers had organized a fundraising gathering in Port Stanley that afternoon at five, so I spent the day in town. I wrote letters, called my grandma and grandpa Herman, and walked around town. By four o'clock, I had grown tired of being a tourist and went for a short paddle up Kettle Creek. When I returned, I was met by a group of cancer society volunteers, a crew with CKNX TV from London, and two local newspaper reporters. By the time the interviews were finished, the volunteers had collected five hundred and fifty dollars in donations. We all felt ecstatic from the results.

Up until that point, I really had no idea how the fundraising was going. All I had seen was the money collected from the fundraising events that I had participated in on my stops. I had no idea what was happening with the donation cans in the IGA stores across Ontario, or how many people were mailing cheques to the cancer society after reading about me or hearing me on the news. Based on the people I met, I was optimistic that people were going to donate money once they heard about Kayaking for Cancer.

When we finished fundraising, the group took me out for a pickerel dinner at a local restaurant. It hadn't been on my agenda, but it wasn't long into our meal before the group began to share their frustrations that the Toronto office hadn't done enough to publicize my trip. Although I was frustrated, I felt caught in the middle. I had done as much as I could to promote the trip and wanted to focus my energy on getting to Toronto. At each stop, I was forced to endure the same complaints from staff and volunteers and pressured to ask Mark Climie why he hadn't notified the staff about my trip.

When I finally did question Mark Climie by phone, he was defensive and quickly made excuses that staff and volunteers were on summer holidays. When I later presented this argument to cancer society volunteers and staff, they all expressed the same reaction:

"Sure it's the summer, but if we had known about your trip we would have supported you more. This is a great fundraising opportunity for the cancer society. We want to help."

By this point in the trip, though, it really didn't matter to me anymore. Toronto was in my sights, only three weeks away. If large numbers of people were going to start donating, it would have to happen through word of mouth and the media.

TRUE FRIENDS

A FTER DINNER, MY hosts dropped me off at a local grocery store so I could finish my shopping. I had arranged to meet Mark and Cathy at eight that evening, so I picked up some fresh fruit and walked back to the centre of town.

My friends were waiting with smiles when we found each other. After warm hugs, we marched off in search of a place to enjoy a few drinks. We settled in at G. T.'s, a restaurant bar built on the beach with an impressive beach volleyball court and outside patio. Seated at an umbrella-covered table with a backdrop of the lake, we drank beer and exchanged news.

Cathy still worked at the Ministry of Natural Resources office in Parry Sound that I had once worked at, so she carried word from many ex-co-workers who sent their congratulations and best wishes. When I told them about my bout with a stomach bug in Sarnia, and how I had seen human turds floating in Lake Erie, they listened sympathetically. They loved hearing my stories. Mark especially enjoyed hearing about the two topless female sunbathers I happened upon as I floated past a small island on the Detroit River.

"Did you stop and ask them for directions?" Mark asked with a huge grin. Drinking beer with friends felt a bit surreal. Although I was still in Ontario, it felt as though my trip had taken me far from home and everything familiar. To be among friends again seemed odd and out of context.

We stayed and talked until eleven, when Cathy made the responsible suggestion that we call it a night. She must have sensed my disappointment because she was quick to add, "Don't worry, we'll see you tomorrow." Tired from the long drive from Parry Sound, they were ready to make the trip back to Port Burwell Provincial Park where they were camped. Remembering that I had to meet them there in the morning, I reluctantly agreed it was probably a good idea.

The next morning, I left the harbour at 7:45 a.m. under thick fog. I had told my friends that I would be there by eleven, but that was before I had measured the distance on my map. When I realized it was thirty-five kilometres to Port Burwell, I knew I didn't have time to waste.

Even at such an early hour, the air was thick and humid on the lake. Sweat ran down my face as soon as I started to paddle. The humidity made my body feel tired and weak, and it begged me to stop and rest, but my mind was focused on my friends. When I reached Port Bruce at ten, the fog had started to clear, but a haze made visibility poor. The sun baked down on me and created a new challenge as I paddled. Unlike the other lakes, Erie was stifling hot and humid during the day. Uncomfortable from the excessive heat, my body complained bitterly.

This heat is killing me. Let's stop. Driven by a desire to rejoin my friends, I pushed on, only stopping occasionally for a drink of warm water. I arrived at Port Burwell Provincial Park shortly past noon, over an hour late. Uncertain where to look for my friends, I landed on the beach close to a tall red and white navigation tower that resembled a smaller version of a lighthouse. I'm easy to pick out in a crowd, so Mark, Cathy, and Peter ran to greet me as I stepped out of my kayak.

My friends' campsite was a few kilometres away from the beach, so we decided to load the kayak on to Mark's truck and bring it back with us. Once at the campsite, we sat down to a waiting summer picnic. Fresh bakery bread, assorted cheeses and cold meats, pickles, olives, fresh tomatoes and cucumbers, beer and wine adorned the table. It was a delicious feast, yet it was the company of my friends that fed my soul. The fact that they had all made the long trek to support me was a wonderful gift that touched me deeply. We drank, ate, and talked about our summer apart. They told me about baseball tournaments and canoe trips that I had missed, and I told them about my adventures in the *Mai Fleur* and the incredible people I had met.

Later in the day, we went for a hike to explore the nearby nature trails. The park had pockets of Carolinian forest, so I was able to share some of my new knowledge from my outing with Blair at Rondeau. Afterwards, we enjoyed a barbecue with the same feast-like qualities as lunch. Fortified with charcoal briquettes, moose steaks from Peter's freezer, potatoes pre-wrapped in tin foil, and an assortment of stir-fried vegetables, my friends stuffed me like a goose before Christmas. Content around the campfire, we sipped Sambuca and talked long into the night. It was a reunion I would cherish always.

Long Point at Any Cost

T HE SOUND OF high winds blowing through the trees and my
tent shaking violently woke me early the next morning. Judging
from the sound, I imagined that the lake was being whipped up
by a hurricane.

Everyone knew we were saying goodbye that day. No one mentioned
the fact that I was leaving in my kayak, even though we were all conscious
of the wind. After breakfast, we hiked the five kilometres to the beach
where we had met the day before. Endless rows of two-metre waves rolled
onto shore and crashed onto the beach. The sound was deafening, and we
had to yell to make ourselves heard over the roar. Impressed by the raw
energy of the waves, we walked the shore in awe, stopping occasionally
to watch a flock of sandpipers picking at bugs on the beach. The gusting
wind pushed the small birds, forcing them to run to keep up with their
bodies. When it seemed they couldn't run any faster, they opened their
wings and briefly floated off the ground, landing a few metres away only
to repeat the process a few minutes later. The image reminded us of a
group of children holding an umbrella in a windstorm, and we all laughed
out loud.

During our walk, we saw black storm clouds far to the south that
warned us what was coming. Unprepared for rain, we raced back to our
campsite. My friends wanted to get going. They each had long drives
home ahead of them. I, on the other hand, wasn't certain what I would
do. The campground was a few kilometres from the beach, so I needed a
vehicle to transport my kayak and equipment. I was also uncertain about

the weather. The crashing waves on the beach looked big and dangerous, although I convinced myself that I was only concerned with the potential for lightning. Everyone packed up to leave but me. I decided to wait and see what happened with the weather.

When my friends were packed, we agreed to go into town for a farewell lunch. Happy to postpone my decision on whether to leave, I loaded my kayak on Mark's truck, and we drove into Port Burwell. Rain fell hard and fast as we clambered into a local restaurant. The sky turned a dark green, and street lights came on as the rain pounded loudly on the restaurant roof. Thunder and lightning joined in, and the storm continued while we enjoyed our meal.

By the time we had eaten most of the pizza, the storm had moved on, and the sky had brightened to a safer looking shade of grey. It was the sign I had hoped for, and it helped me to make the decision to leave. All morning my friends had made comments that hinted at their concern for my safety and their hopes that I would stay and leave in the morning.

"You know," Cathy offered, "you don't have to go. We'll drive you back to the campground." I recognized that the suggestion made sense, but I wouldn't hear it. I would argue that I didn't want to stay with the burden of figuring out how to get my kayak back to the beach, but that was only partially true. The real truth was that I had made plans to meet Fleur that evening, and I was determined to leave. We had not seen each other since Sault Ste. Marie, and I was desperate to see her. Against my friend's wishes and better judgment, I announced my commitment to go.

It was two o'clock when I said goodbye to my friends and began to paddle out of the Port Burwell harbour. Even in the sheltered harbour, I could tell I was in for a fight with the wind. As a precaution, I stopped and tied a cord from my paddle shaft to the kayak. I hadn't done this before, but something in the pit of my stomach told me it would be a good idea. Peter, Mark, and Cathy stood on the pier bundled up in their fleece jackets and windbreakers and watched me leave. I could only guess what they thought of my decision. Before I reached the end of the pier, I stopped and waved goodbye. At that moment, a small voice in my head questioned my decision to leave. It would have been much safer to stay and leave in the morning, but there was no reasoning with me that day.

The desire to see Fleur was too strong for reason or common sense. I was set on my decision to go. *I would meet Fleur at Long Point.*

At the end of the pier, the waves looked big: two metres high and blowing crosswise to my heading. As I left the safety of the harbour, I sensed the waves were rougher than any I had ever paddled before. The little voice in my head continued to raise questions of concern.

Why are you out here? What are you trying to prove? Your bravery? Skill? To whom? Committed to my decision, I ignored the voice and continued to paddle. As soon as I left the protection of the harbour and headed east, the wind pushed and pulled at my paddle blades. Defensively, I gripped the shaft tighter and forced my paddle through the wind and into the water. More questions of doubt filled my mind. *What am I up against?* When the voice of doubt gave up on changing my mind, I prepared myself for the long day ahead. As each wave crashed into my kayak, the wind sprayed water, and the gritty sand stung my eyes. Since I had no time to wipe my face, my eyes teared up and blurred my vision. Only minutes into my trip I abandoned all thoughts of comfort. *You must focus on paddling and maintaining your course,* I told myself. *Do not think about the pain.*

When I had paddled for ten minutes, I started to feel less threatened, and my body responded in reaction to the wind and waves by instinct. The subtle nuances of kayaking had become routine. A body tilt here, an extra strong sweep there, each movement happened without thinking, and slowly my confidence returned. *This isn't so bad,* I thought. The waves were big and rough, but not unmanageable. Surprisingly, I was making good time even though I was fighting a crosswind and waves.

Gaining more confidence, my mind rushed ahead to Long Point Provincial Park, where I hoped to meet Fleur that evening. Would she be there? I didn't know for sure, but I felt that she would do everything in her power to be there if she could. Our last visit together seemed like years ago. So much had happened since Sault Ste. Marie, and I yearned to see her face.

While I daydreamed about Fleur, a huge wave crashed down on top of the kayak and jarred me back to reality. Thoughts of seeing Fleur vanished. In an instant, the waves suddenly grew bigger and more difficult to brace against, and my confidence slipped away. For the first time since I had started my trip, I wasn't having fun. I felt uncertain of my skills and whether I should be there in a kayak. As I continued to paddle, the waves grew bigger. Two-metre waves grew to three, charging towards shore with more destructive power than I had ever seen before.

After thirty minutes, my arms were tired, and I was mentally drained. I still felt confident that I could make it to Long Point, as long as the waves didn't get any bigger.

Of course the waves won't get any bigger; they can't! I assured myself. But the waves did get bigger. The entire shoreline from Port Burwell to Long Point was fronted by steep clay cliffs that rose ten metres or higher from the edge of the water. Waves crashed against the cliffs and left no room for escape between Port Burwell and Long Point. The waves moved toward me in irregular patterns. A series of two-metre waves was followed by larger three-metre waves, followed again and again by more waves.

I heard the first *big* wave coming before I ever saw it. It sounded threatening—a roar that grew louder as it approached. I looked in the direction of the sound but couldn't see through the nearest wave. Then the wave rushed past me, and I saw for the first time a wall of water four metres high, only thirty metres away. The wave looked like a driving avalanche of water, with a white curl on top.

At first, I stared in shock and disbelief. Large rolling waves offer no danger to a kayaker. Even a ten-metre high rolling wave simply raises and lowers your boat like you are on a roller coaster. What I saw looked like a tidal wave. Breaking waves are waves that collapse when they reach shallow water on shore or a shoal. I faced a wall of water that moved towards me like a tsunami.

When I realized what was coming, I tried to maneuver my kayak to face the wave. I managed to turn the bow partially before the *Mai Fleur* slid down the backside of a smaller wave and straight into the brown wall of water. The wave crashed into the *Mai Fleur* and I rode up its steep face as it carried me towards shore. Caught in the grip of the waves' curl, my kayak pitched and rocked violently from side to side, then flipped over. Pumped with adrenalin, I righted the boat with a high brace and a twist of my hip and then let out a triumphant, "Yahoo!" While I fought to regain control of my boat a second wave crashed into me, and I struggled to keep the kayak upright with a series of low braces.

This was the start of my battle. As I regained my course towards

Long Point, the waves grew bigger. With no place to go, I wished that I had stayed in Port Burwell. Angry with my decision, I scolded myself at the top of my lungs. "You stupid fuck," I screamed. "You've bitten off more than you can chew this time, Herman." The only safe place to go ashore was at Long Point or back at Port Burwell. Guided by a combination of stubborn pride and determination, I did not consider returning to Port Burwell. My progress toward Long Point was halted. Thoughts of making good time and distance were replaced by fighting off the relentless assault of the advancing waves. Maintaining a direct course to Long Point was impossible. Each time a wave approached, I stopped paddling and turned to face it. There was no time for a break. The line of waves was endless. No wave was less than three metres, and only a few short minutes separated larger waves that seemed solely intent on capsizing my tiny kayak.

My movements were tense and methodical, motivated by a belief that there was no way out of this situation but to continue to paddle. My concentration was focused on my kayak and the waves. I was unaware of everything else. After a while, feelings of danger eased up as I gained more confidence in my ability to handle the waves that were now regularly four metres in height. For a short time, I even enjoyed myself. Buoyed by feelings of success in handling the ocean-sized waves, I relished the challenge.

These feelings quickly vanished, however, with the muffled roar of another giant wave that rushed toward me. The sound was so much louder than anything else I had heard that I stopped paddling and waited expectantly for a glimpse. When the closest wave passed I stared in shock at a wall of water five metres high. The top of the wave was rolling in on itself as a churning boil of whitewater. As it drew nearer, the wave loomed above me and grew bigger until its immense size seemed to block out the world around me.

When the wave finally reached me, it towered so high I thought that I was going to be crushed. Instead, my kayak was swept up to the crest of the wave as it continued its charge toward shore. Caught in the wave's churning white peak, I was rocked sideways and spun violently in circles while I braced wildly from side to side, desperately trying to stay upright. Pummeled from all directions, I couldn't escape. Sometimes I was submerged underwater to my chest and then pitched backward so that the bow of the kayak stood straight up in the air.

The wave had complete control of me, and in a flash, my kayak flipped, and I was upside down. I held my breath and tried to roll up, but the boat thrashed and spun in every direction all at once. Tossed around underwater, I was unable to roll up. Exhausted and out of breath, I grabbed the loop on my spray skirt and ripped open the cockpit. Initially the weight of the wave held me under, and my body completed involuntary somersaults.

Disoriented and confused at first, I couldn't find the surface. Eventually the wave let me go, and my head popped up—saved by my lifejacket. I gulped air hungrily. Immediately aware that I was separated from my kayak, I reached for the *Mai Fleur* as a new wave crashed over my head. I knew that if I was going to get back into my kayak I needed to attach the floatation bags to the hull for stability.

I heard another wave coming and looked up in time to see a wall of water tower above me. I grabbed a handle on the end of the kayak just as the wave crashed on top of me and drove my body underwater. Afraid of losing my kayak, I held on tightly while the *Mai Fleur* dragged me towards shore.

When I surfaced again, I worked quickly to attach the floatation bags to the sides of the cockpit while new waves continued to break and collapse on top of me. When I had finished blowing air into the floatation bags, I scrambled back into the kayak. Before I could close the spray skirt, another wave crashed over me. Thankful that I had tied a safety line to my paddle, I paddled forward into the waves. The *Mai Fleur* moved sluggishly with water in the cockpit, but there was no time to bail.

As I paddled, I repeated loudly to myself over and over, "I'm going to make it, I'm going to make it, I'm going to make it." This was partly as an affirmation, and partly for comfort. The situation seemed so hopeless, I needed to hear something reassuring, even if it was only the sound of my own voice. The wind and waves were merciless in their attack against me, and at times I felt that the lake truly wanted to devour me.

"You can't beat us!" I screamed in defiance.

As I continued to paddle toward Long Point, the waves got bigger and more frequent. The floatation bags worked amazingly well to help stabilize the kayak. When a big wave crashed into me, it was much easier to stay upright. As I paddled, I thanked Heather for installing the strap and clip system that harnessed the extra floatation to the kayak's hull. Sometimes the kayak was vertical while it climbed the face of a steep wave, and I feared that I would be pushed over like a falling tree. Thankfully, that never happened.

My attempt to reach Long Point was slow. Instead of paddling in a direct line, I veered south toward the approaching waves, or stopped paddling altogether and braced in a defensive opposition. Twice more, a large wave crashed into me and knocked me over, but I rolled up and kept paddling.

As time passed, my body grew more tired and hungry. In between rounds, I fantasized about sitting in a warm restaurant eating chocolate cheesecake and drinking strong, dark coffee.

"Where do these thoughts come from?" I asked, almost expecting an answer. I talked steadily to myself out loud for comfort, and focused on meeting Fleur at Long Point alive.

"You're going to make it. You're going to make it," I assured myself over and over. For a short time, the big waves stopped coming and I thought the storm had ended. Then I heard the familiar roar of an approaching wave, and I knew it wasn't over yet. When the wave came closer I couldn't believe what I saw. Larger than all of the others, the wave appeared more than six metres high.

How can waves get this big on an inland lake? This isn't the ocean! I argued, unwilling to accept that what I saw was possible or real. I moved the kayak towards the wave just before it crashed into me. Again, the *Mai Fleur* and I were caught in the clutches of rolling, churning water near the crest of a gargantuan wave. Knocked from side to side three hundred and sixty degrees, I was battered in every direction as though my kayak had been transformed into a mechanical bull or giant Sumo wrestler.

Out matched and overpowered, I was quickly flipped over and held underwater. I tried to roll up again and again, but failed each time. The churning water sucked and pulled at my body to free me from my kayak. Still attached at my waist, my torso thrashed about wildly as though I was trapped in a washing machine. Eventually out of breath, I exited my kayak for the second time and fought my way to the surface. As I gasped to fill my lungs with air, I saw that my kayak was four metres away and headed towards the cliffs on shore.

Afraid of losing the *Mai Fleur,* I swam as quickly as I could, reaching the kayak just as another tower of water crashed on top of me. When the wave had passed me, I scrambled into the cockpit, grabbed my paddle, and braced as another wall of water pushed the kayak speeding backwards towards shore.

At the same time, I noticed that some of the gear that had been stored inside the cockpit was floating in the water. One sandal. Three water bottles. A water filter. The water filter was the closest to me, so I picked it up even as the waves pushed me closer to the cliffs. I saw my sandal floating in the trough between two waves, but I knew that I was already too close to shore to attempt chasing after it.

Fully aware of how close the waves had pushed me towards the cliffs, I began to paddle back through the wall of breaking waves. My arm muscles strained with each stroke as I fought to plough through the barrier of breaking waves. Some waves collapsed on top of me, while others pushed me backwards. My upper body and torso were forced backwards on impact from the breaking waves. I wasn't certain if I could make it through the waves. Frustrated, I shouted at the waves to let me through, and slowly I fought my way forward. It seemed that I would never get past the wall of water, but gradually I broke past the barrier. Near exhaustion, doubt was able to wedge itself into my thoughts, and I wondered how long I could continue.

Michael, can we survive this? Are we going to make it? I asked myself.

My arms ached from the strain, beginning to lose their strength. I desperately wanted to rest, but I knew I couldn't stop paddling. While my mind filled with doubt, I remembered reading about Gerard D'Aborville of France. The Frenchman had rowed across the Atlantic Ocean, solo, in a custom designed row boat. I wondered where *he* had found all of his strength and endurance during his incredible journey. The article that I remembered reading said that he sang the Alan Jackson song "Here in the Real World" to himself each day to raise his spirits. Desperate for anything that would help, I tried singing the country song for a while, but soon gave up and went back to repeating, "I'm going to make it, I'm going to make it, I'm going to make it. I refuse to die, I refuse to die. You've come too far to drown on Lake Erie," I told myself. "Keep going."

For the next few hours, I battled against the waves. Fear of drowning was overtaken by a deep concentration on survival and seeing Fleur. My entire body worked to fend off the monster waves. As evening approached, the waves began to get smaller, one wave at a time. By seven thirty, the waves were small enough that I could open the spray skirt and bail out the water. I had lost my bailer with my sandal and water bottles, so I used a plastic grocery bag that held two slices of pizza from lunch. Starved from hours of physical exertion, I wolfed down one piece and re-wrapped the second slice in tin foil and shoved it into my life jacket pocket.

Bailing with the plastic bag was a slow process. Large waves continued to wash over the bow and occasionally dump water into the cockpit. Eventually, only a shallow puddle remained, so I deflated the floatation bags and began paddling in earnest to reach my destination before it was too dark to see.

While I paddled, a motorboat launched from shore and drove over to ask if I was all right. The two men had seen me from their house and thought I was a windsurfer in trouble. When I told them I was going to Long Point, they assured me I was only three miles away and if I stayed close to shore, I should be okay. I didn't tell them where I had come from, but I wondered afterwards what they had thought of me being out on the lake. Judging by the looks they gave me, I suspected they thought I was a fool—which at that point, I couldn't argue.

The waves became less threatening while I paddled toward the Long Point peninsula. The sky had cleared some time ago, and the sun was a burning orange ball that hung above the lake. Thankful to be alive, I offered prayers of gratitude. The fact that I had survived the day to enjoy a beautiful sunset seemed like a miracle.

After the sun dropped below the horizon, the daylight faded quickly. Light from a lighthouse at the furthest end of the peninsula was my only guide. I didn't know where to go to shore, but I knew it wasn't there. In the darkness my ears focused on the crashing surf. I loved the sound the water made against the sand and gravel. The waves were like a peaceful lullaby. I closed my eyes and listened to the water lap against the shore. When I sensed my body relaxing, I forced my eyes wide open and sat up straighter in my seat.

Now is not the time to fall asleep, Michael, I chided myself. My body longed to relax and slip into a deep sleep, but I knew it wasn't time. First I had to reach land! When I got closer to shore, I noticed a faint pinprick of light in the dark space that was land. I wondered if it was a building, but then the light moved. It must be someone with a flashlight, I reasoned. Now I had a destination to paddle toward. When I got closer, I saw how big the waves were on shore and understood why I could hear them from so far away.

This day isn't over yet, I warned myself. I was a hundred metres from shore, just outside the barrier of breaking waves. My eyes strained to see in the dim light. I studied the waves for a rhythm that would help make my landing safer. Surfing onto shore can be dangerous fun in the daylight, never mind in semi-darkness. Still uncertain of my approach, I paddled closer and stopped seventy-five metres from shore. I back paddled regularly to prevent the waves from pushing me too close to the dangerous surf. The thought of the boat broaching sideways to the waves, or worse, capsizing in the strong undertow near shore, made me nervous.

As eager as I was to reach shore, I was aware of the importance of timing to land the kayak safely. Holding my paddle in front of me, I got ready to move closer. The muscles in my stomach tightened as I drew my boat nearer. The small light that had led me towards shore was gone. I was alone again. I imagined the people with the flashlight had probably walked back to the safety of their campsite.

I didn't like surfing a loaded kayak. I had very little control over the speed. My job was to steer straight enough to prevent the kayak from turning sideways. I took a deep breath and let it out slowly, then dipped the paddle into the water and pulled the blades left, right, left, right. Each paddle stroke brought me closer to the white-crested wall of water.

Out of the darkness a wave came from behind me, and immediately I was speeding recklessly towards shore. The face of the wave was behind me, pushing my kayak faster and faster toward the beach. I couldn't break away from the wave, and I hated the feeling. The kayak wanted to turn sideways constantly, and the sensation reminded me of when I was seven or eight and I peddled my bike down a steep hill for the first time. Gravity pulled me down the hill so fast that my legs couldn't keep up with the rotating pedals, and I struggled to hold the front wheel straight. When the speed became too much, the handlebars wobbled from side to side until I crashed and fell in a pile of scraped metal and skin.

As the kayak sped toward shore, I knew if it turned too far to either side I wouldn't be able to stop it from rolling under the wave and capsizing into the undertow. I pushed down on the rudder pedal and steered from behind with my paddle blade. It was too dark to see where I was going, so all my concentration was focused on steering until the beach was suddenly right in front of me.

The bow touched shore first and the wave pushed the *Mai Fleur* higher onto the beach. Still within reach of the crashing surf, I scrambled to get the spray skirt off before another wave could fall on top of me. Just as I got both legs out of the cockpit, a new wave crashed onto shore and attempted to claw the kayak back into the water. I held onto the *Mai Fleur* in a short-lived tug of war. When the water retreated, I grabbed the bow line and dragged the kayak to higher ground.

Safe at last, I walked a few steps and collapsed in a heap. After resting for a few minutes, I stood up and looked back toward Port Burwell. It was a miracle that I had survived. Later that night I wrote in my journal: *The sun is now resting behind the western horizon and luckily I too will rest in the comfort of my bed for another night. Thank you.*

LONG POINT REUNION

<hr>

IFOUND CAMPSITE three hundred and sixty-two only a few steps away from the beach. Considering the events of the day, it seemed more than luck that an empty site would be waiting for me so close by. Tired beyond words, I worked slowly to move my camping gear and kayak to the site.

While I struggled to light my stove, a park warden came by to inquire if I had a permit. When I explained who I was, he became very friendly and told me that he had been expecting me to arrive that day or the next. Anxious to see Fleur, I asked him if he would inquire whether she had arrived at the park looking for me. She hadn't checked in, so he asked the gate staff to tell Fleur my campsite number.

Uncertain when or if Fleur would arrive, I walked to a pay phone and called my parents. I didn't say much about the day. A phone call didn't seem the right way to tell them what had happened. I asked my mom to call Mark and Peter and tell them that I had arrived safely at Long Point. I knew they would be worried and would want to know that I was okay.

Fleur and her sister Chantal arrived at my campsite at nine thirty that night. Fleur looked more beautiful than I had remembered. Her long hair was bleached golden yellow by the sun, and her body was tanned and fit from a summer spent leading canoe trips. When I wrapped my arms around her, it felt like Christmas morning. Overwhelmed by the emotional strain of the day and the joy of seeing her, I was a Pandora's box of emotions. I buried my face into the hollow of her neck and drank in her scent. The joy I felt from holding Fleur close to me was rapturous.

Conscious that we were not alone, I turned my attention towards Chantal, thanking her repeatedly for driving Fleur to Long Point. It had taken them almost five hours to make the trip from Bradford, yet I was selfishly relieved when Chantal announced that she was not staying. Sensing our need to be alone, Chantal unloaded Fleur's bag and a cooler of food and quickly hugged us each goodbye before driving away.

I was barely able to contain my emotions: joy for a long-awaited reunion, anxiety from insecurities fuelled from being apart, and trauma from my near drowning that afternoon on Lake Erie. I had a burning need to talk about what had happened, but I didn't know how to begin. Instead, I stuffed my feelings down inside me until we were settled inside the tent. Curled up holding each other, I slowly described the events of my day, which had started with me saying goodbye to our friends in Port Burwell. While I related the details about the waves, coming out of my kayak, and moments of doubt whether I would survive, Fleur listened silently and held my hands gently in hers. When I had finished my story there was a long silence. Fleur was the first to speak.

"Michael, I don't know what to say. I wish I had been here when you first arrived." She kissed me with an open mouth, pressing her lips firmly against mine. After a long pause, she pulled away and looked me in the eyes. "Michael, I am so glad you made it here." Her words trailed off without mentioning what could have happened. There was nothing left for me to say. I had shared what I needed, and I had heard all that I needed from her.

We came together that night as a couple with a passion flamed from being apart and the reminder of how fragile our lives really are. We stayed in the tent most of the next day, making love and talking. Occasionally, one of us would dash from the tent to gather food from the cooler and return to the other's waiting arms.

Late in the day, I called Tilley Endurables and left a message on David Kappelle's voice mail, explaining that I had lost another hat. I felt awkward and embarrassed telling him because they had already given me two hats, so I offered to pay for a replacement. With no idea of how to receive a package, I simply told him my campsite number, and that I was camped at Long Point Provincial Park.

When I surveyed my belongings, I realized my losses were more than I had originally thought. When I capsized my kayak, I lost some things that I was wearing and almost everything that was stored in the cockpit. The list of missing items included my Tilley hat, polarized sunglasses, sport sandals, water bottles, lock for the kayak, six metres of rope, and a canvas cockpit cover to keep out the rain at night. Some of the items I could survive without, but the hat, sunglasses, and sandals were essential.

It wasn't until the next day that Fleur and I were ready to leave the tent and explore beyond our campsite. We were almost out of bread and sweets, so we walked the beach to a small variety store where I had found a pay phone the night I arrived. After lunch, we explored the west beach and grassy sand dunes toward the Big Creek National Wildlife Area. Neither of us had been to Long Point before, so the geomorphology and unique ecosystem was fascinating to both of us.

When we returned to our campsite in the afternoon, my new hat from Tilley Endurables had arrived by Purolator. The delivery driver must have had a chuckle when he read the shipping address. Attached to the hat was a personal handwritten note from David wishing me good luck for the remainder of my trip. I also spoke with Mark Climie at the cancer society office in Toronto that afternoon. After he heard that I had lost my sunglasses and sandals, he quickly declared that he would call the manager of the Mountain Equipment Co-op store in Toronto. Mark knew that the MEC was one of my major sponsors, and so he took it upon himself to see if they would replace the lost items for me. My heart swelled from the support I received from everyone. While I was kayaking I felt alone, but to see the evidence that people cared about me and supported what I was doing felt wonderful.

That evening, Fleur and I joined Ron and Maria Content; their daughters, Rachel and Melisa; and family friends Al and Ingrid at their nearby campsite. We had met Ron and Maria earlier in the day and had been invited to join them for a campfire. We roasted marshmallows and talked over the orange flicker of light about our families, finding each other, and our connections to cancer. By the time we left the campfire, Fleur and I each felt like we were among old friends.

As we walked back, Fleur questioned me about the evening. "Does this happen often when you meet people?"

Unsure what she meant, I responded with, "Does what happen often?"

"People opening up to you and talking as though you were family, or a close friend." Connecting with people and sharing intimate details about our lives had become a common occurrence for me. It wasn't until Fleur pointed it out, that I remembered that connections like that didn't happen every day. When Fleur and I had met in Sault Ste. Marie, we spent most of our time alone. Involving *strangers* in my trip hadn't really started. When I left the Sault, the trip had changed, and connecting with people had become the most significant part of my trip. I was glad that Fleur had the chance to experience this part of the trip with me, and I could tell she was too.

We stayed in bed the next morning until the sun's heat turned the tent into a sauna. Al and Ingrid had offered to bring us with them to Port Rowan, and we had gratefully accepted. Still behaving as newlyweds, we raced over to their campsite and arrived just in time to leave. Port Rowan was a pretty little lakeside town that each of us vowed we would like to return to for a weekend getaway. After we bought some groceries, we sat in the shade of an umbrella table and devoured "death by chocolate" ice-cream cones. Both of us were fit from a summer filled with exercise, and we laughed like children, knowing we were breaking some gastronomic rule by eating dessert before lunch.

When we returned to the park, we walked the beach toward the tip of Long Point, drawn by the mystery of what lay at the end of the beach. We had heard that the property past the park boundary was owned by the Canadian Wildlife Service because of its significant waterfowl habitat. We had also heard that walking the beach was the only activity that was allowed. No one was permitted to hike inland off the beach, camp, hunt, or fish in the designated area.

It was the area past this point that intrigued us most. According to other campers, at the end of the government boundary line, the land was owned by a private American corporation that banned all access for any reason. I was told that there were even rumors that people had been charged with trespassing simply for boating close to shore. The area was so contentious, the owners had a fence across the beach that stretched out into the water to keep people out. We didn't walk that far, but the idea of a fence seemed outrageous to me, and I wondered if this would affect my kayaking around the tip.

The next morning brought grey skies and a knot in the pit of my stomach. It was our last morning together, and I dreaded saying goodbye. We had talked a lot about our future together, and we had decided to share an apartment in Thunder Bay when I finished my trip. We both knew it could take a couple of months before we would be together again. I didn't ask Fleur to meet me in Toronto at the end of my trip. I knew that a plane ticket was not possible on her student budget. I simply accepted that she could not be there when I finished my trip, and left it at that.

We spent most of the day in the tent talking. We wanted to be close to each other for every minute that we had left together. Unfortunately, the time passed too quickly. It felt like we had just arrived, and then it was time for Fleur to leave. Chantal arrived at eight that evening to pick up Fleur and take her away. Fleur cried while we hugged and kissed good bye. She never mentioned my foolhardy decision to leave Port Burwell in a storm, but she did tell me repeatedly to be careful. I did not cry, but I wished I had. I wanted Fleur to know beyond words that I was sad about saying goodbye too. I had become so immune to goodbyes that tears would not come, even when I willed them.

Later that evening, park staff delivered a package from the Mountain Equipment Co-op filled with energy bars, sunglasses, and sport sandals. To my amazement, Mark had come through on his promise to find me replacements for my lost items. Newly equipped, I was ready to go again.

Feeling a bit glum, I joined my new best friends, Ron and Maria and company, around an evening campfire. We talked late into the night under a starry sky, but thoughts of Fleur never left me.

ERIE'S WOODEN BENCHES

I SPENT THE next day making plans about how to get around Long Point. I had heard enough controversy that I didn't know if it was a good idea to continue with my plans to kayak around the tip. After I talked with John, the park superintendent, I decided it would be prudent to avoid a possible conflict; instead I would simply shuttle across the base of the peninsula. This was a difficult decision for me to make, because I didn't want to appear to be shortening the trip unless it was clearly unavoidable, like at Niagara Falls.

John was a great help to me. He called the park superintendent at Selkirk Provincial Park, approximately sixty kilometres away by water, and arranged permission for me to camp there after the park was closed. I had missed the fact that it was the start of Labour Day weekend, and in three days, the provincial parks would all close for the summer.

I woke early the next day, eager to get moving. It was easier to get up when I was alone. I had enjoyed a leisurely stop, but my body was ready to go back to work. Accustomed to the strain of paddling six hours a day, my body craved physical exercise like a drug. Ron had insisted the night before that he would make me breakfast and help move my kayak. I woke too early to visit Ron and Maria, so I sat on the beach and watched a burning red sunrise.

We loaded my kayak into the back of Ron's truck and made the short shuttle across to Long Point Bay. Ron and Maria stayed with me while I packed the kayak, determined to see me off. I left Long Point Bay at eleven o'clock under clear skies with a light breeze. As much as I

247

enjoyed making new friends, I loved the feeling of moving on, and held a deeper understanding of the Willie Nelson song "On the Road Again." Thinking back to my childhood, I wondered if I had been born for a gypsy life.

I arrived in front of a lakeside restaurant at Port Dover a few minutes before five. The beach and patio bar were busy with tourists. While I sat in my kayak deciding whether to go ashore, someone from the patio yelled out: "Hey, where're you coming from?"

When I called back, "Thunder Bay," the same voice asked if I was the guy he had seen on TV. Unsure, I answered, "Maybe," and then the voice invited me to come ashore so that he could buy me a beer.

The voice belonged to Roger Chandler, a comic with Canada's Yuk Yuk's comedy clubs. He was there with his wife, Karen, and their friend, Rick, from Regina. Roger told me that he had been in Thunder Bay the day that I started my trip, but had missed my launch, then saw me on TV in Windsor and had hoped to see me in Toronto when I finished. We all laughed at the coincidence of meeting in Port Dover, but to me there was no coincidence. Roger just *happened* to have friends in Port Dover, so before rushing to perform at a show in Toronto, he found me a place to store my kayak and set up my tent for the night.

Following a hand-drawn map on a bar napkin, I paddled up a river to a local boat yard. A collection of sailboats and fishing vessels all in need of repair littered the yard. It was a scene from an east coast fishing town: a parking lot of various sized boats with names like *Fishing Fever, Emerald Skyes,* and *Big Catch.* I tied my kayak up to a five-slip dock nestled among two large cabin cruisers and unloaded some food and dry clothes for the night.

I cooked pasta on my portable stove and ate a quiet supper on the dock. Port Dover, I learned, had been a tourist destination for over a hundred years. Back in the heyday of train travel, people from Toronto would come to Port Dover for its world-famous Lake Erie pickerel. Today, people still came by car or boat to buy, or dine on, local Erie fish. When I finished cleaning my dishes, I walked into town and discovered a vibrant and busy main street with numerous restaurants advertising fresh fish caught today. Already filled up with pasta, I settled for reading the daily menus posted in restaurant windows or on streetside placards. I had little money for buying luxury dinners, and moments like this made me feel like a penniless vagabond. It was no fun to be a tourist without any money, so I walked back to my kayak to write in my journal.

The shipyard where I left my kayak was a mess. The lot was barren of anything green, and the ground was stained with oil. Decomposed wood, rusted metal boats, and piles of garbage were spewn everywhere. When I couldn't find a suitable place to set up my tent, I settled for sleeping on the dock. This proved to be a big mistake. The dock was only slightly wider than my shoulders, and each time I moved to get more comfortable I woke, worried that I would roll into the water.

The dreadful night ended early with the happy chatter of songbirds hidden in the trees across the river. My body was stiff and tired, but I felt no pleasure from staying in my sleeping bag. Resigned to an early start, I ate a peasant breakfast of stale bread and jam, and then walked to the beach.

I sat near the water and wrote postcards to family and friends while the sun came up. When I had finished writing all of my postcards, I explored the beach. What I found was disturbing. Spaced by some order of design were wooden benches sponsored by local families and organizations. Carved into the wood were the names of fishermen who had drowned in Lake Erie. When I discovered the first bench, I thought it was a unique monument left by the town as a reminder of the men who gave their lives to feed their families. As I continued my walk along the shore, I realized there were many other benches with dozens of names of sons, husbands, brothers and dads who had been lost to the lake. When I read the names, I thought about my day between Port Burwell and Long Point, and how close I had come to joining the list.

At noon, I phoned Roger as we had planned, and he picked me up to go sailing at Turkey Point. Roger, Karen, and Rick welcomed me into their group like an old school friend, and we talked easily on the drive. When we arrived at Turkey Point, Roger and Karen's sailing friends announced it was too calm to sail, so we enjoyed a day on the beach. They were all interesting people to talk with. Roger had been in the comedy business for sixteen years and had also spent some time as a rafting guide on the Fraser River in British Columbia. Rick was a professor at Regina University, with a master's degree in art from Oxford.

We ended our day together with a stop at a historic Port Dover landmark called the Norfolk Tavern.

"You have to see this place," was all that Roger told me as we got out of the car. Steeped in history dating back to the early 1800s and the War of 1812, the Norfolk Tavern looked like a small museum converted into a modern-day pub. Seated at a corner table sipping cold pints of beer, we talked about the possibility of meeting up in Niagara Falls. Roger and Karen were recreational kayakers and were excited about the chance to kayak with me on the Niagara River. When we said goodbye, I had a strong feeling we were going to see each other again.

When I arrived back at my kayak, it was too late to look for a new place to sleep. I didn't have money to go to a motel, so I spent another wakeful night on the narrow dock.

I woke early the next morning, feeling both thankful and ready to leave. When I had planned my trip itinerary in the winter and set my arrival date for Toronto, I really had no idea how fast a pace I would need to travel each day. Now that the trip was drawing to a close, my daily schedule was run more by fundraising opportunities and a set arrival date in Toronto than by how many kilometres I could paddle each a day. Although I enjoyed the spontaneous excursions with new friends, I was nostalgic for days alone on Lake Superior.

While I packed my sleeping bag, a man named Tom came by to say hello. Tom was Roger's friend who had made arrangements for me to sleep on the dock at the Port Dover Boat Works. We talked about my trip and the violent storm that I had paddled through the previous Sunday. Tom confirmed my belief that the waves on Lake Erie had been more than six metres in height.

Until my conversation with Tom, I hadn't spoken to anyone who had any knowledge of the waves that day. Tom told me that a couple of commercial fishermen he knew had told him that they had seen twenty footers, and that nobody went out that day to fish during the storm.

Prior to meeting Tom, I had started to doubt the size of the waves that day. I knew that kayakers had a tendency to overestimate the size of waves because of how low they sat on the water. For some reason, Tom's confirmation about the size of the waves unnerved me. Knowing the truth reminded me that regardless of the success I'd had on the other lakes, I still had two Great Lakes to paddle before reaching Toronto.

Tom worked as a boat restorer at the Port Dover Boat Works. When he noticed that one of the plastic eye hooks on the top deck of my kayak was cracked, he offered to help with the repair. The plastic hook was one of many that attached a rope on the top of the kayak for emergency rescues. I had an extra hook from Seaward Kayaks in my repair bag, so with some of Tom's marine silicone, we fixed the small problem in a jiffy. The needed repair had not been a serious threat to the *Mai Fleur*, but I welcomed Tom's help. I knew it was a symbolic gesture of his desire to be a part of my trip, and I greatly appreciated his time and effort.

I paddled the shoreline from Port Dover to Selkirk Provincial Park without any problems. When I arrived, I could see that the shoreline was extremely shallow. Anxious about the rocks, I gingerly paddled the *Mai Fleur* close to shore, wincing at the sound of rock scraping on fiberglass.

I set up my tent and cooked my spaghetti supper while perched on a grassy ledge overlooking the lake. It was the first night the campground was closed, but it already had a graveyard mood. While I washed my dishes, a cyclist came in on a road bike loaded down with bulging saddle bags from wheel to wheel. He had the entire campground to choose from, yet he set up his tent within talking distance of me. I took that as a sign that he was friendly, so I walked over and said hello.

Rick was a tall, muscular bike traveller from Florida, who had legs almost as thick as my torso. Rick explained that he had been on the road for five weeks, headed for the Rockies. After commenting that he found the evenings cool for the beginning of September, Rick asked me if I thought he would see snow in Alberta. His nose turned up when I told him there was a chance that he could see snow before he reached Manitoba.

When he showed me his road maps, I understood why. To save space and weight, he had chosen one large road map to guide him across Canada. Although Rick had come a long way, I doubted whether he understood how big Ontario was, or what the highway around Lake Superior looked like. When I asked him if he owned warmer clothes he said no, explaining that he had planned to finish his trip before it started to snow. Our conversation ended shortly afterward. I sensed that he didn't appreciate my cold weather forecast.

The sun was warm and bright when I woke the next day. While I prepared my breakfast, Rick prepared himself for a new day on the road. We shared pleasant greetings, but our conversation ended there. I felt bad for dispensing gloomy news to a fellow traveller, so I walked over and offered him a parting gift. Reaching out, I handed Rick a full bottle of sunscreen.

"Here's hoping the sun's warm, and that you have the wind at your back," I offered. Rick accepted my gift with a smile and a handshake.

"The same to you," he responded. "And thanks for the heads-up last night about the prospect of snow," he added with a grin. I could tell he meant what he said, and I felt better about myself as an Ontario ambassador.

More Wind and Waves

T HE LAKE WAS calm, with no hint of a breeze, as I paddled away from the Selkirk shore. My paddle to Port Maitland was quiet and uneventful. When I arrived at the mouth of the Grand River, it didn't appear that the town offered any amenities near the lake. There were no stores or people that I could see. The buildings near the water seemed only involved in ship building or repairs.

In need of groceries and curious about the famous Grand River, I paddled upstream towards the town of Dunnville. There was no boat traffic on the river, but an ocean vessel sat anchored in the river channel not far from the lake. I paddled my kayak alongside the rusted metal hull that rose up from the water like a boat-shaped skyscraper. It was the biggest ship I had ever seen, and the monstrous structure looked out of place on the river. Seated in my tiny boat, I felt dwarfed by its height.

I arrived in Dunnville at four o'clock, left my kayak at the Dunnville Boat Club, and went shopping for groceries. When I returned, the manager of the boat club let me sleep on the floor of their building. It wasn't the best offer that I had received on my trip, but compared to sleeping outside on a narrow dock, it was safe and dry.

The next morning, I woke before 7:00 a.m. to sunshine and strong winds. I decided to get an early start in case it might be a tough paddle to Port Colborne. A group of cancer society volunteers had organized a welcome party for me in the afternoon, and I didn't want to be late.

By eight fifteen I had paddled back down the Grand River with the help of a modest current. When I reached the lake, I saw that Erie had

253

already turned rough, with white-capped waves everywhere. Expecting another challenge, I stopped and prepared myself mentally, storing a few loose items inside the cockpit. I kept only one water bottle within reach.

At the mouth of the river, I saw a legion of metre-high waves with white crests moving across the lake. The muscles in my stomach tightened as I left the shelter of the river and navigated my kayak into the rough water. I wasn't scared, but I *was* nervous. The experience of paddling from Port Burwell was still fresh in my mind, a reminder of what the lake was capable of doing to a small boat.

The paddle to Port Colborne was a grinding struggle. The conditions were not as threatening as the day I had paddled to Long Point, but fear of what could come was ever present. While I paddled, the height of the waves grew, and they became steeper and more pushy. Near points of land, rebound waves from shore collided with onshore waves, creating rough and dangerous water. To avoid the dangers near Rock and Mohawk Points, I paddled far away from the security of shore.

As the waves grew, my kayak was pushed at unnerving speeds that I was helpless to stop. Wave after wave rushed in from behind, picked up the *Mai Fleur*, and carried me forward, racing out of control. Each time I felt the telltale sign of the stern rise, my heart beat quickened and I struggled to steer the kayak straight without flipping over. Sometimes while I surfed down the steep face of a wave, the bow dipped below the surface and peeled a spray of water into my face. The experience was both exhilarating and frightening all at once. I loved the speed, but I understood the consequences, and that took away much of the fun.

I arrived safely in Port Colborne at Sugarloaf Marina at two thirty. I was met by a group of cancer society volunteers, the town mayor, and two newspaper reporters. When I had finished the interview with the two reporters, I sat with some of the cancer volunteers and talked about my trip. Someone had either invited or encouraged one of the reporters to join us, which made me feel uncomfortable. I had grown wary and untrusting of reporters, so I was guarded when I spoke in their presence. I didn't feel I could talk freely, not knowing what would end up in print.

When the reporter finally left, I confided with my hosts why I had been quiet and reserved. The group didn't understand my concerns, promising me that I didn't have to worry about their reporter friend. I didn't believe they understood reporters. I was convinced that when there was a story, all reporters were looking for a fresh angle to write about.

Dick and Dorothy McCaffrey were volunteers with the cancer society who invited me to stay in their home for the night. I enjoyed a wonderful dinner and evening with them and other volunteers from the cancer society at a local restaurant. The restaurant dinners held a sense of celebration for me, providing a connection with people I admired for their community involvement. The dinners had become an honour I cherished dearly during the last days of my trip.

The next morning, I stayed in my room and quietly wrote in my journal while my hosts slept. Dorothy had warned me the night before that she was not an early riser, so I patiently waited, resigning myself to a late start. When she did wake, Dorothy prepared a platter of French toast and homemade fruit salad with the enthusiasm of a great aunt.

When I had finished breakfast, Dorothy called Ron Brown, a cancer society volunteer in Crystal Beach, for advice on how I would get around the Niagara River. During the previous night's dinner, I had admitted that I didn't have a clear idea of how I was going to get past Niagara Falls. Dorothy thought Ron could help. Ron explained over the phone that when I reached Fort Erie and the Niagara River, I must exit into the Chippewa Channel. Ron also offered me a place to stay when I got to Fort Erie, but it was his last words that I remembered most.

"Don't miss the Chippewa exit."

When Dorothy and I arrived at the marina, a crowd of supporters was waiting for me, concerned about the weather. The sky was blue, but there was a strong wind and several people warned that the waves were big. When I walked to the end of the sheltered marina, I saw that the wind and waves did look bigger than the previous day, but they looked manageable. The experience of paddling to Long Point was ever present on my mind, but I wasn't going to let it make me fear the lake.

Whether you crash your car, or encounter near death on the lake while kayaking, we all have to climb back on the proverbial horse, I reasoned with myself. Once I had packed my kayak, I slipped eagerly into the lake at eleven thirty, destined for Fort Erie.

My experience paddling to Fort Erie was a repeat of the day before. Big waves pushed me at uncontrollable speeds until I was certain that it was only a matter of time before my kayak would flip, and I would be swimming again. To prevent this, I steered the kayak with my paddle blade by pulling or pushing water toward or away from the stern with cautious precision. I knew that any over-correction to steer straight would cause the boat to turn sharply and flip.

The area around Point Albino was the most treacherous. Refracting waves and odd water currents travelled around the point, mixed with the wind-driven waves, creating an angry maelstrom of towering water. Knowing that I didn't want to fight my way through the waves, I altered my course and paddled on its fringe. This course was safer, but not entirely innocent.

While I paddled past the point, a big wave rushed in from behind and surfed my kayak at breakneck speeds over a shallow water shoal littered with boulders just below the surface. My kayak crossed over the rocks without touching, but once again I knew that I had cheated disaster. Without enough water to offer any cushion, capsizing over the rocks would have been disastrous.

Once passed Point Albino, I fixed my gaze toward the end of the lake. I had given a lot of thought about the dangers of paddling Lake Superior, but Lake Erie had given me the most trouble. Although many people knew of the dangers that surrounded Lake Superior, little was said of Erie, or the fact that it had taken more ships than any other great lake. I now understood why. Long, narrow, and shallow, it didn't take much of a wind to stir it up and create waves too big for a lake. I looked forward to getting off Erie. I had had enough, and would forever think of Erie as "the nasty lake."

Niagara Falls Detour

I APPROACHED FORT Erie with giddy excitement. I knew that when my paddle blades touched the Niagara River, I would have only one lake left to paddle. From my kayak seat, I saw two bridges on either side of the lake. I wasn't sure which way to go, but I assumed that I had been heading for the American side, so I changed my course and paddled to the left shore. This change in direction placed my kayak broadside to the strong winds, which pushed me sideways towards the head of the Niagara River.

I fought my way across the lake. Muscles strained against the wind and waves, yet my kayak continued its sideward drift toward the river. By the time I was eighty metres from the Canadian shore, I was at the head of the river; I could feel the river pulling at my kayak. When I realized that I couldn't fight the current, my stomach tightened with a familiar sickening feeling. The swift water was pulling me downstream, and I didn't know what lay ahead.

It had been twenty years since I had been to Niagara Falls, and I had no idea if there were continuous rapids from the lake leading up to the drop. My long sea kayak didn't favour rapids or swift current. Instead of riding over the top of the waves, my kayak plowed through them as I passed under the Peace Bridge. The current was remarkably fast, and because the water was funneled and forced to squeeze through the narrow river, the channel was clogged with metre-high standing waves.

Anxious to get to shore, I tilted the kayak's hull on its side and ferried across the river. When I was free of the main current, I continued downstream, hugging the shoreline while I searched for a place to stop. I passed under another bridge and beached my kayak on a sandy shore.

I had reached Fort Erie, and although there was no one there to greet me, it felt like a good place to stop. My map of the river and falls was tucked out of reach, and I needed to know what lay ahead before I could go on. I felt *done* for the day. When I spotted a pay phone across the road from the river, it was a sign for me to stay put. I pulled my list of contacts out of my map case and called Ted Wood, a cancer society volunteer. Calling a stranger always made me feel a bit awkward and nervous, but when Ted answered the phone on the third ring, his voice was warm and welcoming. Ted had been waiting for my call, and within minutes, he arrived to help.

In the time it took Ted to find me, I had met Dan Prevost, the owner of Precision Auto Glass. Dan's garage was across the river from where I had stopped, and he had offered me space to store my kayak. My trip had lost the adventure I had found on Lake Superior, yet I had grown to enjoy the urban adventure of not knowing exactly how my day would end. Every day was a mystery that simply worked out due to the kindness of others.

Ted was a gracious host who treated me like family while I stayed the night. In the morning, we talked over a leisurely breakfast before I began a whirlwind day. After making plans to meet with a local newspaper, Ted drove me to the Crystal Beach IGA store so I could thank the assistant store manager and staff for supporting the Kayaking for Cancer campaign.

After we left the store, Ted drove me to Fort Erie where I met a reporter for an interview, and then he brought me back to the sand beach where I had stopped the day before. With a warm handshake, Ted and I said goodbye, and I slipped my kayak back into the Niagara River current. The night before, I had made a point to learn more about Niagara River geography. Feeling better prepared for where I was going and what lay ahead, I paddled with an easy calm down the Niagara River.

I didn't see anyone until I noticed Ron Brown standing near the river and waving his arms frantically to get my attention. Since our phone conversation back in Port Colborne, Ron had worried whether I would know how to get around the falls. After a short break to get new directions, Ron said goodbye with a promise to meet me at a gathering down river.

When I reached the river's divide at Grand Island, I detoured onto the Canadian side of the Niagara River, also known as Chippewa Channel. Grand Island was on American soil and the border for Canada and the US. I paddled down the Chippewa Channel for half a kilometre and was met by a group of supporters near Kingsbridge Park. The mayor of Niagara Falls, the local Member of Parliament, cancer society volunteers, and two newspaper reporters all clapped and cheered as I paddled toward the crowded dock.

After a short reception, which included the gift of a pen set from the mayor and interviews with the reporters, I was left alone with the cancer society volunteers. We talked and snacked on refreshments that they had brought. The volunteers felt like my surrogate family wherever I went, providing me with a great sense of comfort and support.

Later that afternoon, Ron brought me to the Chippewa IGA store, where I met the owners, Bob and Marie. Kind, helpful, and supportive are words that describe how I felt about these two people. Before we left, Marie handed Ron a personal cheque for one hundred and fifty dollars for Kayaking for Cancer. Later that day, Ron took me with his family to dinner and then drove me to a motel that was paid for by the owner of the Niagara Falls IGA store. It was midnight by the time I put my head on the pillow. I was exhausted.

The next day was a blur. I spent part of the morning and early afternoon at the Chippewa IGA store. Bob and Marie had organized a fundraising barbecue outside their store, and I was the main attraction. Flipping burgers and hot dogs, I had a chance to meet and speak with numerous locals who had seen my face in their weekly IGA price flyer all summer. It was the kind of event that I had envisioned and hoped for the entire trip. When the barbecue wrapped up, Marie drove me to Niagara Falls so that I could meet Mike Glatt, the owner of the Niagara Falls IGA store. In addition to paying for my motel room, Mike had been a huge supporter of the fundraising, and the donation cans had done exceptionally well in his store.

During the day, Roger Chandler tracked me down through the cancer society and offered to bring me to his comedy show that night at the Yuk Yuk's comedy club in Niagara Falls. Roger had told the club manager about my fundraising trip, and he had promised to donate one dollar from each "shooter" drink sold that night.

Roger and Karen met me late in the afternoon with three bikes, and we went for a sightseeing bike ride from the town of Chippewa to the Rainbow Bridge. I had never visited the Niagara area as a cyclist, and the view of the gorge and falls from this vantage point was spectacular. We were able to see much more than the pedestrians or motorists, yet we still had the luxury to stop when we wanted to snap a picture and enjoy the view.

Later that evening, I sat in the dimly lit comedy club and watched Roger share his self-deprecating brand of humour, which had the crowd in stitches with laughter. It was another moment when I felt like I was living a double life. One minute I was a lone kayaker, and the next I was an ordinary tourist enjoying a comedy act. When Roger left me back at my motel room, my head was swimming with memories after another busy day.

PADDLING AND POLITICS

W HEN I ARRIVED in Fort Erie everyone I met told me that I couldn't kayak the Niagara River below Niagara Falls. "The cops won't let you launch into the gorge," was the common advice. "Not unless you put up a fifty-thousand-dollar bond," someone offered with a chuckle at the IGA barbecue in Chippewa. When I expressed a desire to get on the river as soon after Niagara Falls as possible, the responses were unanimous. "You can't get on the river before Queenstown."

Niagara Falls became my biggest portage of the trip. From a purists' perspective of self-propelled expeditions, many would say that I cheated. I agreed with this point of view, but I also accepted the reality that I wasn't doing the trip entirely on my own. I was one piece of a larger puzzle that involved the cancer society and anyone else who took an interest in me and my trip. I just couldn't see myself trying to portage around Niagara Falls on a busy road with summer tourists. I could see the headlines: "Krazy Kayaker Killed on the Road." That kind of publicity wasn't what I was seeking for myself or the cancer society. To solve the problem, volunteers found a boat trailer long enough for my kayak, and we transported the *Mai Fleur* by road down to Queenstown.

Roger, Karen, and their friend John Wolfenberg met me in Queenstown to kayak the river to Niagara-on-the-Lake. No one had accompanied me since my paddle with Peter from Killbear Provincial Park to Parry Sound, and I liked the prospect of having company.

When I launched my kayak into the river, I marveled at the colour of the water. The river was an emerald green that sparkled and radiated an image of purity. After two weeks of paddling on Lake Erie, the river was uplifting. When I remarked about my feelings toward the green water, John was quick to respond.

"Don't let the colour fool you. You don't want to drink this river water any more than the Detroit." For some reason, the reality of John's words bothered me for the whole day. *Is there no more clean water?* I mused solemnly.

The trip to Niagara-on-the-Lake was an easy paddle aided by a swift current. Our small flotilla arrived in the picturesque town of Niagara-on-the Lake at three o'clock, where we were greeted by a small group of supporters. Ruth Delgat was one of the cancer society volunteers that met me at the marina, and she kindly offered me a place to stay. Saying goodbye to Roger and Karen was once again bittersweet, but I had become accustomed to saying goodbye by then. We parted with hugs and handshakes and exchanged addresses with the promise to stay in touch—more scraps of paper that meant much more than simply a mailing address.

Ruth had a beautiful home in Niagara-on-the-Lake, close to the water. We sat and talked late into the evening about my trip and fundraising efforts. When Ruth started to complain about the lack of support from the Toronto office, I felt as though she had torn away a scab. My arrival in Toronto was six days away, and I had tried to bury my angst with the head brass at Ontario division of the cancer society. Working to complete the trip and organize media contacts and fundraising events had become too much. Out of the need to keep going, I had accepted the situation and focused my efforts on paddling.

I had originally contacted the cancer society to gain help and support with fundraising in each of the towns along my Great Lakes route. What I wanted was a Mark Scissons or Lillian Thompson-style of organization from the cancer society, and I had trusted them to set it up. By the time I started to have concerns, Mark Climie had insisted that the volunteers were too busy on their summer vacations to organize any fundraising for me. All of the volunteers I had met on my trip had flatly refuted that claim, insisting that they were not notified about my trip until a few days before my arrival. "Too late to organize anything properly," they argued.

After discussing the matter with countless volunteers from Lake St. Clair to Lake Ontario, I had reached my own conclusion. I had been caught in the middle of organizational politics. The Terry Fox Run was set for September 18, the day after my arrival in Toronto. Some cancer society insiders that I spoke with suggested that the head office didn't want my fundraising campaign to burn out the volunteers before the Terry Fox Run. Although I understood this rationale, I struggled with my own feelings of disappointment.

The next morning, Ruth helped me contact the local newspaper for an interview before I left for Port Dalousie. I started paddling at noon, and although I had told myself to stop worrying about fundraising, I couldn't stop thinking about it. With nothing else to do but paddle and think, my mind focused on the fact that I was approaching Toronto, and the major Toronto media still hadn't heard about Kayaking for Cancer.

By three in the afternoon, I had paddled close enough to Port Dalousie that a sailboat came out to guide me into the yacht club where I was met by a waiting crowd of supporters, local newspaper reporters, and cable news cameras. Once I had made an "official arrival," Wendy Trottier, a representative from the cancer society, placed calls to two separate radio stations, with hopes of attracting interest and donations. What I remember most was that my arrival and reception felt rather ho-hum and half-interested, no more exciting than if I had simply finished a day's paddle from Niagara Falls.

I was grateful, however, to the Port Dalousie Yacht Club. When the crowd left, the manager offered me floor space in one of their storage buildings for my kayak and sleeping bag. I was also treated to a quiet dinner in the yacht club's restaurant. It was a bizarre situation. On one hand, I was met by a sailboat escort and greeted by newspaper reporters and supporters, yet there I was left in a storage building alone with my kayak and sleeping on the floor. For some reason, it made me think back to my first night on Lake Superior. I had come full circle.

I woke early the next day, eager to be back on the water where I was most comfortable and understood my job. An employee named Bob helped me move my kayak down to the water. I started paddling at 9:00 a.m. and arrived in Grimsby early in the afternoon. It had been an easy day with clear skies and very little wind or waves. Two fishermen directed me to Forans Marina. When I reached the pier, five people, including a reporter from the Grimsby newspaper, were there to greet me.

I stayed on the pier for the remainder of the afternoon, talking with anyone who showed the least amount of interest in my kayak or the little sign I had posted that read "Kayaking for Cancer." At six o'clock, a photographer named Cathy, who worked for the *Hamilton Spectator,* came and took some photographs of me in my kayak. At the time it seemed inconsequential, considering the paper hadn't sent a reporter, but she took a really nice photo. A few days later, a representative from the paper called my parents and sold them an eight-by-ten picture of me. It was the only good photograph ever taken of me in my kayak, and my mom had it framed as a family memento.

After the photographer left, I started to set up my tent, when John Wolfenberg, who I had paddled with on the Niagara River, arrived. He had phoned around and found out where I was and came looking for me to invite me home for the night. When I explained that Joyce and Rex Harrison were taking me out for dinner, he eagerly suggested they bring me to his house later. Grateful for the company after my night alone in Port Dalousie, I was deposited on John's door step around nine. John was very easy-going, and we sat and talked in his living room about work, kayaking, and our families until almost midnight. I went to sleep in the spare room feeling exhausted once again.

On a tight schedule to get to work on time, John left me at my kayak at seven fifteen the next morning. I found a pay phone nearby and called a few radio stations, eventually getting a short interview on CFRB radio. I left by 9:00 a.m. and paddled through dense fog all the way to the Burlington Skyway. I arrived at Hamilton Harbour at half past twelve, and after getting my bearings, reached Spencer Smitt Park at two thirty, where newspaper reporters and a CHCH TV camera crew were waiting.

When the media stepped away, I met the owner of the Burlington IGA store and a representative for the mayor of Hamilton, who gave me a book about the city and a pen. I have no memory of my evening in Hamilton, and my journal is mostly blank except for a few lines detailing that the owner of the Hamilton Venture Inn offered me a room for the night. I also wrote, *For the first time, I'm ready to finish fundraising.*

LILLIAN'S GIFT

T HE NEXT COUPLE of days were similarly anti-climactic. My view of
the Lake Ontario shoreline was a continuous parade of concrete
and steel, while my evenings were spent alone in complimentary
hotel rooms. As I got closer to Toronto, it felt increasingly odd to be left
alone in a city surrounded by people. By Thursday, I was in Oakville,
and the lonely isolation reminded me of my meeting with the Sault Ste.
Marie radio announcer who asked me why anyone would care that I was
kayaking for cancer.

On Friday, I arrived at the Port Credit Yacht club. The major
difference that day was that the *Toronto Sun* newspaper had sent its staff
writer Joe Warmington to interview me on the dock. Joe confessed that
he had "just heard" about my trip, but he promised to help bring some
attention to my arrival in Toronto the next day.

That evening, my cancer society hosts were Kathryn and Ted
Glugosh. Warm and engaging, Kathryn and Ted introduced me to their
friends Ed and Beryl, who had recently returned from a two-year trip by
sailboat to Venezuela. Full of rich stories about ocean storms, dolphins,
sharks, and fears of pirates, their adventure made my trip seem bland by
comparison.

Later the same night, Ron Content, whom I had met at Long Point,
found me at the yacht club and brought me back to his home in Oakville.
When Ron and Maria had made the suggestion that I stay with them
when I reached the city, I thought the offer was simply a sentiment of
the moment, similar to someone saying, "Hey, we should get together

sometime." I should have known better. Ron and Maria were sincere, and they made me feel not just like an honoured guest, but like family. It was a fitting end for the last night of my trip. The whole Content family gathered in their living room and listened intently while I recounted my adventures since we had said goodbye on Lake Erie.

When we finally said good night, I lay awake in bed and thought about all of the people I had met or shared a meal or a roof with since leaving Thunder Bay. When I considered all of the amazing people that I had the pleasure to encounter, I realized that their reactions to me were a testament to the truth that people are good, kind, and care about others. I will never forget the people who reached out and made a connection with me. Because of them, I was never truly alone.

For weeks I had carried the strain and worry that my fundraising dream had failed. When I came up with the idea, it had seemed so simple. Start the trip, ask for donations, and if each person in Ontario gave a quarter, it would add up to a sizeable amount of money.

While I struggled to find meaning in my dream called Kayaking for Cancer, it was the memory of Lillian Thompson and the wisdom that she shared with me in Lion's Head that saved my spirit.

She had asked, "Is the money all that matters Michael? Is that why you are doing this? You know, you will touch people on this trip even if they don't give a donation."

The more I thought about Lillian's words, the more I realized that she was right, and the same was true in my personal life. I had so much to celebrate in my life, and raising money for cancer or having a career with a job title beside my name were ultimately the same thing. What truly matters is our relationships, and the impact we leave on others. That is a person's legacy.

The End of a Dream

O N THE FINAL day of my trip, I woke feeling exhilarated and eternally grateful for everything I had experienced. If I compared my mood of the last few days to that of Charles Dickens' character, Scrooge, I woke on that last day transformed and feeling joyful and light-hearted.

Paddling the thirty kilometres from Oakville to Toronto's Sunnyside Beach seemed effortless. With my mind uncluttered with concerns about raising donations, my thoughts turned to the idea of not stopping. *What if I didn't stop? What if I continued out the St. Lawrence all the way to the Atlantic?* I mused. *Now that would be an adventure!*

After a hundred and twenty-seven days, one might expect that I would be tired of kayaking. The truth was that, although I was tired of my role as a fundraiser, paddling was still a pleasure.

There is no record in my journal of my last day kayaking to Toronto. The page in my journal is blank, and my memory begins the moment I saw the crowd gathered on Sunnyside Beach. It was the biggest reception I had seen, and when the crowd saw me they began to shout my name and cheer.

Spurred on by the welcoming cries, I paddled faster. *One last moment for Kayak Man,* I told myself. The first person my eyes picked out of the crowd was a beautiful young woman with long blonde hair. She was standing on a small spit of sand separate from the main group, looking through a very large telephoto lens perched on a tripod. When the woman stood back from the camera, I was shocked to see that it was

Fleur. Anticipating a busy work load in her second year at university, with little money, Fleur had assured me that she wouldn't be able to meet me in Toronto. In disbelief, I studied the image of the beautiful young woman, thinking that I must be dreaming.

It can't be Fleur, she's in Thunder Bay, I told myself. *She can't afford to fly to Toronto for the weekend.* Her long sun-bleached hair blowing in the wind and her radiant smile convinced me I wasn't dreaming. My best friend had come to support me and celebrate my arrival. I was overjoyed.

I landed my kayak at Sunnyside Beach, Toronto, on Saturday, September 17, 1994. I was immediately swarmed by people. Fleur was the first to hug and congratulate me followed by my parents, family members, friends, and a swelling mass of unknown well-wishers. When the crowd had stopped coming by to say hello and offer their congratulations, David Fraser, a spokesman for the Canadian Cancer Society, addressed the crowd and news reporters. On behalf of the Canadian Cancer Society, David congratulated me and thanked me for my summer dedicated to kayaking for cancer.

When the time came for me to speak I was overwhelmed with emotions I hadn't expected. As I spoke, my words got caught in my throat and I had to wipe tears from my eyes as I talked about how cancer touches all of us in some way, and tried to thank the countless people who had supported me on my journey. When I finished my speech, there was a loud applause, and then I stepped down and joined the crowd. For that moment in time, everyone that was there felt like my family.

What had begun as a dream called Kayaking for Cancer–A Celebration of Life had officially come to an end. I was home.

EPILOGUE

A FEW MONTHS after I had completed my kayak trip, I received a letter from the cancer society. The letter was an official record of the funds raised from the Kayaking for Cancer campaign. After reviewing the money collected from the participating IGA stores across Ontario and private donations, the sum was eighteen thousand, three hundred and twenty two dollars and 26 cents. I never focused on the amount. I was more interested in the next few lines in the letter. "We want to emphasize that we have no way to calculate the true value of your expedition. Many of the cancer society offices near your route reported receiving an increase in donation cheques in the mail after you left the area. However, without a specified link that said this cheque is for Kayaking for Cancer, we cannot confirm that those additional funds were received because of your fundraising expedition."

I read the letter a different way. We have no way to calculate the true human value of your expedition.

ACKNOWLEDGMENTS

═══════════════════

I T IS AN undeniable fact that without help, Kayaking for Cancer would never have happened. It is my sincerest wish to pay tribute with deep gratitude to every person who helped me along my journey. If there is anyone I did not mention, please excuse me, but trust that your connection was no less important. Every smile, nod, or generous helping hand left an indelible mark on my soul that will not fade.

Family, Friends, and Acquaintances

Ron and Brenda Herman, Fleur Pigeon, Pat and Art Herman,
Jennifer Smith, Owen Smith, Alice Train, Jim James,
Mark Knoester, Linda Valente, Deanna Campbell,
Ilene and Walter Hill, Carol and Joe Tambasco,
Cathy Scissons (Novak), Mark Scissons,
Peter Wassermann, Kirk Kinghorn,
Cindy Rusak, Jim Rusak,
Fred Jones, (CBC radio, Thunder Bay),
Rick and Lorraine Halabisky,
Ann, Rudi, Lenard , Joan and Sam (Silver Islet residents)
Beverly Cheadle, Greg Cheadle,
Bill Setch, Madeline Watt,
Joyce and Ellison McKenzie,
Jack LeSarge, Deb and Sue (from Pukaskwa Park)
Gary Fellbaum, Kelly Dugas, Carol and Joel (Michipicoten),

Neville and Doris, Lysanne and Rene,
Terry O'Neil, Cheryl Widdifield,
Dan Greco, Beth Bond, Dr. Dieter Poenn,
John Solomon, Mrs. East, Peggy Murphy,
Heather Metcalf,
Bob and Diane Wilkes,
Bill and Marg Johnston, Bob and Lori Korstanje,
John and Mary Walihura, Gerry and Louanne Murphy,
Anne-Marie McCrae, Bert and Lenora Morrison,

Betty Hendricks, Lou Burns, Dave Grim,
Lillian Thompson, Fred and Naomi Laird, Sjak Breg,
Dave Scott, Jim and Michelle Stokeley,
Ross and Marj Ireland, Harry Little, Ivan Walter, Bill Blacklock,
Jean Meisenhimer, Elaine Palmer, Molly, Mel and Beth Farnsworth,
Jim Bridle, Amber and Rob Kunz, Tim Papps, Jim, Donna and Carrie
Goodman, Ted and Molly Oliver, Paul and Cheryl Henshaw, Judy
Levaseur, Darren, Kim, Tessa and Keean Cavers, Greg Cavers, Steve
Lutsch, Priska, Ron and Ruth Neily, Audrey and Murry Knox, Barb,
Blair, Abby and Martha Pierce, Susan and Sheridan Atkinson, Chantal
Pigeon, Ron and Maria, Rachel and Melisa Content, Al and Ingrid,
Roger and Karen Chandler, Tom (boat builder in Port Dover), Dick
and Dorothy McCaffrey, Ron Brown, Ted Wood, Dan Prevost, Bob and
Marie (owners of Chippewa IGA), Ruth Delgat, Wendy Trottier, John
Wolfenberg, Kathryn and Ted Glugosh.

Financial Support from Family

Ron and Brenda Herman, Pat and Art Herman, Ilene and Walter Hill,
Deanna Campbell, Carol and Joe Tambasco, and Mark Weiss.

Corporate Support

Jim James, IGA Food Stores (Oshawa Foods)
Steve Ree, Seaward Kayaks
Mountain Equipment Co-op
David Kapelle, Tilley Endurables
Hi-Tec Sports

Nimbus Paddles
The Original Bug Shirt Company
Mustang Survival
Effem Foods (Mars candy bar)
Gatorade Sports
Mountain Dreams
Harvest Food Works
Frances Boyes, Smoothwater Outfitters
General Ecology Inc.
Peter Cosentino, Toronto Blue Jays
Tim Ingram, Sea Wing self-rescue kayak sponsons
Mark Knoester, Manager Bolton IGA
Bob Carter, Crown, Cork and Seal

Acknowledgments
about This Book

T HE TASK OF telling this story has been a journey and a process that has taken me literally years. I would like to thank some very important people who helped me find my voice and gave me the confidence to keep writing.

Thanks, Mom, for your patience to listen to my early efforts to write, and for your words of encouragement. Fleur, your unwavering support has kept me going. Thank you for your editorial review of each page, and your willingness to offer critical feedback despite my fragile ego. Thank you, writer Charles Wilkens, for taking the time to read a couple of pages of my early draft, and for offering both encouragement and the best advice I could have received: "Just tell your story."

When the time came to share this story, I needed proof that someone would find the story worth reading, so I asked a select group of book lovers if they would read my manuscript. A few friends, family members, and acquaintances accepted the request, and I am grateful for their feedback and response. For reading my rough draft I thank Crystal Bonnic, Brenda Herman, Ron Herman, Allana Logan, Teresa Emmerson, Denise Swain, Mark Swain, Angela Comeau, Kayla Comeau, Wendy Maltby, Mac Maltby and Ron Nigrini. In addition, I want to thank DeWayne Nikkila, Stacey Schat, and Shirley Farmer for their critical review of the book's content and grammar. Each of your questions, comments, and suggestions was helpful beyond measure.

About the Author

A FORMER INSTRUCTOR with the Outward Bound Wilderness School, Michael Herman has completed numerous wilderness expeditions into northern Ontario, Canada.

Today, Michael and Fleur live outside Powassan, Ontario, with their three children. They are planning a family canoe expedition slated for the summer 2015. You can contact the author at mlionelherman@gmail.com

REFERENCES

Holling, Holling C. *Paddle To The Sea*. Boston: Sandpiper Publishing, 1980.

Jackson, Alan. *Here In The Real World*. Arista Records, compact disk, 1990.

Kesselheim, Alan S. *Water and Sky: Challenging the Northern Wilderness*. New York, New York: Dell Publishing, 1989.

Death of a Legend: Documentary Film, Directed by Bill Mason, Montreal: National Film Board of Canada, 1971.

Waterwalker: Documentary Film, Directed by Bill Mason, Montreal: National Film Board of Canada, 1985.

McGuffin, Gary and Joanie McGuffin. *Where Rivers Run: A 6,000 Mile Exploration of Canada by Canoe*. Toronto: Stoddart Publishing, 1988.

Nordby, Will, ed. *Seekers of the Horizon: Sea Kayaking Voyages From Around the World*. Chester, Connecticut: The Globe Pequot Press, 1989.

Peale, Norman Vincent. *The Power Of Positive Thinking*. New York, New York: Prentice Hall, 1952.

Raffan, James. *Summer North of 60: By Paddle and Portage across the Barren Lands*. Toronto: Key Porter Books, 1990.

APR - - 2013

CPSIA information can be obtained at www.ICGtesting.com
Printed in the USA
LVOW080158170212

269034LV00003B/7/P